CONSTITUTION LAWS
Rights, Liberties and Justice

CONSTITUTION LAWS
Rights, Liberties and Justice

R K Jatain

MD PUBLICATIONS PVT LTD
NEW DELHI
www.mdppl.com

Published by :

MD Publications Pvt Ltd
"MD House", 11, Darya Ganj,
New Delhi - 110002
Phone : +91-11-45355555
E-mail : contact@mdppl.com
Website: www.mdppl.com

ISBN: 978-81-7533-450-2

Published and Printed by Mr. Pranav Gupta on behalf of **MD Publications Pvt Ltd** at Times Press, New Delhi.

PREFACE

The Constitution of India is the Supreme Law of India. It lays down the framework defining fundamental political principles, establishes the structure, procedures, powers, and duties of government institutions, and sets out fundamental rights, directive principles, and the duties of citizens. It is the longest written constitution of any sovereign country in the world, containing 448 articles in 22 parts, 12 schedules and 118 amendments. Besides the English version, there is an official Hindi translation. Dr B.R. Ambedkar is widely regarded as the father of the Indian Constitution.

The Constitution was adopted by the Constituent Assembly on 26 November 1949, and came into effect on 26 January 1950. The date 26 January was chosen to commemorate the Purna Swaraj declaration of independence of 1930. With its adoption, the Union of India officially became the modern and contemporary Republic of India and it replaced the Government of India Act 1935 as the country's fundamental governing document. To ensure constitutional autochthony, the constitutional framers inserted Article 395 in the constitution and by this Article the Indian Independence Act, 1947 was repealed. The Constitution declares India to be a sovereign, socialist, secular, democratic republic, assuring its citizens of justice, equality, and liberty, and endeavours to promote fraternity among them. The words "socialist" and "secular" were added to the definition in 1976 by constitutional amendment(mini constitution). India celebrates the adoption of the constitution on 26 January each year as Republic Day. The major portion of the Indian subcontinent was under British colonial rule from 1757 to 1947. The impact of economic, political and social exploitation during this period helped the gradual rise of the Indian independence movement to gain independence from foreign rule. The movement culminated in the formation of the Dominion of India on 15 August 1947, along with the Dominion of Pakistan. The Constitution of India was adopted on 26 November 1949 and came into effect on 26 January 1950, proclaiming India to be a sovereign, democratic republic. It contained the founding principles of the law of the land which would govern India after its independence from British rule. On the day the constitution came into effect, India ceased to be a dominion of the British Crown. The Indian constitution is the world's longest constitution. At the time of commencement, the constitution had 395 articles in 22 parts and 8 schedules. It consists of almost 80,000 words and took 2 years 11 months and 18 days to build.

The Constitution was drafted by the Constituent Assembly, which was elected by the elected members of the provincial assemblies. Dr B.R. Ambedkar, Sanjay Phakey, Jawaharlal Nehru, C. Rajagopalachari, Rajendra Prasad, Sardar Vallabhbhai Patel, Kanaiyalal Munshi,

Purushottam Mavalankar, Sandipkumar Patel, Maulana Abul Kalam Azad, Shyama Prasad Mukherjee, Nalini Ranjan Ghosh, and Balwantrai Mehta were some important figures in the Assembly. There were more than 30 members of the scheduled classes. Frank Anthony represented the Anglo-Indian community, and the Parsis were represented by H P Modi. The Chairman of the Minorities Committee was Harendra Coomar Mookerjee, a distinguished Christian who represented all Christians other than Anglo-Indians. Ari Bahadur Gururng represented the Gorkha Community. Prominent jurists like Alladi Krishnaswamy Iyer, Benegal Narsing Rau and K M Munshi, Ganesh Mavlankar were also members of the Assembly. Sarojini Naidu, Hansa Mehta, Durgabai Deshmukh, Rajkumari Amrit Kaur and Vijayalakshmi Pandit were important women members. This book has been prepared for lawyers, students, researchers and for all those associated with judicial system of the country.

In preparation of this book, I am thankful to my family, friends and colleagues for their constant support and guidance. I am grateful to Mr Pranav Gupta, Director of MD Publications Pvt Ltd, for his encouragement in preparation of this book.

R K Jatain

CONTENTS

1

The Appropriation (No. 3) Act, 1996

Act No. 31 of 1996 [23rd September, 1996]

AN ACT to authorise payment and appropriation of certain sums from and out of the Consolidated Fund of India for the services of the financial year 1996- 97.

Be it enacted by Parliament in the Forty-seventh Year of the Republic of India as follows:-

1. Short title. This Act may be called the Appropriation (No. 3) Act, 1996.

2. Issue of Rs. 4,65,857,03,00,000 out of the Consolidated Fund of India for the year 1996 - 97. From and out of the Consolidated Fund of India there may be paid and applied sums not exceeding those specified in column 3 of the Schedule amounting in the aggregate [inclusive of the sums specified in column 3 of the Schedule to the Appropriation (Vote on Account) No. 2 Act, 1996] (18 of 1996) to the sum of four lakh sixty-five thousand eight hundred and fifty-seven crores and three lakh rupees towards defraying the several charges which will come in course of payment during the financial year 1996-97 in respect of the services specified in column 2 of the Schedule.

3. Appropriation. The sums authorised to be paid and applied from and out of the Consolidated Fund of India by this Act shall be appropriated for the services and purposes expressed in the Schedule in relation to the said year.

4. Construction of references to Ministries and Departments in the Schedule. References to Ministries or Departments in the Schedule are to such Ministries or Departments as existing immediately before the 28th June, 1996 and shall, on or after that date, be construed as references to the appropriate Ministries or Departments as reconstituted from time to time.

❑❑❑

2

The British Statutes (Repeal) Act, 2004

No. 17 of 2004 [20th February, 2004]

AN ACT to repeal the British Law Ascertainment Act, 1859, the Foreign Law Ascertainment Act, 1861, the Colonial Probates Act, 1892, insofar as they apply to India, and the India (Consequential Provision) Act, 1949.

Be it enacted by Parliament in the Fifty-fifth Year of the Republic of India as follows:-

1. Short title. This Act may be called the British Statutes (Repeal) Act, 2004 .

2. Definition. In this Act, "British Statutes" means the British Law Ascertainment Act, 1859 (22 and 23 Vict. C. 63), the Foreign Law Ascertainment Act, 1861 (24 and 25 Vict. C. 11), the Colonial Probates Act, 1892 (55 and 56 Vict. C. 6), insofar as they apply to India, as the India (Consequential Provision) Act, 1949 (12, 13 and 14 Geor. VI V. 92).

3. Repeal. The British Statutes are hereby repealed.

❑❑❑

3

The Caste Disabilities Removal Act, 1850

Short title given by the Indian Short Title Act, 1897 (14 of 1897).This Act has been extended to Berar by the Berar Laws Act, 1941 (4 of 1941) and has been declared to be in force in all the Provinces of India, except the Scheduled Districts, by the Laws Local Extent Act, 1874 (15 of 1874), s.3.

It has been declared in force in the Santhal Parganas by the Santhal Parganas Settlement Regulation (3 of 1872), s.3.

It has been declared, by notification under s.3 (a) of the Scheduled Districts Act, 1874 (14 of 1874), to be in force in the following Scheduled Districts, namely :—

West Jalpaiguri................See Gazette of India, 1881, Pt. I, p.74.

The Districts of Hazaribagh, Lohardga (now the Ranchi District, See Calcutta Gazette, 1899, Pt.I, p.44), and Manbhum, and Paragana Dhalbhum and the Kolhan in the District of Singhbhum...... Ditto 1881, Pt.I, p. 504

The Scheduled portion of the Mirzapur District..... Ditto 1879, Pt.I, p. 383

Jaunasar Bawar Ditto 1879, Pt. I, p. 382

The District Ditto 1886, Pt. I, p. 301

The Scheduled Districts of the C.P. Ditto 1886 , Pt.I, p. 771

The Scheduled Districts in Ganjam and Vizagapatam Ditto 1898, Pt.I, p. 870

Coorg .... Ditto 1879, Pt.I, p.747

Assam (except the North Lushai Hills) Ditto 1897, Pt.I, p.299

The Porahat Estate in the Singhbhum District Ditto 1897,Pt.I, p.1059

It has been extended by notification under s.5 of the last-mentioned Act, to the following Scheduled Districts.namely :—

Kumaon and Garhwal.......See Gazette of India, 1876, Pt. I, p.606

The Tarai of the Province of Agra Ditto 1876, Pt.I, p.505

It has also been extended to the New Provinces and Merged States, see Act 59 of 1949.

ACT NO. 21 OF 1850

[AS ON 1959]

An Act for extending the principle of Section 9, Regulation VII, 1832 of the Bengal Code throughout {Subs. by Act 3 of 1951, s.3. and Sch., for the 'territories subject to the Government of the East India Company'.} [India].

[11 the April, 1850]

Preamble

WHEREAS it is enacted by Section 9, Regulation VII, 1832, of the Bengal Code, { Rep.by the Bengal Civil Courts Act, 1871 (6 of 1871), which was rep. by the Bengal, North-Western Provinces and Assam Civil Courts Act, 1887 (12 of 1887)} that "whenever in any civil suit the parties to such suit may be of different persuasions, when one party shall be of the Hindu and the other of the Muhammadan persuasion, or where one or more of the parties to the suit shall not be either of the Muhammadan or Hindu persuasions the laws of those religions shall not be permitted to operate to deprive such party or parties of any property to which, but for the operation of such laws, they would have been entitled"; and whereas it will be beneficial to extend the principle of that enactment throughout 893 [India] ; It is enacted as follows :—

1. Law or usage which inflicts forfeiture of, or affects, rights on change of religion or loss of caste to cease to be enforced. So much of any law or usage now in force within {Subs. by Act 3 of 1951, s.3 and Sch. for 'the territories subject to the Government of the East India Company'.} [India] as inflicts on any person forfeiture of rights or property, or may be held in any way to impair or affect any right of inheritance, by reason of his or her renouncing, or having been excluded from the communion of, any religion , or being deprived of caste, shall cease to be enforced as law {Subs. by s.3 and Sch., *ibid.*, for 'in the Courts of the East India Company, and in the Courts established by Royal Charter within the said territories'.}[in any court].

{Added by s.3 and Sch., *ibid.*,

[2. Short title and extent.

(1) This Act may be called the Caste Disabilities Removal Act, 1850.

(2) It extends to the whole of India except the State of Jammu and Kashmir.]

❑❑❑

4

The Census Act, 1948

Act No. 37 of 1948 [As on 1955]

AN ACT to provide for certain matters in connection with the taking of census.

[3rd September, 1948]

WHEREAS it is expedient to provide for the taking of census in {The word "the Provinces and Acceding States" were rep. by the A.O.1950.} India or any part thereof whenever necessary or desirable and to provide for certain matters in connection with the taking of such census;

It is hereby enacted as follows:-

1. Short title and extent.

(1) This Act may be called the Census Act, 1948. {Subs., *ibid.*, for the former sub-section.}

[(2) It extends to the whole of India {Subs.by Act 51 of 1950, s.2, for "except the States of Hyderabad, Jammu and Kashmir, Mysore and Travancore-Cochin".} [except the State of Jammu and Kashmir].]

{Ins., *ibid.*, s.3.The original s.2 was rep. by the A.O. 1950.}

2. Rule of construction respecting enactments not extending to Part B States. Any reference to the Indian Penal Code or the Indian Evidence Act, 1872, shall, in relation to a Part B State, be construed as a reference to the corresponding enactment in force in that State.

3. Central Government to take census. The Central Government may, by notification in the Official Gazette, declare its intention of taking a census in the whole or any part of the territories to which this Act extends, whenever it may consider it necessary or desirable so to do, and thereupon the census shall be taken.

4. Appointment of ceases staff.

(1) The Central Government may appoint a Census Commissioner to supervise the taking of the census throughout the area in which the census is intended to be taken, and Superintendents of Census Operations to supervise the taking of the census within the several States.

(2) The State Government may appoint persons as census-officers to take, or aid in, or supervise the taking of, the census within any specified local area and such persons, when so appointed, shall be bound to serve accordingly.

(3) A declaration in writing, signed by any authority authorised by the State Government in this behalf that any person has been duly appointed a census-officer for any local area shall be conclusive proof of such appointment.

(4) The State Government may delegate to such authority as it thinks fit the power of appointing census-officers conferred by subsection (2).

5. Status of census authorities as public servants. The Census Commissioner, all Superintendents of Census Operations and all census-officers shall be deemed to be public servants within the meaning of the Indian Penal Code.

6. Discharge of duties of census officers in certain cases.

(1) Where the District Magistrate, or such authority as the State Government may appoint in this behalf, by a written order so directs -

(a) every officer in command of any body of men belonging to the naval, military or air forces, or of any vessel of war, of India;

(b) every person (except a pilot or harbourmaster) having charge or control of a vessel;

(c) every person in charge of a lunatic asylum, hospital, workhouse, prison, reformatory or lock-up or of any public, charitable, religious or educational institution;

(d) every keeper, secretary or manager of any sarai, hotel, boarding-house, lodging-house, emigration depot or club;

(e) every manager or officer of a railway or any commercial or industrial establishment; and

(f) every occupant of immovable property wherein at the time of the taking of the census persons are living, shall perform such of the duties of a census-officer in relation to the persons who at the time of the taking of the census are under his command or charge, or are inmates of his house, or are present on or in such immovable property or are employed under him as may be specified in the order.

(2) All the provisions of this Act relating to census-officers shall apply, so far as may be, to all persons while performing such duties under this section, and any person refusing or neglecting to perform any duty which under this section he is directed to perform shall be deemed to have committed an offence under section 187 of the Indian Penal Code.

7. Powers call upon certain persons to assistance. The District Magistrate, or such authority as the State Government may appoint in this behalf for any local area, may, by written order which shall have effect throughout the extent of his district or of such local area, as the case may be, call upon-

(a) all owners and occupiers of land, tenure-holders, and farmers and assignees of land revenue, or their agents;

(b) all members of the district, municipal, panchayat and other local authorities and officers and servants of such authorities; and

(c) all officers and members of staff of any factory, firm or establishment, to give such assistance as shall be specified in the order towards the taking of a census of the persons who are, at the time of the taking of the census, on the lands of such owners, occupiers, tenure-holders, farmers and assignees, or in the premises of factories, firms and other establishments, or within the areas for which such local authorities are established, as the case may be, and the persons to whom an order under this section is directed shall be bound to obey it and shall, while acting in pursuance of such order, be deemed to be public servants within the meaning of the Indian Penal Code.

8. Asking of questions and obligation to answer.

(1) A census-officer may ask all such questions of all persons within the limits of the local area for which he is appointed as, by instructions issued in this behalf by the State Government and of published in the Official Gazette, he may be directed to ask.

(2) Every person of whom any question is asked under sub-section (1) shall be legally bound to answer such question to the best of his knowledge or belief:

Provided that no person shall be bound to state the name of any female member of his household, and no woman shall be bound to state the name of her husband or deceased husband or of any other person whose name she is forbidden by custom to mention.

9. Occupier to permit access and affixing of numbers. Every person occupying any house, enclosure, vessel or other place shall allow census-officers such access thereto as they may require for the purposes of the census and as, having regard to the customs of the country, may be reasonable, and shall allow them to paint on, or affix to, the place such letters, marks or numbers as may be necessary for the purposes of the census.

10. Occupier or manager to fill up schedule.

(1) Subject to such orders as the State Government may issue in this behalf, a census-officer may, within the local area for which he is appointed, leave or cause to be left a schedule at any dwelling house or with the manager or any officer of any commercial or industrial establishment, for the purpose of its being filled up by the occupier of such house or of any specified part thereof or by such manager or officer with such particulars as the State Government may direct regarding the inmates of such house or part thereof, or the persons employed under such manager or officer, as the case may be, at the time of the taking of the census.

(2) When such schedule has been so left, the said occupier, manager or officer, as the case may be, shall it up or cause it to be filled up to the best of his knowledge or belief so far as regards the inmates of such house or part thereof or the persons employed under him as the case may be, at the time aforesaid, and shall sign his name thereto and, when so required, shall deliver the schedule so filled up and signed to the census-officer or to such person as the census-officer may direct.

11. Penalties.

(1) (a) Any census-officer or any person lawfully required to give assistance towards the taking of a census who refuses or neglects to use reasonable diligence in performing any duty imposed upon him or in obeying any order issued to him in accordance with this Act or any rule made thereunder, or any person who hinders or obstructs another person in performing any such duty or in obeying any such order; or

(b) any census-officer who intentionally puts any offensive or improper question or knowingly makes any false return or, without the previous sanction of the Central Government or the State Government, discloses any information which he has received by means of, or for the purposes of, a census return; or

(c) any sorter, compiler or other member of the census staff who removes, secretes, damages or destroys any census document or deals with any census document in a manner likely to falsify or impair the tabulations of census results; or

(d) any person who intentionally gives a false answer to, or refuses to answer to the best of his knowledge or belief, any question asked of him by a census-officer which he is legally bound by section 8 to answer; or

(e) any person occupying any house, enclosure, vessel or other place who refuses to allow a census-officer such reasonable access thereto as he is required by section 9 to allow; or

(f) any person who removes, obliterates, alters, or damages any letters, marks or numbers which have been painted or affixed for the purposes of the census; or

(g) any person who, having been required under section 10 to fill up a schedule, knowingly and without sufficient cause fails to comply with the provisions of that section, or makes any false return thereunder; or

(h) any person who trespasses into a census office, shall be punishable with fine which may extend to one thousand rupees and in case of a conviction under part (b) or (c) shall also be punishable with imprisonment which may extend to six months.

(2) Whoever abets any offence under sub-section (1) shall be punishable with fine which may extend to one thousand rupees.

12. Sanction required for prosecutions. No prosecution under this Act shall be instituted except with the previous sanction of the State Government or of an authority authorised in this behalf by the State Government.

13. Operation of other laws not barred. Nothing in this Act shall be deemed to prevent any person from being prosecuted under any other law for any act or omission which constitutes an offence under this Act:

Provided that no such prosecution shall be instituted except with the previous sanction referred to in section 12.

14. Jurisdiction. No court inferior to that of a Presidency Magistrate or a Magistrate of the second class {Ins.by Act 51 of 1950, s.4.} [or in a Part B State, a Magistrate corresponding to a Magistrate of the second class] shall try, whether under this Act or under any other law, any act or omission which constitutes an offence under this Act.

15. Records of census not open to inspection nor admissible in evidence. No person shall have a right to inspect any book, register or record made by a census-officer in the discharge of his duty as such, or any schedule delivered under section 10, and notwithstanding anything to the contrary in the Indian Evidence Act, 1872, no entry in any such book, register, record or schedule shall be admissible evidence in any civil proceeding whatsoever or in any criminal proceeding other than a prosecution under this Act or any other law for any act or omission which constitutes an offence under this Act.

16. Temporary suspension of other laws as to mode of taking census in municipalities. Notwithstanding anything in any enactment or rule with respect to the mode in which a census is to be taken in any municipality, the municipal authority, in consultation with the Superintendent of Census Operations or with such other authority as the State Government may authorize in this behalf, shall, at the time it appointed for the taking of any census cause the census of the municipality to be taken wholly or in part by any method authorised by or under this Act.

17. Grant of statistical abstracts. The Census Commissioner or any Superintendent of Census Operations or such person as the State Government may authorizes in this behalf may, if he so thinks fit, at the request and cost (to be determined by him) of any local authority or person, cause abstracts to be prepared and supplied containing any such statistical information as can be derived from the census returns for India or any State, as the case may be, being information which is not contained in any published report and which in his opinion it is reasonable for that authority or person to require.

18. Power to make rules.

(1) The Central Government may make rules for carrying out the purposes of this Act.

(2) In particular, and without prejudice to the generality of the foregoing power, the Central Government may make rules providing for the appointment of census-officers and of persons to perform any of the duties of census-officers or to give assistance towards the taking of a census, and for the general instructions to be issued to such officers and persons.

❑❑❑

5

The Central Laws (Extension to Arunachal Pradesh) Act, 1993

[Act No. 44 of 1993] [27th May 1993]

AN ACT to Provide for the extension of certain Central laws to the State of Arunachal Pradesh.

Be it enacted by Parliament in the Forty Fourth Year of the Republic of India as follows:-

1. Extension of certain laws. The Acts mentioned in the Schedule and all rules orders, regulations and schemes made thereunder are hereby extended to and shall be in force in the State of Arunachal Pradesh.

2. Construction of references to laws not in force in Arunachal Pradesh. Any reference in any Act mentioned in the Schedule to a law which is not in force in the State of Arunachal Pradesh shall in relation to that State be construed as a reference to the corresponding law if any in force in that State.

3. Construction of references to authorities where new authorities have been constituted. Any reference by whatever form of words in any law for the time being in force in the State of Arunachal Pradesh to any authority competent at the date of the passing of that law to exercise any power or discharge any functions in that State shall where a corresponding new authority has been constituted or under any law now extended to that State have effect as if it were a reference to the new authority.

4. Power to remove difficulties.

(1) If any difficulty arises in giving effect to the provisions of any Act now extended to the State of Arunachal Pradesh the Central Government may by order notified

in the Official Gazette make such provisions or give such directions as appear to it necessary for the removal of the difficulty.

(2) In particular and without prejudice to the generality of the foregoing power any such notified order may -

(a) specify the corresponding authorities within the meaning of Section 4 Power to remove difficulties;

(b) provide for the transfer of any matter pending immediately before the commencement of this Act before any court tribunal or other authority to any corresponding court tribunal or other authority for disposal.

Provided that no such order shall be made after the expiry of two years from the date of commencement of this Act.

(3) Every order made under this section shall be laid before each House of Parliament.

THE SCHEDULE
(See Section 2)

Year	No	Short title
1	2	3
1862	3	The Government Seal Act, 1862
1873	5	The Government Savings Banks Act, 1873
1874	4	The Foreign Recruiting Act, 1874
1881	26	The Negotiable Instruments Act, 1881
1884	4	The Explosive Act, 1884
1885	13	The Indian Telegraph Act, 1885
1888	4	The Indian Reserve Forces Act, 1888
1905	4	The Indian Railway Board Act, 1905
1908	6	The Explosive Substances Act, 1908
1938	5	The Manoeuvres, Field Firing and Artillary Practice Act, 1938
1941	25	The Railways (Local Authorities Taxation) Act, 1941
1948	31	The National Cadet Corps Act, 1948
1948	37	The Census Act, 1948
1948	46	The Coal Mines Provident Fund and Miscellaneous Provisions Act, 1948

□□□

6

The Central Provinces Laws Act, 1875

ACT NO. 20 OF 1875 [AS ON 1956]

SCHEDULE

(See section 3)

A. BENGAL REGULATIONS {So much of Act 20 of 1875 as relates to the following Bengal Regulations was rep.by the Act noted against each:-

{Ben. Reg.1 of 1798 - Transfer of Property Act, 1882 (4 of 1882).

Ben. Reg.10 of 1804 - Special Laws Repeal Act, 1922 (4 of 1922).

Ben. Reg.17 of 1806 - Transfer of Property Act, 1882 (4 of 1882).

Ben. Reg.20 of 1810 - Cantonments Act, 1889 (13 of 1889).

Ben. Reg.5 of 1817 - Indian Treasure-trove Act, 1878 (6 of 1878).

Ben. Reg.20 of 1825 - Code of Criminal Procedure, 1882 (10 of 1882).

Ben. Reg.6 of 1819 was rep. in the C.P.by Act 17 of 1878, and later generally, by Act 12 of 1891.}

Number and Subject Extent of operation Power to duties how to year of be exercised or performed Regulations

1 2 3 4

{So much of Act 20 of 1875 as relates to the following Bengal Regulations was rep.by the Act noted against each:-

{Ben. Reg.1 of 1798 —Transfer of Property Act, 1882 (4 of 1882).

Ben. Reg.10 of 1804 —Special Laws Repeal Act, 1922 (4 of 1922).

Ben. Reg.17 of 1806 —Transfer of Property Act, 1882 (4 of 1882).

Ben. Reg.20 of 1810 —Cantonments Act, 1889 (13 of 1889).

Ben. Reg.5 of 1817 — Indian Treasure-trove Act, 1878 (6 of 1878).

Ben. Reg.20 of 1825 — Code of Criminal Procedure, 1882 (10 of 1882).

Ben. Reg.6 of 1819 was rep. in the C.P. by Act 17 of 1878, and later generally, by Act 12 of 1891.}

V of 1799 Estates of Intestates. {Subs.by C.P.Act {Subs. by C.P. Act 9 of 1923, s.2, for 9 of 1923, s.2, for the original entries.} [Sections 4, 5, 6, and [The functions of the 7.] Court of "Sadr Diwani Adalat" and Of "the Board of Revenue" shall be performed respectively by the {See however the C.}

P. Courts Act, 1917 (C.P.1 of 1917), s. 31.} Judicial Commissioner and by the State Government.]

{So much of Act 20 of 1875 as relates to the following Bengal Regulations was rep.by the Act noted against each:-

{Ben. Reg.1 of 1798 — Transfer of Property Act, 1882 (4 of 1882).

Ben. Reg.10 of 1804 — Special Laws Repeal Act, 1922 (4 of 1922).

Ben. Reg.17 of 1806 — Transfer of Property Act, 1882 (4 of 1882).

Ben. Reg.20 of 1810 — Cantonments Act, 1889 (13 of 1889).

Ben. Reg.5 of 1817 — Indian Treasure-trove Act, 1878 (6 of 1878).

Ben. Reg.20 of 1825 — Code of Criminal Procedure, 1882 (10 of 1882).

Ben. Reg.6 of 1819 was rep.in the C.P. by Act 17 of 1878, and later generally, by Act 12 of 1891.}

{The entry relating to Reg.11 of 1806 was rep.by M.P.Act 15 of 1950, s.2.}

SCHEDULE-concld.

Number and year Subject Extent of operation Powers or duties how to be of Regulation exercised or performed

1 2 3 4

{See footnote 1 on prepare}

XI of 1812 Foreign. So much as has not been the powers of the "Nizamat Immigrants repealed Adalat" shall be exercised by the {See however the C.P. Courts Act, 1917 (C.P. 1 of 1917), s. 31.} Judicial Commissioner. {See footnote 1 on prepare.}

III of 1818 State Prisoners. So much as has not been repealed.

{See footnote 1 on prepage.}

{The entry relating to Reg.6 of 1825 was rep.by M.P.Act 15 of 1950, s.2.}

XI of 1825 Alluvion and The whole...Diluvion.

V of 1827 Administration of so much as has not The powers of the Landed property been repealed, except the "Board of Revenue" words and figures "and shall be exercised Clauses 5 and 6, Section by the {Subs.by the XVI, regulation III, 1803". A.O.1937 for "Chief Commissioner"} State Government].

B. ACTS OF THE GOVERNMENT GENERAL IN COUNCIL

Number and year Subject Extent of operation of Act

1 2 3

VIII of 1851. Tolls on Roads and Bridges The whole Act, except section 1, and the schedule.

{The entry relating to Act 18 of 1853 (Sale of Spirits in Cantonments) was rep. by Act 12 of 1891.

XIII of 1857. Opium...... Sections 21, 22, 23, 25, 26, 27, 28, 29.

{The entry relating to the Minors Act, 1858 (40 of 1859), was rep. by Act 8 of 1890.}

XV of 1864. Tolls..... The whole Act.

CENTRAL PROVINCES LAWS ACT, 1875
ACT No.20 OF 1875
[As on 1956]

An Act to declare and amend the law in force in the Central Provinces.

Comment: The purpose of the Act is to declare and amend certain portions of law in force in the Central Provinces

Preamble. Whereas it is expedient to declare and amend certain portions of law in force in the Central Provinces; It is hereby enacted as follows:-

1. Short title. This Act may be called the Central Provinces Laws Act, 1875:

Local extent. It extends to the territories now under the administration of the state Government of the Central Provinces.

Commencement. And it shall come into force on the passing thereof.

2. Repeal of enactments and rules. On and from the date on which this Act comes into force the following shall be repealed, that is to say-

(a) all Bengal Regulations except the Regulations or parts of Regulations hereinafter declared to be in force;

(b) all {Subs. by the A O. 1950 for "Acts of the Central Legislature".} [Central Acts] (except the Acts mentioned in the schedule hereto annexed) which do not expressly or by necessary implication extend to the said territories or any part thereof, and have not been extended thereto in exercise of a power conferred by a {Subs., *ibid*, for "Act of the Central Legislature".} [Central Act];

(c) all rules, regulations and enactments not being Statutes, Bengal Regulations, {Subs. by the A.O. 1950 for "Acts of the Central Legislature".} [Central Acts], or rules or regulations made in exercise of a power conferred by a Statute, Bengal Regulation or {Subs., *ibid.*, for "Act of the Central Legislature".} [Central Act].

{The proviso as to the law relating to land-revenue and Courts of Wards was rep. by Act 12 of 1891.}

3. Certain enactments to be deemed to be in force. On and from the said date the enactments specified in the schedule hereto annexed shall be deemed to be in force throughout the said territories to the extent mentioned in the third column of the said schedule.

But the powers and duties incident to the operation of the same enactments, so far as such powers and duties are referred to in the fourth column of the said schedule, shall be exercised and performed y the authorities mentioned in that column. Nothing in this section shall be deemed to affect the operation of any enactment not mentioned in the said schedule.

4. Confirmation of existing Acts. Every {Subs.by the A.O. 1950 for "Act of the Central Legislature"} [Central Act] which extends, or can by notification be extended, to the territories which were under the administration of the State Government at the time of the passing thereof.shall extend, or may by notification be extended, as the case may be to all the territories now under the administration of the said State Government.

{The provisions of this section have been repealed insofar as they are inconsistent with the provisions of the Muslim Personal Law (Shariat) Application Act 1937 (26 of 1937); see s.6 of that Act.}

5. Rule of decision in cases of certain classes. In questions regarding inheritance, special property of females, betrothal, marriage, dower, adoption guardianship, minority, bastardy, family relations wills, legacies, gifts, partitions or any religious usage or institution, the rule of decision shall be the Muhammadan law in cases where the parties are Muhammadans, and the in Hindu law in cases where the parties are Hindus, except insofar as such law has been by legislative enactment altered or abolished, or is opposed to the provisions of this Act:

> *Provided that when among any class or body of persons or among the members of any family any custom prevails which is inconsistent the law applicable between such persons under this section, and which, if not inconsistent with such law, would have been given effect to as legally binding, such custom shall, notwithstanding anything herein contained, be given effect to.*

6. Rules in cases not expressly provided for. In cases not provided for by Section 5, or by any other law for the time being in force, the Courts shall act according to justice equity and good conscience.

7. Articles exempt from attachment. Implements of husbandry and cattle for agricultural purposes and implements of trade are exam executed from attachment and sale in execution of decrees of the Civil Courts.

8. Power to make subsidiary rules. The said State Government may from time to time make rules consistent with this Act as to the following matters -

(a) the maintenance of watch and ward and the establishment of proper system of conservancy and sanitation at fairs and other large public assemblies;

(b) the imposition of taxes for the purposes mentioned in clause (a) of this section on persons holding or joining any of the assemblies therein referred to;

(c) the custody of judicial records, civil and criminal; {The words "and the destruction from time to time of such of the said records as it may be deemed unnecessary to keep" rep.by Act 3 of 1879.}

{Cl.(d) relating to the appointment, duties, punishment, suspension and dismissal of all ministerial officers was rep.by the A.O. 1937.}

9. Penalty for breach of rules. The State Government may, in making any rule under this Act attach to the breach of it, in addition to any other consequences that would ensue from such breach a punishment, on conviction before a Magistrate, not exceeding one month's imprisonment, or two hundred rupees fine, or both.

10. Publication of rules. Force of rules. All rules made under this Act shall {The words "when sanctioned by the G.G.in C". rep. by Act 38 of 1920, s.2 and Sch.I.} be published in the {Subs.by the A.O.1937 for "C.P.Gazette".} [Official Gazette] and shall thereupon have the force of law.

11. Local repeal in part of Code of Civil Procedure. Sections 184, 185 and 189 of the Code of Civil Procedure {See now the Code of Civil Procedure, 1908 (5 of 1908), Sch.I, Order XVIII, Rules 8, 9 and 13.} are hereby repealed.]

12. Sections substituted in same Code. For sections 182, 190 and 191 of the same Code701 the following shall be substituted (namely):-

Note of evidence to be taken. "182. A note of the essential points of the evidence of each witness shall be made at the time.and in the course of oral examination, by the Judge, in his own language, or English if he is sufficiently acquainted with- that language, and such notes shall be filed with, ancl form part of the record of the case".

Judge unable to make note to record reason of his inability. "190. If the Judge be prevented from making a note as above required, he shall record the reason of his inability to do so, and shall cause such note to be made in writing from his dictation in open Court, and shall sign the same, and such note shall form part of the record".

Power to use note made by Judge dying or removed before conclusion of suit. "191.When the Judge making a note of the evidence, or causing one to be made as above required, dies or is removed from the Court before the conclusion of the suit, his successor may, if he thinks fit, deal with such note as if he himself had made it or caused it to be made."]

❑❑❑

7

The Citizenship (Amendment) Act, 2003

No. 6 of 2004 [7th January, 2004]

AN ACT further to amend the Citizenship Act, 1955.

Be it enacted by Parliament in the Fifty-fourth Year of the Republic of India as follows:-

1. Short title and commencement.

(1) This Act may be called the Citizenship (Amendment) Act, 2003.

(2) It shall come into force on such date as the Central Government may, by notification in the Official Gazette, appoint:

Provided that different dates may be appointed for different provisions of this Act and any reference in any such provision to the commencement of this Act shall be construed as a reference to the commencement of that provision.

2. Amendment of Section 2. In Section 2 of the Citizenship Act, 1955 (57 of 1955) (hereinafter referred to as the principal Act), in sub-section (1),-

(a) for clauses (b) and (c) and the proviso to clause (c), the following clause shall be substituted, namely:-

(b) "illegal migrant" means a foreigner who has entered into India-

(i) without a valid passport or other travel documents and such other document or authority as may be prescribed by or under any law in that behalf; or

(ii) with a valid passport or other travel documents and such other document or authority as may be prescribed by or under any law in that behalf but remains therein beyond the permitted period of time;

(c) after clause (e), the following clause shall be inserted, namely:-

(ee) "overseas citizen of India" means a person who-

(i) is of Indian origin being a citizen of a specified country, or

(ii) was a citizen of India immediately before becoming a citizen of a specified country, and is registered as an overseas citizen of India by the Central Government under sub-section (1) of Section 7A;

(iii) after clause (g), the following clause shall be inserted, namely:-

(gg) "specified country" means a country specified in the Fourth Schedule:

Provided that the Central Government may, by notification in the Official Gazette, amend the said Schedule by way of addition or omission of any entry therein:

Provided further that every notification issued under this clause shall, as soon as may be, after it is made, be laid before each House of Parliament;.

3. Substitution of new Section for Section 3. For Section 3 of the principal Act, the following Section shall be substituted, namely:-

"3. Citizenship by birth.

(1) Except as provided in sub-section (2), every person born in India-

(a) on or after the 26th day of January, 1950, but before the 1st day of July, 1987;

(b) on or after the 1st day of July, 1987, but before the commencement of the Citizenship (Amendment) Act, 2003 and either of whose parents is a citizen of India at the time of his birth;

(c) on or after the commencement of the Citizenship (Amendment) Act, 2003, where-

(i) both of his parents are citizens of India; or

(ii) one of whose parents is a citizen of India and the other is not an illegal migrant at the time of his birth, shall be a citizen of India by birth.

(2) A person shall not be a citizen of India by virtue of this section if at the time of his birth-

(a) either his father or mother possesses such immunity from suits and legal process as is accorded to an envoy of a foreign sovereign power accredited to the President of India and he or she, as the case may be, is not a citizen of India; or

(b) his father or mother is an enemy alien and the birth occurs in a place then under occupation by the enemy."

4. Amendment of Section 4. In Section 4 of the principal Act, for sub-section (1), the following sub-sections shall be substituted, namely:-

"(1) A person born outside India shall be a citizen of India by descent,-

(a) on or after the 26th day of January, 1950, but before the 10th day of December, 1992, if his father is a citizen of India at the time of his birth; or

(b) on or after the 10th day of December, 1992, if either of his parents is a citizen of India at the time of his birth:

Provided that if the father of a person referred to in clause (a) was a citizen of India by descent only, that person shall not be a citizen of India by virtue of this section unless-

(a) his birth is registered at an Indian consulate within one year of its occurrence or the commencement of this Act, whichever is later, or, with the permission of the Central Government, after the expiry of the said period; or

(b) his father is, at the time of his birth, in service under a Government in India:

Provided further that if either of the parents of a person referred to in clause (b) was a citizen of India by descent only, that person shall not be a citizen of India by virtue of this section, unless-

(a) his birth is registered at an Indian consulate within one year of its occurrence or on or after the 10th day of December, 1992, whichever is later, or, with the permission of the Central Government, after the expiry of the said period; or

(b) either of his parents is, at the time of his birth, in service under a Government in India:

Provided also that on or after the commencement of the Citizenship (Amendment) Act, 2003, a person shall not be a citizen of India by virtue of this section, unless his birth is registered at an Indian consulate in such form and in such manner, as may be prescribed,-

(i) within one year of its occurrence or the commencement of the Citizenship (Amendment) Act, 2003, whichever is later; or

(ii) with the permission of the Central Government, after the expiry of the said period:

Provided also that no such birth shall be registered unless the parents of such person declare, in such form and in such manner as may be prescribed, that the minor does not hold the passport of another country.

(1A) A minor who is a citizen of India by virtue of this section and is also a citizen of any other country shall cease to be a citizen of India if he does not renounce the citizenship or nationality of another country within six months of attaining full age.

5. Amendment of Section 5. In Section 5 of the principal Act,-

(a) for sub-section (1), the following shall be substituted, namely:-

"(1) Subject to the provisions of this section and such other conditions and restrictions as may be prescribed, the Central Government may, on an application made in this behalf, register as a citizen of India any person not being an illegal migrant who is not already such citizen by virtue of the Constitution or of any other provision of this Act if he belongs to any of the following categories, namely:-

(a) a person of Indian origin who is ordinarily resident in India for seven years before making an application for registration;

(b) a person of Indian origin who is ordinarily resident in any country or place outside undivided India;

(c) a person who is married to a citizen of India and is ordinarily resident in India for seven years before making an application for registration;

(d) minor children of persons who are citizens of India;

(e) a person of full age and capacity whose parents are registered as citizens of India under clause (a) of this sub-section or sub-section (1) of Section 6;

(f) a person of full age and capacity who, or either of his parents, was earlier citizen of independent India, and has been residing in India for one year immediately before making an application for registration;

(g) a person of full age and capacity who has been registered as an overseas citizen of India for five years, and who has been residing in India for two years before making an application for registration.

EXPLANATION 1: For the purposes of clauses (a) and (c), an applicant shall be deemed to be ordinarily resident in India if-

(i) he has resided in India throughout the period of twelve months immediately before making an application for registration; and

(ii) he has resided in India during the eight years immediately preceding the said period of twelve months for a period of not less than six years.

EXPLANATION 2: For the purposes of this sub-section, a person shall be deemed to be of Indian origin if he, or either of his parents, was born in undivided India or in such other territory which became part of India after the 15th day of August, 1947."

(b) after sub-section (5), the following sub-section shall be inserted, namely:-

"(6) If the Central Government is satisfied that circumstances exist which render it necessary to grant exemption from the residential requirement under clause (c) of sub-section (1) to any person or a class of persons, it may, for reasons to be recorded in writing, grant such exemption.".

6. Amendment of Section 6. In Section 6 of the principal Act, in sub-section (1), for the words "who is not a citizen of a country specified in the First Schedule", the words "not being an illegal migrant" shall be substituted.

7. Insertion of heading and new Sections 7A, 7B, 7D and 7D. After Section 7 of the principal Act, the following heading and sections shall be inserted, namely:-

OVERSEAS CITIZENSHIP

7A. Registration of overseas citizens.

(1) The Central Government may, subject to such conditions and restrictions including the condition of reciprocity as may be prescribed, on an application made in this behalf, register any person as an overseas citizen of India if-

(a) that person is of Indian origin of full age and capacity who is a citizen of a specified country; or

(b) that person is of full age and capacity who has obtained the citizenship of a specified country on or after the commencement of the Citizenship (Amendment) Act, 2003 and who was a citizen of India immediately before such commencement; or

(c) that person is a minor of a person mentioned in clause (a) or clause (b).

(2) The person registered as an overseas citizen of India under sub-section (1) shall be an overseas citizen of India as from the date on which he is so registered.

(3) No person who has been deprived of his Indian citizenship under this Act shall be registered as an overseas citizen of India under sub-section (1) except by an order of the Central Government.

EXPLANATION. For the purposes of this Section and Sections 7B, 7C and 7D, the expression "person of Indian origin" shall mean a citizen of another country who-

(i) was eligible to become a citizen of India at the time of the commencement of the Constitution;

(ii) belonged to a territory that became part of India after the 15th day of August, 1947; and

(iii) the children and grand-children of a person covered under clauses (i) and (ii), but does not include a person who is or had been at any time a citizen of Pakistan, Bangladesh or such other country as the Central Government may, by notification in the Official Gazette, specify.

7B. Conferment of rights on overseas citizens of India.

(1) Notwithstanding anything contained in any other law for the time being in force, an overseas citizen of India shall be entitled to such rights [other than the rights specified under sub-section (2)] as the Central Government may, by notification in the Official Gazette, specify in this behalf.

(2) An overseas citizen of India shall not be entitled to the rights conferred on a citizen of India-

(a) under article 16 of the Constitution with regard to equality of opportunity in matters of public employment;

(b) under article 58 of the Constitution for election as President;

(c) under article 66 of the Constitution for election of Vice-President;

(d) under article 124 of the Constitution for appointment as a Judge of the Supreme Court;

(e) under article 217 of the Constitution for appointment as a Judge of the High Court;

(f) under Section 16 of the Representation of the People Act, 1950 (43 of 1950) in regard to registration as a voter;

(g) under Sections 3 and 4 of the Representation of the People Act, 1951 (43 of 1951) with regard to the eligibility for being a member of the House of the People or of the Council of States, as the case may be;

(h) under Sections 5, 5A and 6 of the Representation of the People Act, 1951 (43 of 1951) with regard to the eligibility for being a member of the Legislative Assembly or a Legislative Council, as the case may be, of a State;

(i) for appointment to public services and posts in connection with the affairs of the Union or of any State except for appointment in such services and posts as the Central Government may by special order in that behalf specify.

(3) Every notification issued under sub-section (1) shall be laid before each House of Parliament.

7C. Renunciation of overseas citizenship.

(1) If any overseas citizen of India of full age and capacity makes in the prescribed manner a declaration renouncing his overseas citizenship of India, the declaration shall be registered by the Central Government, and upon such registration, that person shall cease to be an overseas citizen of India.

(2) Where a person ceases to be an overseas citizen of India under sub-section (1), every minor child of that person registered as an overseas citizen of India, shall thereupon cease to be an overseas citizen of India.

7D. Cancellation of registration as overseas citizen of India. The Central Government may, by order, cancel the registration granted under sub-section (1) of Section 7A if it is satisfied that-

(a) the registration as an overseas citizen of India was obtained by means of fraud, false representation or the concealment of any material fact; or

(b) the overseas citizen of India has shown disaffection towards the Constitution of India as by law established; or

(c) the overseas citizen of India has, during any war in which India may be engaged, unlawfully traded or communicated with an enemy or been engaged in, or associated with, any business or commercial activity that was to his knowledge carried on in such manner as to assist an enemy in that war; or

(d) the overseas citizen of India has, within five years after registration under sub-section (1) of Section 7A has been sentenced to imprisonment for a term of not less than two years; or

(e) it is necessary so to do in the interest of the sovereignty and integrity of India, the security of India, friendly relations of India with any foreign country, or in the interests of the general public.

8. Amendment of Section 8. In Section 8 of the principal Act,-

(a) in sub-section (1), the words "who is also a citizen or national of another country" shall be omitted;

(b) in the proviso to sub-section (2), after the word "declaration", the words "in the prescribed form and manner" shall be inserted;

(c) sub-section (3) shall be omitted.

9. Amendment of Section 9. In Section 9 of the principal Act, in sub- section (2), for the word "person", the words "citizen of India" shall be substituted.

10. Omission of Sections 11 and 12. Sections 11 and 12 of the principal Act shall be omitted.

11. Amendment of Section 14. In Secion 14 of the principal Act, for the words and figures "Sections 5 and 6", the words, figures and letter "Sections 5, 6 and 7A" shall be substituted.

12. Insertion of new Section 14A. After Section 14 of the principal Act, the following Section shall be inserted, namely:-

"14A. Issue of national identity cards.

(1) The Central Government may compulsorily register every citizen of India and issue national identity card to him.

(2) The Central Government may maintain a National Register of Indian Citizens and for that purpose establish a National Registration Authority.

(3) On and from the date of commencement of the Citizenship (Amendment) Act, 2003, the Registrar General, India, appointed under sub-section (1) of Section 3 of the Registration of Births and Deaths Act, 1969 (18 of 1969) shall act as the National Registration Authority and he shall function as the Registrar General of Citizen Registration.

(4) The Central Government may appoint such other officers and staff as may be required to assist the Registrar General of Citizen Registration in discharging his functions and responsibilities.

(5) The procedure to be followed in compulsory registration of the citizens of India shall be such as may be prescribed.

13. Insertion of new Section 15A. After Section 15 of the principal Act, the following Section shall be inserted, namely:-

"15A. Review.

(1) Any person aggrieved by an order made by the Central Government, may, within thirty days from the date of such order, make an application for review of such order:

Provided that the Central Government may entertain an application after the expiry of the said period of thirty days, if it is satisfied that the applicant was prevented by sufficient cause from making the application in time:

Provided further that an application for a review of an order passed in terms of the provisions of Section 14A shall be disposed of in the manner provided for in the procedure as may be laid down under clause (ia) of sub-section (2) of Section 18.

(2) On receipt of an application under sub-section (1), the Central Government shall, make such order as it deems fit, and the decision of the Central Government on such review shall be final."

14. Amendment of Section 17. In Section 17 of the principal Act,-

(a) for the words "six months", the words "five years" shall be substituted;

(b) for the words "with fine", the words "with fine which may extend to fifty thousand rupees" shall be substituted.

15. Amendment of Section 18. In Section 18 of the principal Act,-

(i) in sub-section (2),-

(a) after clause (a), the following clause shall be inserted, namely:-

"(aa) the form and manner in which a declaration under sub-section (1) of Section 4 shall be made;";

(b) after clause (i), the following clause shall be inserted, namely:-

"(ia) the procedure to be followed in compulsory registration of the citizens of India under sub-section (5) of Section 14A;";

(ii) in sub-section (3), the following proviso shall be inserted, namely:-

"Provided that any rule made in respect of a matter specified in clause (ia) of sub-section (2) may provide that a breach thereof shall be punishable with imprisonment for a term which may extend to three months, or with fine which may extend to five thousand rupees, or with both.".

16. Omission of First Schedule. The First Schedule to the principal Act shall be omitted.

17. Substitution of Second Schedule by a new Schedule. For the Second Schedule to the principal Act, the following Schedule shall be substituted, namely:-

THE SECOND SCHEDULE
OATH OF ALLEGIANCE

[See Sections 5(2) and 6(2)]

I, A/B....................do solemnly affirm (or swear) that I will bear true faith and allegiance to the Constitution of India as by law established, and that I will faithfully observe the laws of India and fulfil my duties as a citizen of India.".

18. Amendment of Third Schedule. In the Third Schedule to the principal Act,-

(a) in the opening portion, the words "who is not a citizen of a country specified in the First Schedule" shall be omitted;

(b) in clause (b), for the words "he has renounced the citizenship of that country in accordance with the law therein in force in that behalf and has notified such renunciation to the Central Government", the words "he undertakes to renounce the citizenship of that country in the event of his application for Indian citizenship being accepted" shall be substituted;

(c) in clause (d),-

(i) for the words "twelve years", the words "fourteen years" shall be substituted;

(ii) for the words "nine years", the words "eleven years" shall be substituted;

(d) in the proviso, in clause (ii), for the words "thirteen years", the words "fifteen years" shall be substituted.

19. Insertion of new Fourth Schedule. After the Third Schedule to the principal Act, the following Schedule shall be inserted, namely:-

THE FOURTH SCHEDULE

[See Section 2(1)(gg)]

1. Australia.
2. Canada.
3. Finland.
4. France.
5. Greece.
6. Ireland.
7. Israei.
8. Italy.
9. Netherlands.
10. New Zealand.
11. Portugal.
12. Republic of Cyprus.
13. Sweden.
14. Switzerland.
15. United Kingdom.
16. United States of America.".

□□□

8

The Citizenship (Amendment) Act, 2005

1. Short title and commencement.

(1) This Act may be called the Citizenship (Amendment) Act, 2005.

(2) It shall be deemed to have come into force on the 28th day of June, 2005.

2. Amendment of Section 2. In Section 2 of the Citizenship Act, 1955 (57 of 1955) (hereinafter referred to as the principal Act), in sub-section (1),-

(a) for clause (ee), the following clause shall be substituted, namely:-

(ee) "overseas citizen of India" means a person registered as an overseas citizen of India by the Central Government under section 7A;

(b) clause (gg) shall be omitted.

3. Amendment of Section 5. In Section 5 of the principal Act, in sub-section (1), in clause (g), for the words "two years", the words "one year"shall be substituted.

4. Substitution of new Section for Section 7A. For Section 7A of the principal Act, the following Section shall be substituted, namely:-

"7A. Registration of overseas citizens of India.-The Central Government may, subject to such conditions and restrictions as may be prescribed, on an application made in this behalf, register as an overseas citizen of India-

(a) any person of full age and capacity,-

(i) who is citizen of another country, but was a citizen of India at the time of, or at any time after, the commencement of the Constitution; or

(ii) who is citizen of another country, but was eligible to become a citizen of India at the time of the commencement of the Constitution; or

(iii) who is citizen of another country, but belonged to a territory that became part of India after the 15th day of August, 1947; or

(iv) who is a child or a grand-child of such a citizen; or

(b) a person, who is a minor child of a person mentioned in clause (a):

Provided that no person, who is or had been a citizen of Pakistan, Bangladesh or such other country as the Central Government may, by notification in the Official Gazette, specify, shall be eligible for registration as an overseas citizen of India.".

5. Omission of Fourth Schedule. The Fourth Schedule to the principal Act shall be omitted.

6. Repeal and saving.

(1) The Citizenship (Amendment) Ordinance, 2005 (Ord. 2 of 2005) is hereby repealed.

(2) Notwithstanding such repeal, anything done or any action taken under the principal Act, as amended by the said Ordinance, shall be deemed to have been done or taken under the principal Act, as amended by this Act.

❑❑❑

9

The Citizenship Act, 1955

[Act No. 57 of Year 1955 Dated 30th December, 1955]

AN ACT to provide for the acquisition and determination of Indian citizenship.

Comment: From the resume of the aforementioned provisions of the Constitution and the Citizenship Act, it becomes clear that whenever any authority is called upon to decide even for the limited purpose of another law, whether a person is or is not a citizen of India, the authority must carefully examine the question and the provisions of the Citizenship Act extracted hereinbefore. Lal Babu Hussain and others, *Petitioners* v. *Electoral Registration Officer*, AIR 1995 SUPREME COURT, 1189.

Be it enacted by Parliament in the Sixth Year of the Republic of India as follows: -

1. Short title. This Act may be called the Citizenship Act, 1955.

2. Interpretation.

(1) In this Act, unless the context otherwise requires,-

(a) "a Government in India" means the Central Government or a State Government.

(b) "citizen" in relation to a country specified in Schedule I, means a person who, under the citizenship or nationality law for the time being in force in that country, is a citizen or national of that country;

(c) "citizenship or nationality law" in relation to a country specified in Schedule I, means an enactment of the Legislature of that country which, at the request of the government of that country, the Central Government may, by notification in the Official Gazette, have declared to be an enactment making provision for the citizenship or nationality of that country:

Provided that no such notification shall be issued in relation to the Union of South Africa except with the previous approval of both Houses of Parliament.

(d) "Indian consulate" means the office of any consular officer of the Government of India where a register of births is kept, or where there is no such office, such office as may be prescribed;

(e) "minor" means a person who has not attained the age of eighteen years;

(f) "person" does not include any company or association or body of individuals, whether incorporated or not;

(g) "prescribed" means prescribed by rules made under this Act;

(h) "undivided India" means India as defined in the Government of India Act, 1935, as originally enacted.

(2) For the purposes of this Act, a person born aboard a registered ship or aircraft, or aboard an unregistered ship or aircraft of the government of any country shall be deemed to have been born in the place in which the ship or aircraft was registered or, as the case may be, in that country.

(3) Any reference in this Act to the status or description of the father of a person at the time of that person's birth shall, in relation to a person born after the death of his father, be construed as a reference to the status or description of the father at the time of the father's death; and where that death occurred before, and the birth occurs after the commencement of this Act, the status or description which would have been applicable to the father had he died after the commencement of this Act shall be deemed to be the status or description applicable to him at the time of his death.

(4) For the purposes of this Act, a person shall be deemed to be of full age if he is not a minor, and of full capacity if he is not of unsound mind.

ACQUISITION OF CITIZENSHIP

3. Citizenship by birth.

[1][(1) Except as provided in sub-section (2), every person born in India :-

(a) on or after the 26th day of January, 1950, but before the commencement of the Citizenship (Amendment) Act, 1986;

(b) on or after such commencement and either of whose parents is a citizen of India at the time of his birth, shall be a citizen of India by birth.]

(2) A person shall not be such a citizen by virtue of this section if at the time of his birth:-

(a) his father possesses such immunity from suits and legal process as is accorded to an envoy of a foreign sovereign power accredited to the President of India and is not a citizen of India; or

(b) his father is an enemy alien and the birth occurs in a place then under occupation by the enemy.

[2][4. Citizenship by descent.

(1) A person born outside India :-

(a) on or after the 26th January, 1950, but before the commencement of the Citizenship (Amendment) Act, 1992, shall be a citizen of India by descent if his father is a citizen of India at the time of his birth; or

(b) on after such commencement, shall be a citizen of India by descent if either of his parents is a citizen of India at the time of his birth:]

Provided that if the father of such a person [3][referred to clause (a)] was a citizen of India by descent only, that person shall not be a citizen of India by virtue of this section unless-

(a) his birth is registered at an Indian consulate within one year of its occurrence or the commencement of this Act, whichever is later, or, with the permission of the Central Government, after the expiry of the said period; or

(b) his father is, at the time of his birth, in service under a Government in India:

[3][Provided further that if either of the parents of such a person referred to in clause (b) was a citizen of India by descent only, that person shall not be a citizen of India by virtue of this section, unless-

(a) his birth is registered at an Indian consulate within one year of its occurrence or the commencement of the Citizenship (Amendment) Act, 1992, whichever is later, or with the permission of the Central Government, after the expiry of the said period; or

(b) either of his parents is, at the time of his birth, in service under a Government in India.

(2) If the Central Government so directs, a birth shall be deemed for the purposes of this section to have been registered with its permission, notwithstanding that its permission was not obtained before the registration.

(3) For the purposes of the proviso to sub-section (1), [4][any person] born outside undivided India who was, or was deemed to be, a citizen of India at the commencement of the Constitution shall be deemed to be a citizen of India by descent only.

5. Citizenship by registration.

(1) Subject to the provisions of this section and such conditions and restrictions as may be prescribed, the prescribed authority may, on application made in this behalf, register as a citizen of India any person who is not already such citizen by virtue of the Constitution or by virtue of any of the other provisions of this Act and belongs to any of the following categories,-

(a) persons of Indian origin who are ordinarily resident in India and have been resident for five years immediately before making an application for registration;

(b) persons of Indian origin who are ordinarily resident in any country or place outside undivided India;

(c) persons who are, or have been, married to citizens of India and are ordinarily resident in India and have been so resident for five years immediately before making an application for registration.

(d) minor children of persons who are citizens of India; and

(e) persons of full age and capacity who are citizens of a country specified in Schedule I:

Provided that in prescribing the conditions and restrictions subject to which persons of any such country may be registered as citizens of India under this clause, the Central Government shall have due regard to the conditions subject to which citizens of India may, by law or practice of that country, become citizens of that country by registration.

EXPLANATION: For the purposes of this sub-section, a person shall be deemed to be of Indian origin if he, or either of his parents, was born in undivided India.

(2) No person being of full age shall be registered as a citizen of India under sub-section (1) until he has taken the oath of allegiance in the form specified in Schedule II.

(3) No person who has renounced, or has been deprived of his, Indian citizenship, or whose Indian citizenship has terminated, under this Act shall be registered as a citizen of India under sub-section (1) except by order of the Central Government.

(4) The Central Government may, if satisfied that there are special circumstances justifying such registration, cause any minor to be registered as a citizen of India.

(5) A person registered under this section shall be a citizen of India by registration as from the date on which he is so registered; and a person registered under the provisions of clause (b)(ii) of Article 6 or Article 8 of the Constitution shall be deemed to be a citizen of India by registration as from the commencement of the Constitution or the date on which he was so registered, whichever may be later.

6. Citizenship by naturalisation.

(1) Where an application is made in the prescribed manner by any person of full age and capacity who is not a citizen of a country specified in Schedule I for the grant of a certificate of naturalisation to him, the Central Government may, if satisfied that the applicant is qualified for naturalisation under the provisions of Schedule III, grant to him, a certificate of naturalisation:

Provided that, if in the opinion of the Central Government, the applicant is a person who has rendered distinguished service to the cause of science, philosophy, art, literature, world peace or human progress generally, it may waive all or any of the conditions specified in Third Schedule III.

(2) The person to whom a certificate of naturalisation is granted under sub-section (1) shall, on taking the oath of allegiance in the form specified in Schedule II, be a citizen of India by naturalisation as from the date on which that certificate is granted.

[5][**6A. Special provisions as to citizenship of persons covered by the Assam Accord**

(1) For the purposes of this section-

(a) "Assam" means the territories included in the State of Assam immediately before the commencement of the Citizenship (Amendment) Act, 1985;

(b) "detected to be a foreigner" means detected to be a foreigner in accordance with the provisions of the Foreigners Act, 1946 (31 of 1946) and the Foreigners (Tribunals) Order, 1964 by a Tribunal constituted under the said Order;

(c) "specified territory" means the territories included in Bangladesh immediately before the commencement of the Citizenship (Amendment) Act, 1985;

(d) a person shall be deemed to be Indian origin, if he, or either of his parents or any of his grandparents was born in India;

(e) a person shall be deemed to have been detected to be a foreigner on the date on which a Tribunal constituted under the Foreigners (Tribunals) Order, 1964 submits its opinion to the effect that he is a foreigner to the officer or authority concerned.

(2) Subject to the provisions of sub-sections (6) and (7), all persons of Indian origin who came before the lst day of January, 1966 to Assam from the specified territory (including such of those whose names were included in the electoral rolls used for the purposes of the General Election to the House of the People held in 1967) and who have been ordinarily resident in Assam since the dates of their entry into Assam shall be deemed to be citizens of India as from the lst day of January, 1966.

(3) Subject to the provisions of sub-sections (6) and (7), every person of Indian origin who-

(a) came to Assam on or after the lst day of January, 1966 but before the 25th day of March, 1971 from the specified territory; and

(b) has, since the date of his entry into Assam, been ordinarily resident in Assam; and

(c) has been detected to be a foreigner;

shall register himself in accordance with the rules made by the Central Government in this behalf under section 18 with such authority (thereafter in this sub-section referred to as the registering authority) as may be specified in such rules and if his name is included in any electoral roll for any Assembly or Parliamentary Constituency in force on the date of such detection, his name shall be deleted therefrom.

EXPLANATION: In the case of every person seeking registration under this sub-section, the opinion of the Tribunal constituted under the Foreigners (Tribunals) Order, 1964 holding such person to be a foreigner, shall be deemed to be sufficient proof of the requirement under clause (c) of this sub-section and if any question arises as to whether such person complies with any other requirement under this sub-section, the registering authority shall -

(i) if such opinion contains a finding with respect to such other requirement, decide the question in conformity with such finding;

(ii) if such opinion does not contain a finding with respect to such other requirement, refer the question to a Tribunal constituted under the said Order having jurisdiction in accordance with such rules as the Central Government may make in this behalf under section 18 and decide the question in conformity with the opinion received on such reference.

(4) A person registered under sub-section (3) shall have, as from the date on which he has been detected to be a foreigner and till the expiry of a period of ten years from that date, the same rights and obligations as a citizen of India (including the right to obtain a passport under the Passport Act, 1967 (15 of 1967) and the obligations connected therewith), but shall not entitled to have his name included in any electoral roll for any Assembly or Parliamentary constituency at any time before the expiry of the said period of ten years.

(5) A person registered under sub-section (3) shall be deemed to be a citizen of India for all purposes as from the date of expiry of a period of ten years from the date on which he has been detected to be a foreigner.

(6) Without prejudice to the provisions of section 8,-

(a) if any person referred to in sub-section (2) submits in the prescribed manner and form and to the prescribed authority within sixty days from the date of commencement of the Citizenship (Amendment) Act, 1985, a declaration that he does not wish to be a citizen of India, such person shall not be deemed to have become a citizen of India under that sub-section;

(b) if any person referred to in sub-section (3) submits in the prescribed manner and form and to the prescribed authority within sixty days from the date of commencement of the Citizenship (Amendment) Act, 1985 for year or from the date on which he has been detected to be a foreigner, whichever is later, a declaration that he does not wish to be governed by the provisions of that sub-section and sub-sections (4) and (5), it shall not be necessary for such person to register himself under sub-section (3).

EXPLANATION: Where a person required to file a declaration under this sub-section does not have the capacity to enter into a contract, such declaration may be filed on his behalf by any person competent under the law for the time being in force, to act in his behalf.

(7) Nothing in sub-sections (2) to (6) shall apply in relation to any person-

(a) who, immediately, before the commencement of the Citizenship (Amendment) Act, 1985, for year is a citizen of India;

(b) who was expelled from India, before the commencement of the Citizenship (Amendment) Act, 1985, for year under the Foreigners Act, 1946 for year.

(8) Save as otherwise expressly provided in this section, the provisions of this section shall have effect notwithstanding anything contained in any other law for the time being in force.]

7. Citizenship by incorporation of territory.

(1) If any territory becomes a part of India, the Central Government may, by order notified in the Official Gazette, specify the persons who shall be citizens of India by reason of their connection with that territory; and those persons shall be citizens of India as from the date to be specified in the order.

TERMINATION OF CITIZENSHIP

8. Renunciation of citizenship.

(1) If any citizen of India of full age and capacity, who is also a citizen or national of another country, makes in the prescribed manner a declaration renouncing his Indian citizenship, the declaration shall be registered by the prescribed authority, and, upon such registration, that person shall cease to be a citizen of India:

Provided that if any such declaration is made during any war in which India may be engaged, registration thereof shall be withheld until the Central Government otherwise directs.

(2) Where [6][a person] ceases to be a citizen of India under sub-section (1) every minor child of that person shall thereupon cease to be a citizen of India:

Provided that any such child may, within one year after attaining full age, make a declaration that he wishes to resume Indian citizenship and shall thereupon again become a citizen of India.

(3) For the purposes of this section, any woman who is, or has been, married shall be deemed to be of full age.

9. Termination of citizenship.

(1) Any citizen of India who by naturalisation, registration or otherwise voluntarily acquires, or has at any time between the 26th January, 1950 and the commencement of this Act voluntarily acquired, the citizenship of another country shall, upon such acquisition or, as the case may be, such commencement, cease to be a citizen of India:

Provided that nothing in this sub-section shall apply to a citizen of India who, during any war in which India may be engaged, voluntarily acquires the citizenship of another country, until the Central Government otherwise directs.

(2) If any question arises as to whether, when or how any person has acquired the citizenship of another country, it shall be determined by such authority, in such manner, and having regard to such rules of evidence, as may be prescribed in this behalf.

10. Deprivation of citizenship.

(1) A citizen of India who is such by naturalisation or by virtue only of clause (c) of Article 5 of the Constitution or by registration otherwise than under clause

(b)(ii) of Article 6 of the Constitution or clause (a) of sub-section (1) of Section 5 of this Act shall cease to be a citizen of India, if he is deprived of that citizenship by an order of the Central Government under this section.

(2) Subject to the provisions of this section, the Central Government may, by order, deprive any such citizen of Indian citizenship, if it is satisfied that-

- (a) the registration or certificate of naturalisation was obtained by means of fraud, false representation or the concealment of any material fact; or
- (b) that citizen has shown himself by act or speech to be disloyal or disaffected towards the Constitution of India as by law established; or
- (c) that citizen has, during any war in which India may be engaged, unlawfully traded or communicated with an enemy or been engaged in, or associated with, any business that was to his knowledge carried on in such manner as to assist an enemy in that war; or
- (d) that citizen has, within five years after registration or naturalisation, been sentenced in any country to imprisonment for a term of not less than two years; or
- (e) that citizen has been ordinarily resident, out of India for a continuous period of seven years, and during that period, has neither been at any time a student of any educational institution in a country outside India or in the service of a Government in India or of an international organisation of which India is a member, not registered annually in the prescribed manner at an Indian consulate his intention to retain his citizenship of India.

(3) The Central Government shall not deprive a person of citizenship under this section unless it is satisfied that it is not conducive to the public good that person should continue to be a citizen of India.

(4) Before making an order under this section, the Central Government shall give the person against whom the order is proposed to be made, notice in writing informing him of the ground on which it is proposed to be made and, if the order is proposed to be made on any of the grounds specified in sub-section (2) other than clause (e) thereof, of his right, upon making application therefor in the prescribed manner, to have his case referred to a committee of inquiry under this section.

(5) If the order is proposed to be made against a person or any of the grounds specified in sub-section (2) other than clause (e) thereof and that person so applies in the prescribed manner, the Central Government shall, and in any other case it may, refer the case to a Committee of Inquiry consisting of a Chairman (being a person who has for at least ten years held a judicial office) and two other members appointed by the Central Government in this behalf.

(6) The Committee of Inquiry shall, on such reference, hold the inquiry in such manner as may be prescribed and submit its report to the Central Government, and the Central Government shall ordinarily be guided by such report in making an order under this section.

SUPPLEMENTAL

11. Commonwealth citizenship. Every person who is a citizen of a Commonwealth country specified in Schedule I shall, by virtue of that citizenship, have the status of a Commonwealth citizen of India.

12. Power to confer rights of Indian citizen on citizens of certain countries.

(1) The Central Government may, by order notified in the Official Gazette, make provisions on a basis of reciprocity for the conferment of all or any of the rights of a citizen of India on the citizens of any country specified in Schedule I.

(2) Any order made under sub-section (1) shall have effect notwithstanding anything inconsistent therewith contained in any law other than the Constitution of India or this Act.

13. Certificate of citizenship in case of doubt. The Central Government may, in such cases as it thinks fit, certify that a person with respect to whose citizenship of India a doubt exists, is a citizen of India; and a certificate issued under this section shall, unless it is proved that it was obtained by means of fraud, false representation or concealment of any material fact, be conclusive evidence that that person was such a citizen on the date thereof, but without prejudice to any evidence that he was such a citizen at an earlier date.

14. Disposal of application under sections 5 and 6.

(1) The prescribed authority or the Central Government may, in its discretion, grant or refuse an application under section 5 or section 6 and shall not be required to assign any reasons for such grant or refusal.

(2) Subject to the provisions of section 15, the decision of the prescribed authority or the Central Government on any such application as aforesaid shall be final and shall not be called in any court.

15. Revision.

(1) Any person aggrieved by an order made under this Act by the prescribed authority or any officer or other authority (other than the Central Government) may, within a period of thirty days from the date of the order, make an application to the Central Government for revision of that order:

Provided that the Central Government may entertain the application after the expiry of the said period of thirty days, if it is satisfied that the applicant was prevented by sufficient cause from making the application in time.

(2) On receipt of any such application under sub-section (1), the Central Government shall, after considering the application of the aggrieved person and any report thereon which the officer or authority making the order may submit, make such order in relation to the application as it deems fit, and the decision of the Central Government shall be final.

16. Delegation of powers. The Central Government may, by order, direct that any power which is conferred on it by any of the provisions of this Act other than those of section 10 and section 18 shall, in such circumstances and under such conditions, if any, as may be specified in the order, be exercisable also by such officer or authority as may be so specified.

17. Offences. Any person who, for the purpose of procuring anything to be done or not to be done under this Act, knowingly makes any representation which is false in a material particular shall be punishable with imprisonment for a term which may extend to six months, or with fine, or with both.

18. Power to make rules.

(1) The Central Government may, by notification in the Official Gazette, make rules to carry out the purposes of this Act.

(2) In particular and without prejudice to the generality of the foregoing power, such rules may provide for-

(a) the registration of anything required or authorised under this Act to be registered, and the conditions and restrictions in regard to such registration;

(b) the forms to be used and the registers to be maintained under this Act;

(c) the administration and taking of oaths of allegiance under this Act, and the time within which, and the manner in which, such oaths shall be taken and recorded;

(d) the giving of any notice required or authorised to be given by any person under this Act;

(e) the cancellation of the registration of, and the cancellation and amendment of certificates of naturalisation relating to, persons deprived of citizenship under this Act, and the delivering up of such certificates for those purposes;

(ee) the manner and form in which and the authority to whom declarations referred to in clauses (a) and (b) of sub-section (6) of section 6A shall be submitted and other matters connected with such declarations;

(f) the registration at Indian consulates of the births and deaths of persons of any class or description born or dying outside India;

(g) the levy and collection of fees in respect of applications, registrations, declarations and certificates under this Act, in respect of the taking of an oath of allegiance, and in respect of the supply of certified or other copies of documents;

(h) the authority to determine the question of acquisition of citizenship of another country, the procedure to be followed by such authority and rules of evidence relating to such cases;

(i) the procedure to be followed by the committees of inquiry appointed under section 10 and the conferment on such committees of any of the powers, rights and privileges of civil courts;

(j) the manner in which applications for revision may be made and the procedure to be followed by the Central Government in dealing with such applications; and

(k) any other matter which is to be, or may be, prescribed under the Act.

(3) In making any rule under this section, the Central Government may provide that breach thereof shall be punishable with fine which may extend to one thousand rupees.

(4) Every rule made under this section shall be laid, as soon as may be after it is made before each House of Parliament, while it is in session, for a total period of thirty days which may be comprised in one session or in two or more successive sessions, and if, before the expiry of the session immediately following the session or the successive sessions aforesaid, both Houses agree in making any modification in the rule or both Houses agree that the rule should not be made, the rule shall thereafter have effect only in such modified form or be of no effect, as the case may be; so, however, that any such modification or annulment shall be without prejudice to the validity of anything previously done under that rule.

19. Repeals. *[Repealed by the Repealing and Amending Act, 1960 (58 of 1960)].*

SCHEDULE I

[Sections 2(1)(b) and 5(1)(e)]

A. The following Commonwealth countries:

1. United Kingdom
2. Canada
3. Commonwealth of Australia
4. New Zealand
5. Union of South Africa
6. Pakistan
7. Ceylon
8. Federation of Rhodesia and Nyasaland
9. Ghana
10. Federation of Malaya
11. Singapore

B. The Republic of Ireland

EXPLANATION: In this Schedule, "United Kingdom" means the United Kingdom of Great Britain and Northern Ireland, and includes the Channel Islands, the Isle of Man and all Colonies; and "Commonwealth of Australia" includes the territories of Papua and the territory of Norfolk Island.

SCHEDULE - II : OATH OF ALLEGIANCE

[Sections 5(2) and 6(2)]

I, A. B. _________ do solemnly affirm (or swear) that I will bear true faith and allegiance to the Constitution of India as by law established, and that I will faithfully observe the laws of India and fulfil my duties as a citizen of India.

SCHEDULE - III : QUALIFICATIONS FOR NATURALISATION

[Section 6(1)]

The qualifications for naturalisation of a person who is not a citizen of a country specified in Schedule I are:-

(a) that he is not a subject or citizen of any country where citizens of India are prevented by law or practice of that country from becoming subjects or citizens or that country by naturalisation;

(b) that, if he is a citizen of any country he has renounced the citizenship of that country in accordance with the law therein in force in that behalf and has notified such renunciation to the Central Government;

(c) that he has either resided in India or been in the service of a Government in India or partly the one and partly the other, throughout the period of twelve months immediately preceding the date of the application;

(d) that during the twelve years immediately preceding the said period of twelve months, he has either resided in India or been in the service of a Government in India, or partly the one and partly the other, for periods amounting in the aggregate to not less than nine years;

(e) that he is of good character;

(f) that he has an adequate knowledge of a language specified in Schedule VIII to the Constitution; and

(g) that in the event of a certificate of naturalisation being granted to him, he intends to reside in India, or to enter into, or continue in, service under a Government in India or under an international organisation of which India is a member or under a society, company or body of persons established in India:

Provided that the Central Government may, if in the special circumstances of any particular case it thinks fit,-

(i) allow a continuous period of twelve months ending not more than six months before the date of the application to be reckoned, for the purposes of clause (c) above, as if it had immediately preceded that date;

(ii) allow periods of residence or service earlier than thirteen years before the date of the application to be reckoned in computing the aggregate mentioned in clause (d) above.

❑❑❑

10

The Constitution (Scheduled Castes) Orders (Second Amendment) Act, 2002

ACT NO. 61 OF 2002 [17TH DECEMBER, 2002]

AN ACT further to amend the Constitution (Scheduled Castes) Order, 1950, the Constitution (Scheduled Castes) (Union Territories) Order, 1951, the Constitution (Jammu and Kashmir) Scheduled Castes Order, 1956, the Constitution (Dadra and Nagar Haveli) Scheduled Castes Order, 1962 and the Constitution (Pondicherry) Scheduled Castes Order, 1964.

Be it enacted by Parliament in the Fifty- third Year of the Republic of India as follows:-

1. Short title. This Act may be called the Constitution (Scheduled Castes) Orders (Second Amendment) Act, 2002.

2. Amendment of Scheduled Castes Orders.

(1) The Schedule to the Constitution (Scheduled Castes) Order, 1950 is hereby amended in the manner and to the extent specified in Schedule I.

(2) The Schedule to the Constitution (Scheduled Castes) (Union Territories) Order, 1951 is hereby amended in the manner and to the extent specified in Schedule II.

(3) The Constitution (Jammu and Kashmir) Scheduled Castes Order, 1956 is hereby amended in the manner and to the extent specified in Schedule III.

(4) The Constitution (Dadra and Nagar Haveli) Scheduled Castes Order, 1962 is hereby amended in the manner and to the extent specified in Schedule IV.

(5) The Constitution (Pondicherry) Scheduled Castes Order, 1964 is hereby amended in the manner and to the extent specified in Schedule V.

❑❑❑

11

The Constitution (Scheduled Tribes) Order (Amendment) Act, 2003

No. 47 of 2003 [19th September, 2003]

AN ACT further to amend the Constitution (Scheduled Tribes) Order, 1950 to modify the list of Scheduled Tribes in the State of Assam.

Be it enacted by Parliament in the Fifty-fourth Year of the Republic of India as follows:-

1. Short title. This Act may be called the Constitution (Scheduled Tribes) Order (Amendment) Act, 2003.

2. Amendment of the Constitution (Scheduled Tribes) Order, 1950. In the Schedule to the Constitution (Scheduled Tribes) Order, 1950, in Part II, Assam -

(i) for the sub-part heading I. "In the autonomous districts", the following shall be substituted, namely:-

"I. In the autonomous districts of Karbi Anglong and North Cachar Hills";

(ii) for the sub-part heading "II. In the State of Assam excluding the autonomous districts", the following shall be substituted, namely:-

"II. In the State of Assam including the Bodoland Territorial Areas District and excluding the autonomous districts of Karbi Anglong and North Cachar Hills."

❑❑❑

12

The Constitution (Scheduled Tribes) Order Amendment Act, 2006

No. 48 of 2006 [12th December, 2006]

AN ACT further to amend the Constitution (Scheduled Tribes) Order, 1950 to modify the list of Scheduled Tribes in the State of Bihar.

Be it enacted by Parliament in the Fifty-seventh Year of the Republic of India as follows:-

1. Short title. This Act may be called the Constitution (Scheduled Tribes) Order Amendment Act, 2006.

2. Amendment of the Constitution (Scheduled Tribes) Order, 1950, as amended by the Scheduled Castes and Scheduled Tribes Order (Amendment) Act, 1976. In the Constitution (Scheduled Tribes) Order, 1950, as amended by the Scheduled Castes and Scheduled Tribes Order (Amendment) Act, 1976, in the Schedule, in Part III relating to Bihar, for item 22 (since renumbered as item 21), as appearing in the Hindi version of the said Act, the following shall be substituted, namely:- “21. Lohara, Lohra”

❑❑❑

13

The Election Laws (Amendment) Act, 2003

ACT NO. 24 OF 2003 [22ND MARCH, 2003]

AN ACT further to amend the Representation of the People Act, 1951 and the Indian Penal Code.

Be it enacted by Parliament in the Fifty- fourth Year of the Republic of India as follows:-

CHAPTER - I : PRELIMINARY

1. Short title and commencement.

(1) This Act may be called the Election Laws (Amendment) Act, 2003 .

(2) It shall come into force on such date as the Central Government may, by notification in the Official Gazette, appoint. CHAPTER I. AMENDMENT TO THE REPRESENTATION OF THE PROPLE ACT, 1951; CHAPTER II. AMENDMENT TO THE REPRESENTATION OF THE PEOPLE ACT, 1951.

2. Amendment of Section 59. In the Representation of the People Act, 1951 (43 of 1951) (hereafter in this Chapter referred to as the principal Act), in Section 59, for the words, "and no votes shall be received by proxy", the words and, "save as expressl provided by this Act, no votes shall be received by proxy" shall be substituted.

3. Substitution of new Section for Section 60.- For Section 60 of the principal Act, the following Section shall be substituted, namely:-"

60. Special procedure for voting by certain classes of persons.- Without prejudice to the generality of the provisions contained in Section 59, provision may be made, by rules made under this Act, for enabling-

(a) any of the persons as is referred to in clause (a) or clause (b) of sub-section (8) of Section 20 of the Representation of the People Act, 1950 (43 of 1950) (hereafter in this section referred to as the 1950 Act) to give his vote either in person or by postal ballot or by proxy, and not in any other manner, at an election in a constituency where poll is taken;

(b) any of the following persons to give his vote either in person or by postal ballot, and not in any other manner, at an election in a constituency where a poll is taken, namely:-

(i) any person as is referred to in clause (c) or clause (d) of sub-section (8) of Section 20 of the 1950-Act;

(ii) the wife of any such person to whom the provisions of sub-section (3) of Section 20 of the 1950-Act apply and such wife being ordinarily residing with that person in terms of sub-section (6) of that section;

(c) any person belonging to a class of persons notified by the Election Commission in consultation with the Government to give his vote by postal ballot and not in any other manner, at an election in a constituency where a poll is taken subject to the fu filment of such requirements as may be specified in those rules;

(d) any person subjected to preventive detention under any law for the time being in force to give his vote by postal ballot, and not in any other manner, at an election in a constituency where a poll is taken, subject to the fulfilment of such requireme ts as may be specified in those rules."

4. Amendment of Section 62. In Section 62 of the principal Act, after sub-section (5), the following sub-section shall be inserted, namely:-

"(6) Nothing contained in sub-sections (3) and (4) shall apply to a person who has been authorised to vote as proxy for an elector under this Act in so far as he votes as a proxy for such elector."

CHAPTER - III : AMENDMENT TO THE INDIAN PENAL CODE

5. Amendment of Section 171D. In Section 171D of the Indian Penal Code (43 of 1860), the following proviso shall be inserted at the end, namely:-

"Provided that nothing in this section shall apply to a person who has been authorised to vote as proxy for an elector under any law for the time being in force insofar as he votes as a proxy for such elector."

❏❏❏

14

The Election Laws (Extension to Sikkim) Act, 1976

No.10 Of 1976 [25th January, 1976]

AN ACT to provide for the extension of the Representation of the People Act, 1950 and the Representation of the People Act, 1951, to the State of Sikkim.

Be it enacted by Parliament in the Twenty-sixth Year of the Republic of India as follows:-

1. Extension and amendment of election laws.

(1) The Acts mentioned in the Schedule are hereby extended to, and shall be in force in, the State of Sikkim.

(2) With effect from the commencement of this Act, the Acts mentioned in the Schedule shall be amended as specified therein.

(3) Any reference in the Acts mentioned in the Schedule to a law not in force, or to a functionary not in existence, in the State of Sikkim shall be construed as a reference to the corresponding law in force, or to the corresponding functionary in existence, in that State;

Provided that if any question arises as to who such corresponding functionary is, or if there is no such corresponding functionary, the Central Government shall decide as to who such functionary will be and the decision of the Central Government shall be final.

2. Repeal and saving.

(1) The Election Laws (Extension to Sikkim) Ordinance, 1975 (9 of 1975), is hereby repealed.

(2) Notwithstanding such repeal, anything done or any action taken under or by virtue of the said Ordinance shall be deemed to have been done or taken under or by virtue of this Act.

SCHEDULE : THE REPRESENTATION OF THE PEOPLE ACT, 1950

THE SCHEDULE

[See section 2]

THE REPRESENTATION OF THE PEOPLE ACT, 1950

[43 of 1950]

Section 7A. After Section 7, insert:—

"7A. Total number of seats in the Legislative Assembly of Sikkim and Assembly constituencies.

(1) Notwithstanding anything contained in Section 7, in the Legislative Assembly of the State of Sikkim [deemed under the Constitution (Thirty-sixth Amendment) Act, 1975 to be the Legislative Assembly of that State duly constituted], the total number of seats to be filled by persons chosen by direct election from Assembly constituencies shall be 32.

(2) Every Assembly constituency referred to in sub-section (1) shall be a single-member constituency.

(3) In the Legislative Assembly so deemed to be duly constituted, the extent of each constituency and the reservation of seats shall be as provided for immediately before the commencement of the Constitution (Thirty-sixth Amendment) Act, 1975."

Section 25A. In Part III, after Section 25, insert:

"25A. Conditions of registration as elector in Sangha constituency in Sikkim. Notwithstanding anything contained in sections 15 and 19, for the Sangha constituency in the State of Sikkim, only the Sanghas belonging to monasteries, recognised for the purpose of the elections held in Sikkim in April, 1974, for forming the Assembly for Sikkim, shall be entitled to be registered in the electoral roll, and the said electoral roll shall, subject to the provisions of sections 21 to 25, be prepared or revised in such manner as may be directed by the Election Commission, in consultation with the Government of Sikkim."

The First Schedule. In the First Schedule, under the heading "I.STATES", after serial number 15 and the entries relating thereto, insert:—

"**15A.** Sikkim.. .. .. .. 1 .."

THE REPRESENTATION OF THE PEOPLE ACT, 1951
[43 of 1951]

Section 4. In Section 4, omit "and" at the end of clause (cc) and after that clause, insert:—

"(ccc) in the case of the seat allotted to the State of Sikkim, he is an elector for the Parliamentary constituency for Sikkim;".

Section 5A. After Section 5, insert:—

"5A. Qualifications for membership of Legislative Assembly of Sikkim. Notwithstanding anything contained in Section 5, a person shall not be qualified to be chosen to fill a seat in the Legislative Assembly of Sikkim (deemed to be the Legislative Assembly of that State duly constituted under the Constitution) unless-

(a) In the case of a seat reserved for Sikkimese of Bhutia-Lepcha origin, he is a person either of Bhutia or Lepcha origin and is an elector for an Assembly constituency in the State other than the constituency reserved for the Sanghas;

(b) In the case of a seat reserved for Sikkimese of Nepali origin, he is a person of Nepali origin and is an elector for any Assembly constituency in the State;

(c) In the case of a seat reserved for Scheduled Castes, he is a member of any of the castes specified in the Representation of Sikkim Subjects Act, 1974 and is an elector for any Assembly constituency in the State; and

(d) In the case of a seat reserved for Sanghas, he is an elector of the Sangha constituency."

Section 12A. After Section 12, insert:—

"12A. Notification for election to fill the seat allotted to the State of Sikkim in the Council of States. For the purpose of filling for the first time the seat allotted to the State of Sikkim by the Constitution (Thirty-sixth Amendment) Act, 1975 in the Council of States, the President shall, by a notification published in the Gazette of India, on such date as may be recommended by Election Commission, call upon the elected members of the Legislative Assembly of the State of Sikkim to elect a member in accordance with the provisions of this Act and of the rules and orders made thereunder and the election so held shall for all purposes and intent be deemed to have been held under Section 12."

Section 14A. After Section 14, insert:—

"14A. Notification for electing the representative of the State of Sikkim to the existing House of the People. For the purpose of electing a representative of the State of Sikkim to the House of the People, specified in the clause (e) of article 371F of the Constitution, the Election Commission shall call upon the members of the Legislative Assembly of the State of Sikkim to elect the representative in accordance with such of the provisions of this Act, and the rules and orders made thereunder, as are applicable to the election of the members of the Council of States."

Section 33. In Section 33, after sub-section (1), insert:—

"(1A) Notwithstanding anything contained in sub-section (1), for election to the Legislative Assembly of Sikkim (deemed to be the Legislative Assembly of that State duly constituted under the Constitution), the nomination paper to be delivered to the returning officer shall be in such form and manner as may be prescribed:

Provided that the said nomination paper shall be subscribed by the candidate as assenting to the nomination, and-

(a) In the case of a seat reserved for Sikkimese of Bhutia-Lepcha origin, also by at least twenty electors of the constituency as proposers and twenty electors of the constituency as seconders;

(b) In the case of a seat reserved for Sanghas, also by at least twenty electors of the constituency as proposers and at least twenty electors of the constituency as seconders;

(c) In the case of a seat reserved for Sikkimese of Nepali origin, by an elector of the constituency as proposer:

Provided further that no nomination paper shall be delivered to the returning officer on a day which is a public holiday.".

Section 34. In Section 34, in sub-section (2), for "under sub-section (1) of the Section 33", substitute "under sub-section (1) or, as the case may be, sub-section (1A) of Section 33".

Section 35. In Section 35, for "under sub-section (1)", substitute "under sub-section (1) or, as the case may be, sub-section (1A)".

❒❒❒

15

The Emblems and Names (Prevention of Improper Use) Act, 1950

AN ACT to prevent the improper use of certain emblems and names for professional and commercial purposes.

Be it enacted by Parliament as follows:

1. Short title, extent, application and commencement.

(1) This Act may be called the Emblems and Names (Prevention of Improper Use) Act, 1950.

(2) It extends to the whole of India, and also applies to citizens of India outside India.

(3) It shall come into force on such **1[1]** [dates] as the Central Government may, by notification in the Official Gazette, appoint.

2. Definition. In this Act, unless the context otherwise requires,

(a) *emblem* means any emblem, seal, flag, insignia, coat-of-arms or pictorial representation specified in the Schedule;

(b) *competent authority* means any authority competent under any law for the time being in force to register any company, firm or other body of persons or any trade mark or design or to grant a patent;

(c) *name* includes any abbreviation of a name.

3. Prohibition of improper use of certain emblems and names. Notwithstanding anything contained in any law for the time being in force, no person shall, except in such cases and under such conditions as may be prescribed by the Central Government, use, or continue to use, for the purpose of any trade, business, calling or profession, or in the title of any patent, or in any trade mark or design, any name or emblem specified in the

Schedule or any colourable imitation thereof without the previous permission of the Central Government or of such officer of Government as may be authorised in this behalf by the Central Government.

4. Prohibition of registration of certain companies, etc.

(1) Notwithstanding anything contained in any law for the time being in force, no competent authority shall,

(a) register any company, firm or other body of persons which bears any name; or

(b) register a trade mark or design which bears any emblem or name; or

(c) grant a patent in respect of an invention which bears a title containing any emblem or name, if the use of such name or emblem is in contravention of Section 3.

(2) If any question arises before a competent authority whether any emblem is an emblem specified in the Schedule or a colourable imitation thereof, the competent authority, may refer the question to the Central Government, and the decision of the Central Government thereon shall be final.

5. Penalty. Any person who contravenes the provisions of Section 3 shall be punishable with fine which may extend to five hundred rupees.

6. Previous sanction for prosecution. No prosecution for any offence punishable under this Act shall be instituted, except with the previous sanction of the Central Government or of any officer authorised in this behalf by general or special order of the Central Government.

7. Savings. Nothing in this Act shall exempt any person from any suit or other proceedings which might, apart from this Act, be brought against him.

8. Power of the Central Government to amend the Schedule. The Central Government may, by notification in the Official Gazette, add to or alter the Schedule, and any such addition or alteration shall have effect as if it had been made by this Act.

9. Power to make rules. The Central Government may, by notification in the Official Gazette, make rules to carry out the purposes of this Act.

THE SCHEDULE

[*See* Sections 2 (a) and 3]

1. The name, emblem or official seal of the United Nations Organisation.
2. The name, emblem or official seal of the World Health Organisation.
3. The Indian National Flag.
4. The name, emblem or official seal of the Government of India or of any State, or any other insignia or coat-of-arms used by any such Government or by a Department of any such Government.
5. The emblems of the St. John Ambulance Association (India), and the St. John Ambulance Brigade (India), consisting of the device of a white eight pointed cross embellished in the four principal angles, whether or not the device is surrounded or accompanied by concentric circles or other decoration or by lettering.
6. The name, emblem or official seal of the President, Governor, Sadar-i-Riyasat or Republic or Union of India.
7. Any name which may suggest or be calculated to suggest -
   (i) the patronage of the Government of India or the Government of a State; or
   (ii) connection with any local authority or any corporation or body constituted by the Government under any law for the time being in force.
8. The name, emblem or official seal of the United Nations Educational, Scientific and Cultural Organisation.
9. The name or pictorial representation of Rashtrapati, Rashtrapati Bhavan, Raj Bhavan.
   9-A. The name of pictorial representation of Mahatma Gandhi, Pandit Jawaharlal Nehru, Chhatrapati Shivaji Maharaj or the Prime Minister of India or the words Gandhi, Nehru or Shivaji, except the pictorial use thereof on calendars where only the names of the manufacturers and printers of the calendars are given and the calendars are not used for advertising goods.
10. The medals, badges or decorations instituted by the Government from time to time or the miniatures or replicas of such medals, badges or decorations or the names of such medals, badges or decorations or of the miniatures or replicas thereof.
11. The name, emblem or official seal of the International Civil Aviation Organisation.
12. The word Interpol which is an integral part of the International Criminal Police Organisation.
13. The name, emblem or official seal of the World Meteorological Organisation.
14. The name, emblem of the Tuberculosis Association of India.

15. The name, emblem and official seal of the International Atomic Agency.
16. The names Ashoka Chakra or Dharma Chakra or the pictorial representation of Ashoka Chakra as used in the India National Flag or in the official seal or emblem of the Government of India or of any State Government or of a Department of any such Government.
17. The name of the Parliament or the Legislature of any State, or the Supreme Court, or the High Court of any State, or the Central Secretariat, or the Secretariat of any State Government or any other Government Office or the pictorial representation of any building occupied by any of the aforesaid institutions.
18. The name and emblem of the Rama Krishna Math and Ramakrishna Mission consisting of a Swan floating on waters, with a lotus in the foreground and the rising sun in the background, the whole being encircled by a hooded serpent, with the words superimposed on the bottom portion.
19. The names and emblems of the Sri Sarada Math and Ramakrishna Sarada Mission consisting of a Swan (facing right) floating on water, with a Lotus in the foreground and the rising sun in the background, the whole being encircled by a wild serpent (facing right) with the words superimposed on the bottom portion.
20. The name of 'The Bharat Scouts and Guides' with its 'Emblem'.
21. The name and emblem of the International Olympic Committee consisting of five interlaced rings.

❑❑❑

16

The Government of Part C States Act, 1951

The Government of Part C States Act, 1951. Act No. 49 of 1951. Repealed by the States Reorganization Act, 1956 (37 of 1956), s. 130 (w.e.f. 1st November, 1956).

❑❑❑

17

The Government of Union Territories Act, 1963

ACT NO. 20 OF 1963 [10TH MAY, 1963]

AN ACT to provide for Legislative Assemblies and Councils of Ministers for certain Union territories and for certain other matters.

Be it enacted by Parliament in the Fourteenth Year of the Republic of India as follows:—

PART - I : PRELIMINARY

1. Short title and commencement.

(1) This Act may be called the Government of Union Territories Act, 1963.

(2) It shall come into force on such date[1] as the Central Government may, by notification in the Official Gazette, appoint:

> [2][*Provided that it shall come into force in the Union territory of Mizoram on such date, being a date not earlier than the date of commencement of the Government of Union Territories (Amendment) Act, 1971 (83 of 1971), as the Central Government may, by notification in the Official Gazette, appoint:*]

> [3][*Provided further that it shall come into force in the Union territory of Arunachal Pradesh on such date, being a date not earlier than the date of commencement of the Government of Union Territories (Amendment) Act, 1975 (29 of 1975), as the Central Government may, by notification in the Official Gazette, appoint:*]

> [4][*Provided also that, subject to the preceding provisos,*] *different dates* may be appointed for different provisions of this Act and for different Union territories and any reference in*

any such provision to the commencement of this Act shall be construed as a reference to the coming into force of that provision.

2. Definitions and interpretation.

(1) In this Act, unless the context otherwise requires,—

(a) "Administrator" means the administrator of [5][the Union territory] appointed by the President under artcle 239;

(b) "article" means an article of the Constitution;

(c) "assembly constituency" means a constituency provided under this Act for the purpose of elections to the Legislative Assembly of [5][the Union territory] ;

(d) "Election Commission" means the Election Commission appointed by the President under article 324;

(e) "Judicial Commissioner" includes an Additional Judicial Commissioner;

(f) "scheduled castes" in relation to [5][the Union territory] mean such castes, races or tribes or parts of or groups within such castes, races or tribes as are deemed under article 341 to be scheduled castes in relation to that Union territory;

(g) "scheduled tribes" in relation to [5][the Union territory] mean such tribes or tribal communities or parts of or groups within such tribes or tribal communities as are deemed under article 342 to be scheduled tribes in relation to that Union territory;

[6][(h) "Union territory" means the Union territory of Pondicherry.]

(2) Any reference in this Act to laws made by Parliament shall be construed as including a reference to Ordinances promulgated by the President under article 123 and a reference to Regulations made by the President under article 240.

PART - II : LEGISLATIVE ASSEMBLIES

3. Legislative Assemblies for Union territories and their composition.

(1) There shall be a Legislative Assembly for each Union territory.

[7][(2) The total number of seats in the Legislative Assembly of [6][the Union territory] to be filled by persons chosen by direct election shall be thirty.]

(3) The Central Government may nominate not more than three persons, not being persons in the service of Government, to be members of the Legislative Assembly of [6][the Union territory].

[6][(4) Seats shall be reserved for the Scheduled Castes in the Legislative Assembly of the Union territory.]

(5) The number of seats reserved for the scheduled castes or the scheduled tribes in the Legislative Assembly [8][of [6][the Union territory]] under sub-section (4) shall bear, as nearly as may be, the same proportion to the total number of seats in the Assembly as the population of the scheduled castes in the Union territory or of the scheduled tribes in the Union territory, as the case may be,

in respect of which seats are so reserved, bears to the total population of the Union territory.

[9]['*EXPLANATION.* In this sub-section, the expression "population" means the population as ascertained at the last preceding census of which the relevant figures have been published.

Provided that the reference in this Explanation to the last preceding census of which the relevant figures have been published shall, until the relevant figures for the first census taken after the year 2000 have been published, be construed as a reference to the 1971 census.']

[10][(6) Notwithstanding anything in sub-section (4), the reservation of seats for the Scheduled Castes in the Legislative Assembly of the Union territory shall cease to have effect on the same date on which the reservation of seats for the Scheduled Castes in the House of the People shall cease to have effect under article 334:

Provided that nothing in this sub-section shall affect any representation in the Legislative Assembly of the Union territory until the dissolution of the then existing Assembly.]

4. Qualification for membership of Legislative Assembly. A person shall not be qualified to be chosen to fill a seat in the Legislative Assembly of [10][the Union territory] unless he-

(a) is a citizen of India and makes and subscribes before some person authorised in that behalf by the Election Commission an oath or affirmation according to the form set out for the purpose in the First Schedule;

(b) is not less than twenty-five years of age; and

(c) possesses such other qualifications as may be prescribed in that behalf by or under any law.

5. Duration of Legislative Assemblies. The Legislative Assembly of [10][the Union territory], unless sooner dissolved, shall continue for five years from the date appointed for its first meeting and no longer, and the expiration of the said period of five years shall operate as a dissolution of the Assembly:

Provided that the said period may, while a Proclamation of Emergency issued under clause (1) of Article 352 is in operation, be extended by the President by order for a period not exceeding one year at a time and not extending in any case beyond a period of six months after the Proclamation has ceased to operate.

6. Sessions of Legislative Assembly, prorogation and dissolution.

(1) The Administrator shall, from time to time, summon the Legislative Assembly to meet at such time and place as he thinks fit, but six months shall not intervene between its last sitting in one session and the date appointed for its first sitting in the next session.

(2) The Administrator may, from time to time,–

(a) prorogue the Assembly;

(b) dissolve the Assembly.

7. Speaker and Deputy Speaker of Legislative Assembly.

(1) Every Legislative Assembly shall, as soon as may be, choose two members of the Assembly to be respectively Speaker and Deputy Speaker thereof and, so often as the office of Speaker or Deputy Speaker becomes vacant, the Assembly shall choose another member to be Speaker or Deputy Speaker, as the case may be.

(2) A member holding office as Speaker or Deputy Speaker of an Assembly–

(a) shall vacate his office if he ceases to be a member of the Assembly;

(b) may at any time by writing under his hand addressed, if such member is the Speaker, to the Deputy Speaker, and if such member is the Deputy Speaker, to the Speaker, resign his office;

(c) may be removed from his office by a resolution of the Assembly passed by a majority of all the then members of the Assembly:

Provided that no resolution for the purpose of clause (c) shall be moved unless at least fourteen days' notice has been given of the intention to move the resolution:

Provided further that whenever the Assembly is dissolved, the Speaker shall not vacate his office until immediately before the first meeting of the Assembly after the dissolution.

(3) While the office of Speaker is vacant, the duties of the office shall be performed by the Deputy Speaker or, if the office of Deputy Speaker is also vacant, by such member of the Assembly as may be determined by the rules of procedure of the Assembly.

(4) During the absence of the Speaker from any sitting of the Assembly, the Deputy Speaker, or, if he is also absent, such person as may be determined by the rules of procedure of the Assembly, or, if no such person is present, such other person as may be determined by the Assembly, shall act as Speaker.

(5) There shall be paid to the Speaker and the Deputy Speaker of the Legislative Assembly such salaries and allowances as may be respectively fixed by the Legislative Assembly of the Union territory by law and, until provision in that behalf is so made, such salaries and allowances as the Administrator may, with the approval of the President, by order determine.

8. Speaker or Deputy Speaker not to preside while a resolution for his removal from office is under consideration.

(1) At any sitting of the Legislative Assembly, while any resolution for the removal of the Speaker from his office is under consideration, the Speaker, or while any resolution for the removal of the Deputy Speaker from his office is under consideration, the Deputy Speaker, shall not, though he is present, preside and the provisions of sub-section (4) of Section 7 shall apply in relation to every such sitting as they apply in relation to a sitting from which the Speaker or, as the case may be, the Deputy Speaker is absent.

(2) The Speaker shall have the right to speak in, and otherwise to take part in the proceedings of, the Legislative Assembly while any resolution for his removal

from office is under consideration in the Assembly and shall, notwithstanding anything in Section 12, be entitled to vote only in the first instance on such resolution or on any other matter during such proceedings but not in the case of an equality of votes.

9. Right of Administrator to address and send messages to Legislative Assembly.

(1) The Administrator may address the Legislative Assembly and may for that purpose require the attendance of members.

(2) The Administrator may also send messages to the Assembly whether with respect to a Bill then pending in the Assembly or otherwise, and when a message is so sent, the Assembly shall with all convenient despatch consider any matter required by the message to be taken into consideration.

10. Rights of Ministers as respects Legislative Assembly. Every Minister shall have the right to speak in, and otherwise to take part in the proceedings of, the Legislative Assembly of the Union territory, and to speak in, and otherwise to take part in the proceedings of, any committee of the Legislative Assembly of which he may be named a member, but shall not by virtue of this Section be entitled to vote.

11. Oath or affirmation by members. Every member of the Legislative Assembly of [11][the Union territory] shall, before taking his seat, make and subscribe before the Administrator, or some person appointed in that behalf by him, an oath or affirmation according to the form set out for the purpose in the First Schedule.

12. Voting in Assembly, power of Assembly to act notwithstanding vacancies and quorum.

(1) Save as otherwise provided in this Act, all questions at any sitting of the Legislative Assembly of [11][the Union territory] shall be determined by a majority of votes of the members present and voting other than the Speaker or person acting as such.

(2) The Speaker or person acting as such shall not vote in the first instance but shall have and exercise a casting vote in the case of an equality of votes.

(3) The Legislative Assembly of [11][the Union territory] shall have power to act notwithstanding any vacancy in the membership thereof, and any proceedings in the Legislative Assembly of a [11][the Union territory] shall be valid notwithstanding that it is discovered subsequently that some person who was not entitled so to do, sat or voted or otherwise took part in the proceedings.

(4) The quorum to constitute a meeting of the Legislative Assembly of [11][the Union territory] shall be one-third of the total number of members of the Assembly.

(5) If at any time during a meeting of the Legislative Assembly of [11][the Union territory] there is no quorum, it shall be the duty of the Speaker, or person acting as such, either to adjourn the Assembly or to suspend the meeting until there is a quorum.

13. Vacation of seats.

(1) No person shall be a member both of Parliament and of the Legislative Assembly of [11][the Union territory] and if a person is chosen a member both of Parliament

and of such Assembly, then, at the expiration of such period as may be specified in the rules made by the President, that person's seat in Parliament shall become vacant, unless he has previously resigned his seat in the Legislative Assembly of the Union territory.

(2) If a member of the Legislative Assembly of [11][the Union territory]--

(a) becomes subject to any disqualification mentioned in [12][Section 14 or Section 14A] for membership of the Assembly, or

(b) resigns his seat by writing under his hand addressed to the Speaker, his seat shall thereupon become vacant.

(3) If for a period of sixty days a member of the Legislative Assembly of [11][the union territory] is without permission of the Assembly absent from all meetings thereof, the Assembly may declare his seat vacant:

Provided that in computing the said period of sixty days, no account shall be taken of any period during which the Assembly is prorogued or is adjourned for more than four consecutive days.

14. Disqualifications for membership.

(1) A person shall be disqualified for being chosen as, and for being, a member of the Legislative Assembly of [13][the Union territory]--

(a) if he holds any office of profit under the Government of India or the Government of any State or the Government of [13][the Union territory] other than an office declared by law made by Parliament or by the Legislative Assembly of the Union territory not to disqualify its holder; or

(b) if he is for the time being disqualified for being chosen as, and for being, a member of either House of Parliament under the provisions of sub-clause (b), sub- clause (c) or sub-clause (d) of clause (1) of article 102 or of any law made in pursuance of that article.

(2) For the purposes of this section, a person shall not be deemed to hold an office of profit under the Government of India or the Government of any State or the Government of [13][the Union territory] by reason only that he is a Minister either for the Union or for such State or Union territory.

(3) If any question arises as to whether a member of the Legislative Assembly of [13][the Union territory] has become disqualified for being such a member under the provisions of sub-section (1), the question shall be referred for the decision of the President and his decision shall be final.

(4) Before giving any decision on any such question, the President shall obtain the opinion of the Election Commission and shall act according to such opinion.

[14][**14A. Disqualification on ground of defection for being a member.** The provisions of the Tenth Schedule to the Constitution shall, subject to the necessary modifications (including modifications for construing references therein to the Legislative Assembly of a State, article 188, article 194 and article 212 as references, respectively, to the Legislative Assembly of [13][the Union territory], Section 11, Section 16 and Section 37 of

this Act), apply to and in relation to the members of the Legislative Assembly of [13][the Union territory] as they apply to and in relation to the members of the Legislative Assembly of a State, and accordingly,—

(a) the said Tenth Schedule as so modified shall be deemed to form part of this Act; and

(b) a person shall be disqualified for being a member of the Legislative Assembly of [13][the Union territory] if he is so disqualified under the said Tenth Schedule as so modified.]

15. Penalty for sitting and voting before making oath or affirmation or when not qualified or when disqualified. If a person sits or votes as a member of the Legislative Assembly of [13][the Union territory] before he has complied with the requirements of Section 11 or when he knows that he is not qualified or that he is disqualified for membership thereof, he shall be liable in respect of each day on which he so sits or votes to a penalty of five hundred rupees to be recovered as a debt due to the Union.

16. Powers, privileges, etc., of members.

(1) Subject to the provisions of this Act and to the rules and standing orders regulating the procedure of the Legislative Assembly, there shall be freedom of speech in the Legislative Assembly of [13][the Union territory].

(2) No member of the Legislative Assembly of [13][the Union territory] shall be liable to any proceedings in any court in respect of anything said or any vote given by him in the Assembly or any committee thereof, and no person shall be so liable in respect of the publication by or under the authority of such Assembly of any report, paper, votes or proceedings.

(3) In other respects, the powers, privileges and immunities of the Legislative Assembly of [13][the Union territory] and of the members and the committees thereof shall be such as are for the time being enjoyed by the House of the People and its members and committees.

(4) The provisions of sub-sections (1), (2) and (3) shall apply in relation to persons who by virtue of this Act have the right to speak in, and otherwise to take part in the proceedings of,. the Legislative Assembly of [13][the Union territory] or any committee thereof as they apply in relation to members of that Assembly.

17. Salaries and allowances of members. Members of the Legislative Assembly of [13][the Union territory] shall be entitled to receive such salaries and allowances as may from time to time be determined by the Legislative Assembly of the Union territory by law and, until provision in that behalf is so made, such salaries and allowances as the Administrator may, with the approval of the President, by order determine.

18. Extent of legislative power.

(1) Subject to the provisions of this Act, the Legislative Assembly of [13][the Union territory] may make laws for the whole or any part of the Union territory with respect to any of the matters enumerated in the State List or the Concurrent List in the Seventh Schedule to the Constitution in so far as any such matter is applicable in relation to Union territories.

(2) Nothing in sub-section (1) shall derogate from the powers conferred on Parliament by the Constitution to make laws with respect to any matter for [13][the Union territory] or any part thereof.

19. Exemption of property of the Union from taxation. The property of the Union shall, save in so far as Parliament may by law otherwise provide, be exempted from all taxes imposed by or under any law made by the Legislative Assembly of [13][the Union territory] or by or under any other law in force in [13][the Union territory]:

Provided that nothing in this section shall, until Parliament by law otherwise provides, prevent any authority within [13][the Union territory] from levying any tax on any property of the Union to which such property was immediately before the commencement of the Constitution liable or treated as liable, so long as that tax continues to be levied in that Union territory.

20. Restrictions on laws passed by Legislative Assembly with respect to certain matters.

[15][1] The provisions of article 286, article 287 and article 288 shall apply in relation to any law passed by the Legislative Assembly of [13][the Union territory] with respect to any of the matters referred to in those articles as they apply in relation to any law passed by the Legislature of a State with respect to those matters.

[16][(2) The provisions of article 304 shall, with the necessary modifications, apply in relation to any law passed by the Legislative Assembly of [13][the Union territory] with respect to any of the matters referred to in that article as they apply in relation to any law passed by the Legislature of a State with respect to those matters.]

[17][**21. Inconsistency between laws made by Parliament and laws made by Legislative Assembly.** If any provision of a law made by the Legislative Assembly of [13][the Union territory] with respect to any matter enumerated in the State List in the Seventh Schedule to the Constitution is repugnant to any provision of a law made by Parliament with respect to that matter, whether passed before or after the law made by the Legislative Assembly of the Union territory, or, if any provision of a law made by the Legislative Assembly of [13][the Union territory] with respect to any matter enumerated in the Concurrent List in the Seventh Schedule to the Constitution is repugnant to any provision of any earlier law, other than a law made by the Legislative Assembly of the Union territory, with respect to that matter, then, in either case, the law made by Parliament, or, as the case may be, such earlier law shall prevail and the law made by the Legislative Assembly of the Union territory shall, to the extent of the repugnancy, be void:

Provided that if such law made by the Legislative Assembly of the Union territory has been reserved for the consideration of the President and has received his assent, such law shall prevail in that Union territory:

Provided further that nothing in this section shall prevent Parliament from enacting at any time any law with respect to the same matter including a law adding to, amending, varying or repealing the law so made by the Legislative Assembly of the Union territory.]

22. Sanction of the administrator required for certain legislative proposals. No Bill or amendment shall be introduced into, or moved in, the Legislative Assembly of [13][the Union territory] without the previous sanction of the Administrator, if such Bill or amendment makes provision with respect to any of the following matters, namely:--

(a) constitution and organisation of the court of the Judicial Commissioner;

(b) jurisdiction and powers of the court of the Judicial Commissioner with respect to any of the matters in the State List or the Concurrent list in the Seventh Schedule to the Constitution.

23. Special provisions as to financial Bills.

(1) A Bill or amendment shall not be introduced into, or moved in, the Legislative Assembly of [13][the Union territory] except on the recommendation of the Administrator, if such Bill or amendment makes provision for any of the following matters, namely:-

(a) the imposition, abolition, remission, alteration or regulation of any tax;

(b) the amendment of the law with respect to any financial obligations undertaken or to be undertaken by the Government of the Union territory;

(c) the appropriation of moneys out of the Consolidated Fund of the Union territory;

(d) the declaring of any expenditure to be expenditure charged on the Consolidated Fund of the Union territory or the increasing of the amount of any such expenditure;

[13]e) the receipt of money on account of the Consolidated Fund of the Union territory or the public account of the Union territory or the custody or issue of such money or the audit of the accounts of the Union territory;

Provided that no recommendation shall be required under this sub-section for the moving of an amendment making provision for the reduction or abolition of any tax.

(2) A Bill or amendment shall not be deemed to make provision for any of the matters aforesaid by reason only that it provides for the imposition of fines or other pecuniary penalties, or for the demand or payment of fees for licences or fees for services rendered, or by reason that it provides for the imposition, abolition, remission, alteration or regulation of any tax by any local authority or body for local purposes.

(3) A Bill which, if enacted and brought into operation, would involve expenditure from the Consolidated Fund of [18][the Union territory] shall not be passed by the Legislative Assembly of the Union territory unless the Administrator has recommended to that Assembly the consideration of the Bill.

24. Procedure as to lapsing of Bills.

(1) A Bill pending in the Legislative Assembly of the Union territory shall not lapse by reason of the prorogation of the Assembly.

(2) A Bill which is pending in the Legislative Assembly of [13][the Union territory] shall lapse on a dissolution of the Assembly.

[19][**25. Assent to Bills.** When a Bill has been passed by the Legislative Assembly of the Union territory, it shall be presented to the Administrator and the Administrator shall declare either that he assents to the Bill or that he withholds assent therefrom or that he reserves the Bill for the consideration of the President:

Provided that the Administrator may, as soon as possible after the presentation of the Bill to him for assent, return the Bill if it is not a Money Bill together with a message requesting that the Assembly will reconsider the Bill or any specified provisions thereof, and, in particular, will consider the desirability of introducing any such amendments as he may recommend in his message and, when a Bill is so returned, the Assembly will reconsider the Bill accordingly, and if the Bill is passed again with or without amendment and presented to the Administrator for assent, the Administrator shall declare either that he assents to the Bill or that he reserves the Bill for the consideration of the President:

Provided further that the Administrator shall not assent to, but shall reserve for the consideration of the President, any Bill which,-

(a) in the opinion of the Administrator would, if it became law, so derogate from the powers of the High Court as to endanger the position which that Court is, by the Constitution, designed to fill; or

(b) relates to any of the matters specified in clause (1) of article 31A; or

(c) the President may, by order, direct to be reserved for his consideration; or

(d) relates to matters referred to in sub-section (5) or Section 7 or Section 17 or Section 34 or sub-section (6) of Section 45 or in entry 1 or entry 2 of the State List in the Seventh Schedule to the Constitution:

Provided also that without prejudice to the provisions of the second proviso, the Administrator shall not assent to, but shall reserve for the consideration of the President, any Bill which has been passed by the Legislative Assembly of the Union territory of Mizoram and which relates to any area comprised in any autonomous district in that Union territory under the Sixth Schedule to the Constitution.

EXPLANATION: For the purposes of this Section and Section 25A, a Bill shall be deemed to be a Money Bill if it contains only provisions dealing with all or any of the matters specified in sub-section (1) of Section 23 or any matter incidental to any of those matters and, in either case, there is endorsed thereon the certificate of the Speaker of the Legislative Assembly signed by him that it is a Money Bill.

25A. Bills reserved for consideration. When a Bill is reserved by an Administrator for the consideration of the President, the President shall declare either that he assents to the Bill or that he withholds assent therefrom:

Provided that where the Bill is not a Money Bill, the President may direct the Administrator to return the Bill to the Legislative Assembly together with such a message as is mentioned in the first proviso to Section 25 and, when a Bill is so returned, the Assembly shall reconsider it accordingly within a period of six months from the date of receipt of such message and, if it is again passed by the Assembly with or without amendment, it shall be presented again to the President for his consideration.]

26. Requirements as to sanction and recommendations to be regarded as matters of procedure only. No Act of the Legislative Assembly of the Union territory no provision in any such Act, shall be invalid by reason only that some previous sanction or recommendation required by this Act was not given, if assent to that Act was given by the Administrator, or, on being reserved by the Administrator for the consideration of the President, by the President.

27. Annual financial statement.

(1) The Administrator of each Union territory shall in respect of every financial year cause to be laid before the Legislative Assembly of the Union territory, with the previous approval of the President, a statement of the estimated receipts and expenditure of the Union territory for that year, in this Part referred to as the "annual financial statement".

(2) The estimates of expenditure embodied in the annual financial statement shall show separately–

(a) the sums required to meet expenditure described by this Act as expenditure charged upon the Consolidated Fund of the Union territory, and

(b) the sums required to meet other expenditure proposed to be made from the Consolidated Fund of the Union territory; and shall distinguish expenditure on revenue account from other expenditure.

(3) The following expenditure shall be expenditure charged on the Consolidated Fund of each Union territory:

(a) the emoluments and allowances of the Administrator and other expenditure relating to his office as determined by the President by general or special order;

(b) the charges payable in respect of loans advanced to the Union territory from the Consolidated Fund of India including interest, sinking fund charges and redemption charges, and other expenditure connected therewith;

(c) the salaries and allowances of the Speaker and the Deputy Speaker of the Legislative Assembly;

(d) expenditure in respect of the salaries and allowances of a Judicial Commissioner;

(e) any sums required to satisfy any judgment, decree or award of any court or arbitral tribunal;

(f) expenditure incurred by the Administrator in the discharge of his special responsibility;

(g) any other expenditure declared by the Constitution or by law made by Parliament or by the Legislative Assembly of the Union territory to be so charged.

28. Procedure in Legislative Assembly with respect to estimates.

(1) So much of the estimates as relates to expenditure charged upon the Consolidated Fund of the Union territory shall not be submitted to the vote of

the Legislative Assembly of the Union territory, but nothing in this sub-section shall be construed as preventing the discussion in the Legislative Assembly of any of those estimates.

(2) So much of the said estimates as relates to other expenditure shall be submitted in the form of demands for grants to the Legislative Assembly, and the Legislative Assembly shall have power to assent, or to refuse to assent, to any demand, or to assent to any demand subject to a reduction of the amount specified therein.

(3) No demand for a grant shall be made except on the recommendation of the Administrator.

29. Appropriation Bills.

(1) As soon as may be after the grants under Section 28 have been made by the Assembly, there shall be introduced a Bill to provide for the appropriation out of the Consolidated Fund of the Union territory of all moneys required to meet-

(a) the grants so made by the Assembly, and

(b) the expenditure charged on the Consolidated Fund of the Union territory but not exceeding in any case the amount shown in the statement previously laid before the Assembly.

(2) No amendment shall be proposed to any such Bill in the Legislative Assembly which will have the effect of varying the amount or altering the destination of any grant so made or of varying the amount of any expenditure charged on the Consolidated Fund of the Union territory and the decision of the person presiding as to whether an amendment is inadmissible under this sub-section shall be final.

(3) Subject to the other provisions of this Act, no money shall be withdrawn from the Consolidated Fund of the Union territory except under appropriation made by law passed in accordance with the provisions of this section.

30. Supplementary, additional or excess grants.

(1) The Administrator shall—

(a) if the amount authorised by any law made in accordance with the provisions of Section 29 to be expended for a particular service for the current financial year is found to be insufficient for the purposes of that year or when a need has arisen during the current financial year for supplementary or additional expenditure upon some new service not contemplated in the annual financial statement for that year, or

(b) if any money has been spent on any service during a financial year in excess of the amount granted for that service and for that year, cause to be laid before the Legislative Assembly of the Union territory, with the previous approval of the President, another statement showing the estimated amount of that expenditure or cause to be presented to the Legislative Assembly of the Union territory with such previous approval a demand for such excess, as the case may be.

(2) The provisions of sections 27, 28 and 29 shall have effect in relation to any such statement and expenditure or demand and also to any law to be made authorising the appropriation of moneys out of the Consolidated Fund of the Union territory to meet such expenditure or the grant in respect of such demand as they have effect in relation to the annual financial statement and the expenditure mentioned therein or to a demand for a grant and the law to be made for the authorisation of appropriation of moneys out of the Consolidated Fund of the Union territory to meet such expenditure or grant.

31. Votes on account.

(1) Notwithstanding anything in the foregoing provisions of this Part, the Legislative Assembly of the Union territory shall have power to make any grant in advance in respect of the estimated expenditure for a part of any financial year pending the completion of the procedure prescribed in Section 28 for the voting of such grant and the passing of the law in accordance with the provisions of Section 29 in relation to that expenditure and the Legislative Assembly shall have power to authorise by law the withdrawal of moneys from the Consolidated Fund of the Union territory for the purposes for which the said grant is made.

(2) The provisions of sections 28 and 29 shall have effect in relation to the making of any grant under sub-section (1) or to any law to be made under that sub-section as they have effect in relation to the making of a grant with regard to any expenditure mentioned in the annual financial statement and the law to be made for the authorisation of appropriation of moneys out of the Consolidated Fund of the Union territory to meet such expenditure.

32. Authorisation of expenditure pending its sanction by Legislative Assembly. Notwithstanding anything in the foregoing provisions of this Part, the Administrator may authorise such expenditure from the Consolidated Fund of the Union territory as he deems necessary for a period of not more than six months beginning with the date of the constitution of the Consolidated Fund of the Union territory, pending the sanction of such expenditure by the Legislative Assembly of the Union territory.

33. Rules of procedure.

(1) The Legislative Assembly of the union territory may make rules for regulating, subject to the provisions of this Act, its procedure and the conduct of its business:

Provided that the Administrator shall, after consultation with the Speaker of the Legislative Assembly and with the approval of the President, make rules--

(a) for securing the timely completion of financial business;

(b) for regulating the procedure of, and the conduct of business in, the Legislative Assembly in relation to any financial matter or to any Bill for the appropriation of moneys out of the Consolidated Fund of the Union territory;

(c) for prohibiting the discussion of, or the asking of questions on, any matter which affects the discharge of the functions of the Administrator in so far as he is required by this Act to act in his discretion.

(2) Until rules are made under sub-section (1), the rules of procedure and standing orders with respect to the Legislative Assembly of the State of Uttar Pradesh in force immediately before the commencement of this Act in the Union territory shall have effect in relation to the Legislative Assembly of that Union territory subject to such modifications and adaptations as may be made therein by the Administrator.

34. Official language or languages of Union territory and language or languages to be used in Legislative Assembly thereof.

(1) The Legislative Assembly of the Union territory may by law adopt any one or more of the languages in use in the Union territory or Hindi as the official language or languages to be used for all or any of the official purposes of the Union territory:

Provided that so long as the Legislative Assembly of the Union territory of Pondicherry does not decide otherwise, the French language shall continue to be used as an official language of that Union territory for the same official purposes for which it was being used in that territory immediately before the commencement of this Act:

Provided further that the President may be order direct--

(i) that the official language of the Union shall be adopted for such of the official purposes of the Union territory as may be specified in the order;

(ii) that any other language shall also be adopted throughout the Union territory or such part thereof for such of the official purposes of the Union territory as may be specified in the order, if the President is satisfied that a substantial proportion of the population of the Union territory desires the use of that other language for all or any of such purposes.

(2) The business in the Legislative Assembly of the Union territory shall be transacted in the official language or languages of the Union territory or in Hindi or in English:

Provided that the Speaker of the Legislative Assembly or person acting as such, as the case may be, may permit any member who cannot adequately express himself in any of the languages aforesaid to address the Assembly in his mother-tongue.

35. Language to be used for Acts, Bills, etc. Notwithstanding anything contained in Section 34, until Parliament by law otherwise provides, the authoritative texts--

(a) of all Bills to be introduced or amendments thereto to be moved in the Legislative Assembly of the Union territory,

(b) of all Acts passed by the Legislative Assembly of the Union territory, and

(c) of all orders, rules, regulations and bye-laws issued under any law made by the Legislative Assembly of the Union territory, shall be in the English language:

Provided that where the Legislative Assembly of the Union territory has prescribed any language other than the English language for use in Bills introduced in, or Acts passed by, the Legislative Assembly of the Union territory or in any order, rule, regulation or bye-law issued under any law made by the Legislative Assembly of the Union territory, a translation of the same in the English language published under the authority of the Administrator in the Official Gazette shall be deemed to be the authoritative text thereof in the English language.

36. Restriction on discussion in the Legislative Assembly. No discussion shall take place in the Legislative Assembly of the Union territory with respect to the conduct of any Judicial Commissioner or of any judge of the Supreme Court or of a High Court in the discharge of his duties.

37. Courts not to inquire into proceedings of Legislative Assembly.

(1) The validity of any proceedings in the Legislative Assembly of the Union territory shall not be called in question on the ground of any alleged irregularity of procedure.

(2) No officer or member of the Legislative the Union territory in whom powers are vested by or under this Act for regulating procedure or the conduct of business, or for maintaining order in the Legislative Assembly shall be subject to the jurisdiction of any court in respect of the exercise by him of those powers.

PART III: DELIMITATION OF CONSTITUENCIES

38. Definitions. In this Part, unless the context otherwise requires,

(a) "associate member" means a member associated with the Delimitation Commission under Section 42 [20][or with the Election Commission [21][under Section 43A or Section 43C]];

(b) "Delimitation Commission" means the Delimitation Commission constituted under Section 3 of the Delimitation Commission Act, 1962 (61 of 1962);

[20][(bb) "Election Commission" means the Election Commission appointed by the President under article 324;]

(c) "latest census figures" mean the census figures in the Union territory ascertained at the latest census of which the finally published figures are available;

(d) "parliamentary constituency" means a constituency provided by law for the purpose of elections to the House of the People from the Union territory including the Union territory of Delhi.

39. Assembly constituencies. For the purpose of elections to the Legislative Assembly of the Union territory, the Union territory shall be divided into single-member assembly constituencies in accordance with the provisions of this Part in such manner that the population of each of the constituencies shall, so far as practicable, be the same throughout the Union territory.

40. Representation of Pondicherry in the House of the People. There shall be allotted one seat to the Union territory of Pondicherry in the House of the People and that Union territory shall form one parliamentary constituency.

41. Duties of Delimitation Commission.

(1) It shall be the duty of the Delimitation Commission--

(a) to delimit the assembly constituencies in each Union territory, and

(b) to determine, on the basis of the latest census figures, the number of seats to be reserved for the scheduled castes and for the scheduled tribes in the Legislative Assembly of the Union territory other than the Union territory of Goa, Daman and Diu, and the constituencies in which these seats shall be so reserved.

(2) It shall also be the duty of the Delimitation Commission:

(a) to readjust, on the basis of the latest census figures, the division of each of the Union territories of Delhi, Himachal Pradesh, Manipur and Tripura into parliamentary constituencies, [22][the number being 7, 4, 2 and 2];

(b) to determine the constituency in which the seat shall be reserved for the scheduled castes or for the scheduled tribes, as the case may be; and

(c) to divide the Union territory of Goa, Daman and Diu into two single-member parliamentary constituencies.

42. Associate members.

(1) For the purpose of assisting the Delimitation Commission in its duties, the Delimitation Commission shall associate with itself,--

(a) in respect of the Union territory of Delhi, all the members of the House of the People representing that Union territory;

(b) in respect of each of the Union territories of Himachal Pradesh, Manipur and Tripura, all the members of the House of the People representing that Union territory and three members of the Legislative Assembly of that Union territory to be nominated by the Speaker of the Assembly from among the members thereof;

(c) in respect of the Union territory of Goa, Daman and Diu, the two members of the House of the People representing that Union territory;

(d) in respect of the Union territory of Pondicherry, three members of the Legislative Assembly of that Union territory to be nominated by the Speaker of the Assembly from among the members thereof.

(2) The nomination of members of the several Legislative Assemblies under sub-section (1) shall be made by the respective Speakers thereof as soon as practicable and shall be communicated to the Delimitation Commission.

(3) If owing to death or resignation the office of an associate member falls vacant, it shall be filled as soon as practicable under and in accordance with the foregoing provisions of this section.

(4) None of the associate members shall have the right to vote or to sign any decision of the Delimitation Commission.

43. Procedure as to delimitation. The provisions of sections 7, 9, 10 and 11 of the Delimitation Commission Act, 1962 (61 of 1962), shall apply, as far as may be, in relation to the delimitation of parliamentary and assembly constituencies under this Part as they apply in relation to the delimitation of parliamentary and assembly constituencies under that Act.

[23][43A. Special provision for delimitation of constituencies of Mizoram Legislative Assembly.

(1) The provisions of sections 39 to 43 (both inclusive) shall not apply to the delimitation of constituencies for the purpose of elections to the Legislative Assembly of the Union territory of Mizoram.

(2) The Election Commission shall, in the manner herein provided, distribute the seats assigned to the Legislative Assembly of the Union territory of Mizoram under sub-section (2) of Section 3 to single member assembly constituencies and delimit them on the basis of the latest census figures having regard to the provisions of the Constitution and to the following provisions:--

(a) all constituencies shall, as far as practicable, be geographically compact areas;

(b) in delimiting the constituencies, regard shall be had to physical features, existing boundaries of administrative units, facilities of communication and public convenience.

(3) For the purpose of assisting in the performance of its functions under sub-section (2), the Election Commission shall associate with itself as associate members--

(a) all the persons who, having been elected to the Legislative Assembly of the State of Assam from the Lungleh, Aijal East and Aijal West territorial constituencies, are members of that Assembly immediately before the day appointed under clause (b) of Section 2 of the North-Eastern Areas (Reorganisation) Act, 1971 (81 of 1971); and

(b) such three elected members of the District Council of the Mizo District as the Chairman thereof may nominate:

Provided that none of the associate members shall have a right to vote or sign any decision of the Election Commission.

(4) If, owing to death or resignation, the office of an associate member falls vacant, it shall be filled, if practicable, in accordance with the provisions of sub-section (3).

(5) The Election Commission shall—

(a) publish its proposals for the delimitation of constituencies, together with the dissenting proposals, if any, of any associate member who desires publication thereof in the Official Gazette and in such other manner as the Commission may consider fit, together with a notice inviting objections and suggestions in relation to the proposals and specifying a date on or after which the proposals will be further considered by it;

(b) consider all objections and suggestions which may have been received by it before the date so specified;

(c) after consideration of objections and suggestions which may have been received by it before the date so specified, determine by one or more orders the delimitation of constituencies and cause such order or orders to be published in the Official Gazette; and upon such publication, the order or orders shall have the full force of law and shall not be called in question in any court.

(6) The Election Commission may, from time to time, by notification in the Official Gazette,

(a) correct any printing mistake in any order made under sub-section (5) or any error arising therein from inadvertent slip or omission;

(b) where the boundaries or name of any territorial division mentioned in any such order or orders are or is altered, make such amendments as appear to it to be necessary or expedient for bringing such order up-to-date.

(7) Every order made under sub-section (5) and every notification issued under sub-section (6) shall be laid as soon as may be after it is made or issued before the Legislative Assembly of the Union territory of Mizoram.

(8) All things done, and all steps taken, before the commencement of this Act in the Union territory of Mizoram with a view to delimiting the territorial constituencies of that Union territory for purposes of elections to the Legislative Assembly of that Union territory shall, insofar as they are in conformity with the foregoing provisions of this section, be deemed to have been done or taken under those provisions as if those provisions were in force at the time such things were done or such steps were taken.]

[24][**43B. Representation of Arunachal Pradesh in the House of the people.** In the House of the People to be constituted after the general election to that House to be held after the commencement of the Government of Union Territories (Amendment) Act, 1975 (29 of 1975) and thereafter, there shall be allotted two seats to the Union territory of Arunachal Pradesh and the First Schedule to the Representation of the People Act, 1950 (43 of 1950) shall be deemed to have been amended accordingly.

43C. Special provisions for delimitation of parliamentary constituencies in Arunachal Pradesh and constituencies of Arunachal Pradesh Legislative Assembly.

(1) The provisions of sections 39 to 43 (both inclusive) shall not apply to the delimitation of parliamentary constituencies in the Union territory of Arunachal Pradesh or to the delimitation of constituencies for the purpose of elections to the Legislative Assembly of that Union territory.

(2) The Election Commission shall divide the Union territory of Arunachal Pradesh into two single-member parliamentary constituencies on the basis of the latest census figures.

(3) The Election Commission shall also, in the manner herein provided, distribute the seats assigned to the Legislative Assembly of the Union territory of Arunachal Pradesh under sub-section (2) of Section 3 to single-member

assembly constituencies and delimit them on the basis of the latest census figures having regard to the following provisions:--

(a) all constituencies shall, as far as practicable, be geographically compact areas;

(b) every assembly constituency shall be so delimited as to fall only within one parliamentary constituency;

(c) in delimiting the constituencies, regard shall be had to physical features, existing boundaries of administrative units facilities of communication and public convenience.

(4) For the purpose of assisting in the performance of its functions under sub-sections (2) and (3), the Election Commission shall associate with itself as associate members--

(a) the member of the House of the People representing the Union territory of Arunachal Pradesh;

(b) such five members of the Legislative Assembly of the Union territory of Arunachal Pradesh as the Speaker of that Assembly shall, having regard to the composition of the Legislative Assembly, nominate:

Provided that none of the associate members shall have a right to vote or sign any decision of the Election Commission.

(5) If owing to death or resignation, the office of an associate member falls vacant, it shall be filled, if practicable, in accordance with the provisions of sub-section (4).

(6) The Election Commission shall--

(a) publish its proposals for the delimitation of constituencies together with the dissenting proposals, if any, of any associate member who desires publication thereof in the Official Gazette and in such other manner as the Commission may consider fit, together with a notice inviting objections and suggestions in relation to the proposals and specifying a date on or after which the proposals will be further considered by it;

(b) consider all objections and suggestions which may have been received by it before the date so specified;

(c) after consideration of objections and suggestions which may have been received by it before the date so specified, determine by one or more orders the delimitation of constituencies and cause such order or orders to be published in the Official Gazette; and upon such publication, the order or orders shall have the full force of law and shall not be called in question in any court.

(7) The Election Commission may, from time to time, by notification in the Official Gazette,-

(a) correct any printing mistake in any order made under sub-section (6) or any error arising therein from inadvertent slip or omission;

(b) where the boundaries or name of any territorial division mentioned in any such order or orders are or is altered, make such amendments as appear to it to be necessary or expedient for bringing such order up-to-date.

(8) Every order made under sub-section (6) and every notification issued under sub-section (7) shall be laid as soon as may be after it is made or issued before the House of the People and the Legislative Assembly of the Union territory of Arunachal Pradesh.

(9) All things done, and all steps taken, before the commencement of this Act in the Union territory of Arunachal Pradesh with a view to delimiting the territorial constituencies of that Union territory for purposes of elections to the Legislative Assembly of that Union territory shall, insofar as they are in conformity with the foregoing provisions of this section, be deemed to have been done or taken under those provisions as if these provisions were in force at the time such things were done or such steps were taken.]

[25][**43D. Special provision for determination of constituencies in the Legislative Assembly of Goa, Daman and Diu for Scheduled Castes and Scheduled Tribes.**

(1) The Election Commission shall determine on the basis of the latest census figures-

(i) the number of seats to be reserved for the Scheduled Castes and for the Scheduled Tribes in the Legislative Assembly of the Union territory of Goa, Daman and Diu (hereafter in this section referred to as the Legislative Assembly) having regard to the provisions of sub-section (5) of Section 3; and

(ii) the constituencies in which those seats shall be so reserved having regard to the provisions of clause (c), or, as the case may be, clause (d), of sub-section (1) of Section 9 of the Delimitation Act and without altering the extent of any constituency as delimited by the Delimitation Commission.

(2) The Election Commission shall--

(a) publish its proposals for the determination of the constituencies in which seats shall be reserved for the Scheduled Castes or for the Scheduled Tribes, as the case may be, in the Gazette of India and in the Official Gazette of the Union territory of Goa, Daman and Diu and also in such other manner as the Election Commission may consider fit, together with a notice inviting objections and suggestions in relation to the proposals and specifying a date on or after which the proposals will be further considered by it;

(b) consider all objections and suggestions which may have been received by it before the date so specified;

(c) after consideration of objections and suggestions which may have been received by it before the date so specified, determine by one or more orders the number of seats to be reserved for the Scheduled Castes or for the Scheduled Tribes, as the case may be, in the Legislative Assembly and the constituencies in which those seats shall be so reserved and cause such order or orders to be published in the Gazette of India and in the Official Gazette of the Union territory of Goa, Daman and Diu; and upon such publication in the Gazette of India, the order or orders shall have the full force of law and shall not be called in question in any court and the Second Schedule to the Representation of the People Act, 1950 (43 of 1950) and the order made by the Delimitation Commission under Section 9 of the Delimitation Act in relation to the Legislative Assembly shall be deemed to have been amended accordingly.

(3) Subject to the provisions of sub-section (4), the re-adjustment of representation of any territorial constituencies in the Legislative Assembly necessitated by any order made by the Election Commission under this section, shall apply in relation to every election to the Legislative Assembly held after the publication in the Gazette of India, under sub-section (2), of such order.

(4) Nothing contained in the foregoing sub-sections shall affect the representation in the Legislative Assembly existing on the date of publication in the Gazette of India, under sub-section (2), of any order made by the Election Commission.

(5) The Election Commission may, from time to time, by notification in the Gazette of India and in the Official Gazette of the Union territory of Goa, Daman and Diu--

(a) correct any printing mistake in any order made under sub-section (2) or any error arising therein from inadvertent slip or omission;

(b) where the boundaries or name of any territorial division mentioned in any such order are, or is, altered, make such amendments as appear to it to be necessary or expedient for bringing such order up-to-date.

(6) Every order made under sub-section (2) and every notification issued under sub-section (5) shall be laid, as soon as may be, after it is made or issued before the Legislative Assembly.

EXPLANATION: In this section,--

(a) "Delimitation Act" means the Delimitation Act, 1972 (76 of 1972);

(b) "Delimitation Commission" means the Delimitation Commission constituted under Section 3 of the Delimitation Act.]

43E[26]. Special provisions as to readjustment of territorial constituencies. Notwithstanding anything contained in sections 38 to 43D (both inclusive), until the relevant figures for the first census taken after the year 2026 have been published, it shall not be necessary to readjust the division of each Union territory into territorial constituencies and any reference to the "latest census figures" in this Part shall be construed as a reference to the 2001[27] census figures.]

43F[28]. Notwithstanding the publication of orders under sub-section of Section 10 of the Delimitation Act, 2002 or anything containing in sub-section (2) or sub-section (4) of the said section, any readjustment in the division of Union territory into territorial constituencies by the Delimitation Commission under the said Act, on the basis of 2001 census shall take effect from such date as the Central Government may, by order, published in the Official Gazette, specify and until such readjustment takes effect, any election to the Legislative Assembly may be held on the basis of the territorial constituencies existing before such readjustment.

PART - IV : COUNCIL OF MINISTERS

44. Council of Ministers.

(1) There shall be a Council of Ministers in each Union territory with the Chief Minister at the head to aid and advise the Administrator in the exercise of his functions in relation to matters with respect to which the Legislative Assembly of the Union territory has power to make laws except in so far as he is required by or under this Act to act in his discretion or by or under any law to exercise any judicial or quasi-judicial functions:

Provided that, in case of difference of opinion between the Administrator and his Ministers on any matter, the Administrator shall refer it to the President for decision and act according to the decision given thereon by the President, and pending such decision it shall be competent for the Administrator in any case where the matter is in his opinion so urgent that it is necessary for him to take immediate action, to take such action or to give such direction in the matter as he deems necessary:

2* * * * * * *The second proviso omitted by Act 34 of 1986*

(2) Omitted by Act 34 and 69 of 1986 respectively s. 41 (w.e.f. 20-2-1987).

(3) If and insofar as any special responsibility of the Administrator is involved under this Act, he shall, in the exercise of his functions, act in his discretion.

(4) If any question arises as to whether any matter is or is not a matter as respects which the Administrator is by or under this Act required to act in his discretion, the decision of the Administrator thereon shall be final.

(5) If any question arises as to whether any matter is or is not a matter as respects which the Administrator is required by any law to exercise any judicial or quasi-judicial functions, the decision of the Administrator thereon shall be final.

(6) The question whether any, and if so what, advice was tendered by Ministers to the Administrator shall not be inquired into in any court.

45. Other provisions as to Ministers.

(1) The Chief Minister shall be appointed by the President and the other Ministers shall be appointed by the President on the advice of the Chief Ministers.

(2) The Ministers shall hold office during the pleasure of the President.

(3) The Council of Ministers shall be collectively responsible to the Legislative Assembly of the Union territory.

(4) Before a Minister enters upon his office, the Administrator shall administer

to him the oaths of office and of secrecy according to the forms set out for the purpose in the First Schedule.

(5) A Minister who for any period of six consecutive months is not a member of the Legislative Assembly of the Union territory shall at the expiration of that period cease to be a Minister.

(6) The salaries and allowances of Ministers shall be such as the Legislative Assembly of the Union territory may from time to time by law determine, and until the Legislative Assembly so determines, shall be determined by the Administrator with the approval of the President.

46. Conduct of business.

(1) The President shall make rules—

(a) for the allocation of business to the Ministers; and

(b) for the more convenient transaction of business with the Ministers including the procedure to be adopted in the case of a difference of opinion between the Administrator and the Council of Ministers or a Minister.

(2) Save as otherwise provided in this Act, all executive action of the Administrator, whether taken on the advice of his Ministers or otherwise, shall be expressed to be taken in the name of the Administrator.

(3) Orders and other instruments made and executed in the name of the Administrator, shall be authenticated in such manner as may be specified in rules to be made by the Administrator, and the validity of an order or instrument which is so authenticated shall not be called in question on the ground that it is not an order or instrument made or executed by the Administrator.

PART - V : MISCELLANEOUS AND TRANSITIONAL PROVISIONS

47. Consolidated Fund of the Union territory.

(1) As from such Date[29] as the Central Government may, by notification in the Official Gazette, appoint in this behalf, all revenues received in [30][the Union territory] by the Government of India or the Administrator of the Union territory in relation to any matter with respect to which the Legislative Assembly of the Union territory has power to make laws, and all grants made and all loans advanced to the Union territory from the Consolidated Fund of India and all moneys received by the Union territory in repayment of loans shall form one Consolidated Fund to be entitled "the Consolidated Fund of the Union territory".

(2) No moneys out of the Consolidated Fund of [30][the Union territory] shall be appropriated except in accordance with, and for the purposes and in the manner provided in, this Act.

(3) The custody of the Consolidated Fund of [30][the Union territory], the payment of moneys into such Fund, the withdrawal of moneys therefrom and all other matters connected with or ancillary to those matters shall be regulated by rules made by the Administrator with the approval of the President.

[31]47A. Public Account of the Union territory and moneys credited to it.

(1) As from such date as the Central Government may, by notification in the Official Gazette, appoint in this behalf, all other public moneys received by or on behalf of the Administrator shall be credited to a Public Account entitled "the Public Account of the Union territory".

(2) The custody of public moneys, other than those credited to the Consolidated Fund of the Union territory or the Contingency Fund of the Union territory, received by or on behalf of the Administrator, their payment into the Public Account of the Union territory and the withdrawal of moneys from such account and all other matters connected with or ancillary to the aforesaid matters shall be regulated by rules made by the Administrator with the approval of the President.

48. Contingency Fund of the Union territory.

(1) There shall be established a Contingency Fund in the nature of an imprest to be entitled "the Contingency Fund of the Union territory" into which shall be paid from and out of the Consolidated Fund of the Union territory such sums as may, from time to time, be determined by law made by the Legislative Assembly of the Union territory; and the said Fund shall be held by the Administrator to enable advances to be made by him out of such Fund.

(2) No advances shall be made out of the Contingency Fund of the Union territory except for the purposes of meeting unforeseen expenditure pending authorisation of such expenditure by the Legislative Assembly of the Union territory under appropriations made by law.

(3) The Administrator may make rules regulating all matters connected with or ancillary to the custody of, the payment of moneys into, and the withdrawal of moneys from, the Contingency Fund of the Union territory.

[31]48-A. Borrowing upon the security of the Consolidated Fund of the Union territory.

(1) The executive power of the Union extends to borrowing upon the security of the Consolidated Fund of the Union territory within such limits, if any, as may, from time to time, be fixed by Parliament by law and to the giving of guarantees within such limits, if any, as may be so fixed;

Provided that the power exercisable by the Government of India under the sub-section shall also be exercisable by the Administrator subject to such conditions, if any, as the Government of India may think fit to impose.

(2) Any sums required for the purpose of invoking a guarantee shall be charged on the consolidated Fund of the Union territory.

48B. Form of accounts of the Union territory. The accounts of the Union territory shall be kept in such form as the Administrator may, after obtaining advice of the Comptroller and Auditor General of India and with the approval of the President prescribe by rules.

49. Audit reports. The reports of the Comptroller and Auditor- General of India relating to the accounts of [32][the Union territory] for any period subsequent to the date referred to in sub-section (1) of Section 47 shall be submitted to the Administrator who shall cause them to be laid before the Legislative Assembly of the Union territory.

50. Relation of Administrator and his Ministers to President. Notwithstanding anything in this Act, the Administrator and his Council of Ministers shall be under the general control of, and comply with such particular directions, if any, as may from time to time be given by, the President.

51. Provision in case of failure of constitutional machinery. If the President, on receipt of a report from the Administrator of [32][the Union territory] or otherwise, is satisfied,-

(a) that a situation has arisen in which the administration of the Union territory cannot be carried on in accordance with the provisions of this Act, or

(b) that for the proper administration of the Union territory it is necessary or expedient so to do, the President may, by order, suspend the operation of all or any of the provisions of this Act for such period as he thinks fit and make such incidental and consequential provisions as may appear to him to be necessary or expedient for administering the Union territory in accordance with the provisions of article 239.

[33][**52. Authorisation of expenditure by President.** Where the Legislative Assembly of [32][the Union territory] is dissolved, or its functioning as such Assembly remains suspended, on account of an order under Section 51, it shall be competent for the President to authorise when the House of the People is not in session expenditure from the Consolidated Fund of that Union territory pending the sanction of such expenditure by Parliament.]

53. Provisions for election to Parliament from Goa, Daman and Diu, and Pondicherry.

(1) As soon as practicable after the commencement of this Act, elections shall be held in accordance with law--

 (a) to fill the seats in the House of the People allotted to the Union territory of Goa, Daman and Diu; and

 (b) to fill the seat in the House of the People and the seat in the Council of States allotted to the Union territory of Pondicherry.

(2) Notwithstanding anything contained in any other law for the time being in force, the members nominated to represent the Union territory of Goa, Daman and Diu in the House of the People shall continue to be such until the election of the members to fill the two seats in that House allotted to that Union territory:

Provided that where the dates of election of the members are different, the members so nominated shall cease to be members of that House on the earlier of those two dates.

EXPLANATION: In this sub-section, the expression "date of election" has the same meaning as in Section 67A of the Representation of the People Act, 1951 (43 of 1951).

[34][**54. Transitional provisions for administration of justice in certain areas in the Union territory of Mizoram.** On and from the commencement of this Act in the Union territory of Mizoram and until other provisions in this behalf are made by a competent Legislature or other competent authority, the administration of justice in those areas of that Union territory which are not comprised in any autonomous district under the Sixth Schedule to the Constitution shall be carried on, so far as may be, in accordance with the provisions of paragraphs 4 and 5 of that Schedule, as if those areas were comprised in an autonomous district under that Schedule and the provisions of the said paragraphs were in force in those areas and for this purpose,--

(i) all powers and functions of a District Council under the provisions of the said paragraph 4 shall be exercised and discharged by the Administrator or any officer appointed by him in this behalf;

(ii) the said paragraph 5 shall have effect as if references to the District Council, the Regional Council and the courts constituted by the District Council, by whatever form of words, had been omitted therefrom; and

(iii) references to Governor in the said paragraphs 4 and 5 shall be construed as references to the Administrator.]

[35][**54A. Provision as to provisional Legislative Assembly of Arunachal Pradesh.**

(1) Notwithstanding anything contained in this Act (including provisions relating to the strength of the Legislative Assembly of the Union territory of Arunachal Pradesh), until the Legislative Assembly of the Union territory of Arunachal Pradesh has been duly constituted and summoned to meet for the first session under and in accordance with the provisions of this Act, there shall be a provisional Legislative Assembly which shall consist of members, being those persons referred to in clauses (b), (c) and (d) of Section 3 of the North-East Frontier Agency (Administration) Supplementary Regulation, 1971 (4 of 1971) and who are functioning, immediately before the commencement of this Act in the Union territory of Arunachal Pradesh, as members of the Pradesh Council constituted under the said Section 3.

(2) The term of office of the members of the provisional Legislative Assembly shall expire immediately before the first meeting of the Legislative Assembly duly constituted after the first general election to that Assembly.

(3) The provisional Legislative Assembly constituted under this Section shall, for so long as it is in existence, be deemed to be the Legislative Assembly duly constituted under this Act and accordingly the other provisions of this Act, so far as may be, apply in relation to the provisional Legislative Assembly as they apply in relation to the Legislative Assembly.]

55. Contracts and suits. For the removal of doubts it is hereby declared that--

(a) all contracts in connection with the administration of the Union territory are contracts made in the exercise of the executive power of the Union;

(b) all suits and proceedings in connection with the administration of the Union territory shall be instituted by or against the Government of India.

56. Power of President to remove difficulties. If any difficulty arises in relation to the transition from the provisions of any of the laws repealed by this Act or in giving effect to the provisions of this Act and, in particular, in relation to the constitution of the Legislative Assembly for the Union territory, the President may by order do anything not inconsistent with the provisions of this Act which appear to him to be necessary or expedient for the purpose of removing the difficulty.

57. Amendment to certain-enactments.

(1) The enactments specified in the Second Schedule-

(a) shall, together with all rules, notifications and orders made or issued thereunder, extend to and come into force in the Union territories of Goa, Daman and Diu, and Pondicherry; and

(b) shall be subject to the amendments mentioned in the fourth column of the said Schedule.

(2) All things done, and all steps taken, before the commencement of this Act in connection with the preparation or revision of electoral rolls for the purpose of elections to the House of the People from the Union territories of Goa, Daman and Diu, and Pondicherry, and to the Legislative Assemblies of those Union territories shall, insofar as they are in conformity with the provisions of the Representation of the People Act, 1950 (43 of 950), as amended by this Act, be deemed to have been done in accordance with law.

58. Repeal and savings.

(1) The following laws are hereby repealed:-

(a) the Territorial Councils Act, 1956 (103 of 1956);

(b) the Decree No. 46-2381, dated the 25th October, 1946, as subsequently amended, relating to the Representative Assembly of the State of Pondicherry;

(c) the Decree No. 47-1490, dated the 12th August, 1947, as subsequently amended, relating to the setting up of a Council of Government in the State of Pondicherry;

(d) the State of Pondicherry (Representation of the People) Order, 1955, in so far as it relates to the Representative Assembly of Pondicherry.

(2) Notwithstanding the repeal of the Territorial Councils Act, 1956 (103 of 1956),-

(a) every officer and other employee of the Territorial Council of the Union territory serving under the Council immediately before such repeal shall become an officer or other employee of Government and shall be employed in connection with the administration of the Union territory with such designation as the Administrator may determine and shall hold office by the same tenure and at the same remuneration and on the same terms and conditions of service as he would have but for such repeal held the same and shall continue to do so unless and until such tenure, remuneration and terms and conditions are duly altered by the Administrator:

Provided that-

(i) *the tenure, remuneration and terms and conditions of service of any such officer or other employee shall not be altered to his disadvantage without the previous sanction of the Central Government;*

(ii) *any service rendered by any such officer or other employee before such repeal shall be deemed to be service rendered in connection with the administration of the Union territory;*

(iii) *the Administrator may employ any such officer or other employee in the discharge of such functions as the Administrator may think proper and every such officer or other employee shall discharge those functions accordingly;*

(b) anything done or any action taken (including any notification, order, scheme, rule, form, notice or bye-law made or issued, any licence or permission granted) under the repealed Act shall insofar as it is not inconsistent with the provisions of this Act, continue in force unless and until it is superseded by anything done or any action taken in accordance with law;

(c) all debts, obligations and liabilities incurred, all contracts entered into and all matters and things engaged to be done by, with or for the Territorial Council before such repeal shall be deemed to have been incurred, entered into or engaged to be done in exercise of the executive power of the Union for the purposes of the administration of the Union territory;

(d) all assessments, valuations, measurements or divisions made by the Territorial Council shall, insofar as they are not inconsistent with the provisions of this Act, continue in force unless and until they are superseded by any assessment, valuation, measurement or division made by the Administrator in accordance with law;

(e) all properties, movable and immovable, and all interests of whatsoever nature and kind, vested in the Territorial Council immediately before such repeal shall, with all rights of whatsoever description, used, enjoyed or possessed by that Council, vest in the Union for the purposes of the administration of the Union territory;

(f) all rates, taxes, cesses, fees, rents, fares and other charges which immediately before such repeal were being lawfully levied by the Territorial Council shall continue to be levied at the same rate at which they were being levied by the Council immediately before such repeal until provision to the contrary is made by law;

(g) all rates, taxes, cesses, fees, rents, fares and other charges due to the Territorial Council immediately before such repeal shall be deemed to be due to the Union in connection with the administration of the Union territory;

(h) all suits, prosecutions and other legal proceedings instituted or which might have been instituted by or against the Territorial Council may be continued or instituted by or against the Government of India.

THE FIRST SCHEDULE

[See Sections 4 (a), 11 and 45 (4)]

FORMS OF OATHS OR AFFIRMATIONS

I: *Form of Oath or Affirmation to be made by a Candidate for Election to the Legislative Assembly*

"I, A.B., having been nominated as a candidate to fill a seat in the Legislative Assembly of do swear in the name of God/solemnly affirm that I will bear true faith and allegiance to the Constitution of India as by law established and that I will uphold the sovereignty and integrity of India."

II: *Form of Oath or Affirmation to be made by a Member of the Legislative Assembly of a Union territory*

"I, A.B., having been elected (or nominated) a member of the Legislative Assembly of do swear in the name of God/solemnly affirm that I will bear true faith and allegiance to the Constitution of India as by law established, that I will uphold the sovereignty and integrity of India and that I will faithfully discharge the duty upon which I am about to enter."

III: *Form of Oath of Office for a Member of the Council of Ministers of a Union territory*

"I, A.B., do swear in the name of God/solemnly affirm that I will bear true faith and allegiance to the Constitution of India as by law established, that I will uphold the sovereignty and integrity of India, that I will faithfully and conscientiously discharge my duties as a Minister for the Union territory of............., and that I will do right to all manner of people in accordance with the Constitution and the law without fear or favour, affection or ill-will."

IV: *Form of Oath of Secrecy for a Member of the Council of Ministers of a Union territory*

"I, A.B., do swear in the name of God/solemnly affirm that I will not directly or indirectly communicate or reveal to any person or persons any matter which shall be brought under my consideration or shall become known to me as a Minister for the Union territory of ...., except as may be required for the due discharge of my duties as such Minister."

THE SECOND SCHEDULE

[See Section 57]

ENACTMENTS AMENDED [Not printed.]

ENDNOTES

1. Part I, sections 3, 4 and 14 of Part II, Part III, sections 53, 56 and 57 of Part V and First and Second Schedules, so far as they are applicable, came into force in the Union territory of Goa, Daman and Diu, on the 13th May, 1963, by Notifn. No. G.S.R. 814, dated 13-5-1963, see Gazette of India Extraordinary, Pt. II, Sec. 3(i), p. 423 and the remaining provisions of the Act came into force in the Union territory of Goa, Daman and Diu, on 20-12-1963: vide Notifn. No. G.S.R 1922 dt. 16-12-1963, Gaz. of India, Exty., Pt. II, Sec. 3(i), p. 867. Part I, sections 53, 56 and 57 of Part V and the Second Schedule, so far as they are applicable, came into force in the Union territory of Pondicherry of the 13th May, 1963, by Notifn. No. G.S.R. 815, dated 13-5-1963, see ibid., and the remaining provisions came into force on the 1st July, 1963, by Notifn. No. G.S.R. 1025, dated 15-6-1963, see Gazette of India, Extraordinary, Pt. II, Sec. 3(i), p. 471.

   All the provisions came into force in the Union territories of Himachal Pradesh, Manipur and Tripura, and so much of the provisions as apply to the Union territory of Delhi, came into force in that Union territory, on the 1st July, 1963, by Notifn. No. S.O. 1660, dated 14-6-1963, see Gazette of India, Extraordinary, Pt. II. Sec. 3(ii), p. 301.

   So much of the provisions as apply to the Union territory of Dadra and Nagar Haveli came into force in that Union territory, on the 1st July, 1963, by Notifn. No. G.S.R. 1025, dated 15-6-1963, see Gazette of India, Extraordinary, Pt. II, Sec. 3(i), p. 471. Sections 1, 2, 3, 4, 14, 38, 43A and 56 of the Act shall come into force in the Union Territory of Mizoram on 17-2-1972: vide Notifn. No. G.S.R. 81(E) dated 16-2-1972, Gaz. of India, Exty., Pt. II, Sec. 3(i),p. 241.

   All the provisions of the Act, other than those which have already come into force in the Union territory of Mizoram, shall, so far as they are applicable, come into force in that Union territory on 3-51972; vide Notifn. No. G.S.R. 269(E) dated 30-4-1972, Gaz. of India, Exty., Pt. II, Sec. 3(i), p-....
2. Ins. by Act 83 of 1971, s. 2 (w.e.f. 16-2-1972).
3. Ins. by Act 29 of 1975, s. 2 (w.e.f. 15-8-1975).
4. Subs. by s. 2, ibid., for "Provided further that" (w.e.f. 15-8-1975).

* For dates see page 701.

5. Subs. by Act 18 of 1987, s. 65 (w.e.f. 30-5-1987).
6. Subs. by Act 18 of 1987, s. 65 (w.e.f. 30-5-1987).
7. Subs. by the State of Himachal Pradesh (Adaptation of Laws on Union Subjects) Order, 1973, for sub-section (2) (w.e.f. 25-1-1971).
8. Subs. by s. 2, ibid., for "of the Union territory of Pondicherry" (w.e.f. 30-9-1976).
9. Ins by Act 19 of 1984, s. 2.
10. Subs. by Act 18 of 1987, s. 65 (w.e.f. 30-5-1987).
11. Subs. by Act 18 of 1987, s. 65 (w.e.f. 30-5-1987).
12. Subs. by Act 24 of 1985, s. 2.
13. Subs. by Act 18 of 1987, s. 65 (w.e.f. 30-5-1987).
14. Ins. by Act 24 of 1985, s. 3.

15. S. 20 renumbered as sub-section (1) thereof by Act 83 of 1971, s. 5 (w.e.f. 16-2-1972).
16. Ins. by Act 83 of 1971, s. 5 (w.e.f. 16-2-1972).
17. Subs. by Act 29 of 1975, s. 4, for s. 21 (w.e.f. 15-8-1975).
18. substituted by Act 38 of 2001 w.e.f 10.05.06.
19. Subs. by Act 83 of 1971, s. 7, for s. 25 (w.e.f. 16-2-1972).
20. Ins. by Act 83 of 1971, s. 9 (w.e.f. 16-2-1972).
21. Subs. by Act 29 of 1975, s. 7, for "under Section 43A" (w.e.f. 15-8-1975).
22 Subs. by Act 19 of 1966, s. 37, for certain words (w.e.f. 13-6-1966).
23. Ins. by Act 83 of 1971, s. 10 (w.e.f. 16-2-1972).
24. Ins. by Act 29 of 1975, s. 8 (w.e.f. 15-8-1975).
25. Ins. by Act 86 of 1976, s. 3 (w.e.f. 30-9-1976).
26. inserted by Act, 19 of 1984 S.3 w.e.f. 1.3.1984
27. substituted by Act 19 of 2005 w.e.f.21.05.2005]
28. inserted by Act of 2006
29. Substituted by Act 18 of 1987
30. Substituted by Act 38 of 2001 w.e..f. 10.5.2006
31. Inserted by Act 38 of 2001 w.e.f. 10.5.2006
32. Subs. by Act 18 of 1987, s. 65, for "a Union territory" (w.e.f. 30-5-1987).
33. Ins. by Act 1 of 1980, s. 2 (w.e.f. 25-9-1979).
34. Subs. by Act 83 of 1971, s. 12, for s. 54 (w.e.f. 16-2-1972).
35. Ins. by Act 29 of 1975, s. 10.

18

The House of the People (Extension of Duration) Act, 1976

[16TH FEBRUARY, 1976]

AN ACT to provide for the extension of the duration of the present House of the People.

Be it enacted by Parliament in the Twenty-seventh Year of the Republic of India as follows:-

1. Short title. This Act may be called the House of the People (Extension of Duration) Act, 1976.

2. Extension of duration of the present House of the People. The period of five years [being the period for which the, House of the People may, under clause (2) of article 83 of the Constitution, continue from the date appointed for its first meeting] in relation to the present House of the People shall, while the Proclamations of Emergency issued on the 3rd day of December, 1971 and on the 25th day of June, 1975, are both in operation, be extended for a period of 1[two years].

> *1["Provided that if both or either of the said Proclamations cease or ceases to operate before the expiration of the said period of two years, the present House of the People shall, unless previously dissolved under clause (2) of article 85 of the Constitution, continue until six months after the cesser of operation of the said Proclamations or Proclamation but not beyond the said period of two years."]*

❑❑❑

1. Subs. by Act 109 of 1976, s.2 (w.e.f. 24-11-1976).

19

The Indian Short Titles Act, 1897

Act No. 14 of 1897 [1][22nd July, 1897]

AN ACT to facilitate the citation of certain Acts;

WHEREAS it is expedient to facilitate the citation of certain Acts; It is hereby enacted as follows —

1. Short title. This Act may be called the Indian Short Titles Act, 1897.

2. Citation of Acts described in Schedule. Each of the Acts described in the first three coloumns of the Schedule may, without prejudice to any other mode of citation, be cited for all purposes by the short title mentioned in that behalf in the fourth column thereof.

❑❑❑

20

The Legislative Councils Act, 1957

ACT NO. 37 OF 1957 [18TH SEPTEMBER, 1957]

AN ACT to provide for the creation of a Legislative Council for the State of Andhra Pradesh and the increasing of the strength of the Legislative Councils of the States having such Councils and for matters connected therewith.

Be it enacted by Parliament in the Eighth Year of the Republic of India as follows —

1. Short title. This Act may be called the Legislative Councils Act, 1957.

2. Definitions. In this Act, unless the context otherwise requires —

(a) each of the words and expressions defined in the Representation of the People Act, 1950 (43 of 1950), but not defined in this Act, shall have the same meaning as in that Act;

(b) "sitting member" means a person who immediately before the commecement of this Act is a member of a Legislative Council. 1[

3. * * * *

4. Increase in the strength of the Bihar Legislative Council.

(1) The total number of seats in the Legislative Council of Bihar shall be increased from 72 to 96 and of those seats—

(a) the numbers to be filled by persons elected by the electorates referred to in sub-clauses (a), (b) and (c) of clause (3) of article 171 shall be 34, 8 and 8 respectively;

(b) the number to be filled by persons elected by members of the Legislative Assembly of Bihar in accordance with the provisions of sub-clause (d) of the said clause shall be 34; and

(c) the number to be filled by persons nominated by the Governor of Bihar in accordance with the provisions of sub-clause (e) of that clause shall be 12.

(2) The Delimitation of Council Constituencies (Bihar) Order, 1951, shall, until other provision is made by law, have effect subject to the modifications directed by the First Schedule.

(3) As soon as may be after the commencement of this Act, elections shall be held to fill—

(a) the additional seats allotted to the several council constituencies by the said Orders as modified by this Act; and

(b) the additional seats to be filled by the persons referred to in clause (b) of sub-section (1), as if those seats had become vacant.

(4) In order that, as nearly as may be, one-third of the members of the said Council may retire on the 6th May, 1958, and on the expiration of every second year thereafter, the Governor of Bihar shall, after consultation with the Election Commission, make by order such provisions as he thinks fit in regard to the terms of office of the members to be elected to fill the additional seats under sub-section (3).

5. Increase in the strength of the Bombay Legislative Council.

(1) The total number of seats in the Legislative Council of Bombay shall be increased to 108 and of those seats —

(a) the numbers to be filled by persons elected by the electorates referred to in sub-clauses (a), (b) and (c) of clause (3) of article 171 shall be 36, 9 and 9, respectively;

(b) the number to be filled by persons elected by the members of the Legislative Assembly of Bombay in accordance with the provisions of sub-clause (d) of the said clause shall be 42; and

(c) the number to be filled by persons nominated by the Governor of Bombay in accordance with the provisions of sub-clause (e) of that clause shall be 12.

(2) As from the commencement of this Act, the Delimitation of Council Constituencies (Bombay) Order, 1951, shall, until other provision is made by law, have effect subject to the modifications directed by the Second Schedule and in the said Order as so modified, any reference to the State of Bombay shall be construed as a reference to that State as formed by Section 8 of the States Reorganisation Act, 1956 (37 of 1956).

(3) As from the commencement of this Act —

(a) every sitting member of the said Council representing immediately before such commencement any council constituency shall be deemed to have been elected to the said Council by the council constituency immediately before such commencement, he is an elector for an assembly constituency in the State of Bombay.

TABLE

1	2	3
Bombay City (Graduates)	Ahmedabad City (Teachers)	Surat (Local Authorities)
Greater Bombay (Graduates)	Gujarat (Teachers)	East Khandesh (Local Authorities)
Ahmedabad City (Graduates)	Northern Division (Teachers)	Nasik (Local Authorities)
Gujarat (Graduates)	Bombay City (Local Authorities)	Maharashtra North (Authorities)
Northern Division (Graduates)	Greater Bombay-cum-Maharashtra West (Local Authorities)	Ahmednagar-cum-West Khandesh (Local Authorities)
Poona City (Graduates)	Ahmedabad City (Local Authorities)	Poona City (Local Authorities)
Maharashtra (Graduates)	Ahmedabad District (Local Authorities)	Poona (Local Authorities)
Southern Division (Graduates)	Gujarat North (Local Authorities)	Maharashtra South (Local Authorities)
Bombay City (Teachers)	Mehsana-cum-Banas Kantha (Local Authorities)	Sholapur (Local Authorities)
Poona City (Teachers)	Baroda-cum-Amreli (Local Authorities)	North Satara (Local Authorities)
Greater Bombay-cum-Maharashtra (Teachers)	Broach-cum-Panch Mahals (Local Authorities)	Kolaba-cum-Thana (Local Authorities)
Central Division (Teachers)	Gujarat South (Local Authorities)	Ratnagiri-cum-Kanara (Local Authorities)
Southern Division (Teachers)	Kaira (Local Authorities)	Maharashtra North (Local Authorities)

(b) every sitting member of the said Council elected by the members of the Legislative Assembly of the former State of Bombay and every sitting member of the said Council chosen in pursuance of clause (b) of sub-section (2) of Section 34 of the States Reorganisation Act, 1956 (37 of 1956), shall be deemed to have been duly elected by the members of the Legislative Assembly of the present State of Bombay if immediately before such commencement he is an elector for an assembly constituency in the State of Bombay.

(4) Every sitting elected member of the said Council who is not deemed to have been elected thereto by virtue of clause (a) or clause (b) of sub-section (3) shall, as from the commencement of this Act, cease to be a member of the said Council.

(5) As soon as may be after such commencement, elections shall be held to fill such of the seats allotted to the several Council constituencies by the Delimitation of Council Constituencies (Bombay) Order, 1951, as modified by

this Act and such of the seats to be filled by persons referred to in clause (b) of sub-section (1) as are then vacant, as if those seats had then become vacant.

(6) The said Council shall be deemed to have been first constituted on the date on which the Legislative Council of the former State of Bombay was first constituted.

(7) In order that, as nearly as may be, one-third of the members of the said Council may retire on the 24th April, 1958, and on the expiration of every second year thereafter, the Governor of Bombay shall, after consultation with the Election Commission, make by order such provisions as he thinks fit in regard to the terms of office of the sitting members chosen in pursuance of clause (b) of sub-section (2) of Section 34 of the States Reorganisation Act, 1956 (37 of 1956), and of the members to be elected under sub-section (5) of this Section.

(8) Section 34 of the States Reorganisation Act, 1956, shall be amended, and shall be deemed always to have been amended, as follows:--

(a) in sub-section (2), for the words, brackets and figures Until the said Council has been reconstituted in accordance with the provisions of sub-sections (4) and (5) of this Section and summoned to meet for the first time, the words 'Until otherwise provided by law' shall be substituted;

(b) sub-sections (3), (4) and (5) shall be omitted.

(9) In this Section, the expression 'the former State of Bombay' means the State of Bombay as it existed immediately before the 1st day of November, 1956.

6. Increase in the strength of the Madhya Pradesh Legislative Council.

(1) The total number of seats in the Legislative Council for the State of Madhya Pradesh to be constituted under Section 33 of the States Reorganisation Act, 1956 (37 of 1956), shall be increased from 72 as fixed by sub-section (2) of that Section to 90.

(2) The said Section shall be amended as follows:—

(a) in sub-section (2) —

(i) for the figures "72", the figures "90" shall be substituted;

(ii) in clause (a), for the figures and word "24, 6 and 6", the figures and word "31, 8 and 8" shall be substituted;

(iii) in clause (b), for the figures "24", the figures "31" shall be substituted;

(b) in sub-section (3), for the words "this Act", the words and figures "the Legislative Councils Act, 1957" shall be substituted; and

(c) in sub-section (4) —

(i) for the words "the appointed day", the words "such commencement" shall be substituted; and

(ii) the proviso shall be omitted.

7. Increase in the strength of the Madras Legislative Council.

(1) The total number of seats in the Legislative Council of Madras shall be increased from 50 to 63 and of those seats—

(a) the numbers to be filled by persons elected by the electorates referred to in sub-clauses (a), (b) and (c) of clause (3) of article 171 shall be 21, 6 and 6 respectively;

(b) the number to be filled by persons elected by the members of the Legislative Assembly of Madras in accordance with the provisions of sub-clause (d) of the said clause shall be 21; and

(c) the number to be filled by persons nominated by the Governor of Madras in accordance with the provisions of sub-clause (e) of that clause shall be 9.

(2) The Delimitation of Council Constituencies (Madras) Order, 1951, shall, until other provision is made by law, have effect subject to the modifications directed by the Third Schedule.

(3) As soon as may be after the commencement of this Act,—

(a) elections shall be held to fill—

(i) the additional seats allotted to the local authorities' constituencies and the teachers' constituency by the said Order as modified by this Act; and

(ii) the additional seats, to be filled by the persons referred to in clause (b) of sub-section (1), as if those seats had become vacant;

(b) one person shall be nominated by the Governor of Madras to fill the additional seat under clause (c) of the said sub-section.

(4) In order that, as nearly as may be, one-third of the members of the said Council may retire on the 20th April, 1958, and on the expiration of every second year thereafter, the Governor of Madras shall, after consultation with the Election Commission, make by order, such provisions as he thinks fit in regard to the terms of office of the members to be elected under clause (a) of sub-section (3) and of the member to be nominated under clause (b) of that sub-section.

8. Increase in the strength of the Mysore Legislative Council.

(1) The total number of seats in the Legislative Council of Mysore shall be increased to 63 and of those seats—

(a) the numbers to be filled by persons elected by electorates referred to in sub-clauses (a), (b) and (c) of clause (3) of article 171 shall be 21, 6 and 6 respectively;

(b) the number to be filled by persons elected by the members of the Legislative Assembly of Mysore in accordance with the provisions of sub-clause (d) of the said clause shall be 21; and

(c) the number to be filled by persons nominated by the Governor of Mysore in accordance with the provisions of sub-clause (e) of that clause shall be 9.

(2) As from the commencement of this Act, the Delimitation of Council Constituencies (Mysore) Order, 1951, shall, until other provision is made by law, have effect subject to the modifications directed by the Fourth Schedule, and in the said Order as so modified, a reference to the State of Mysore shall be

construed as a reference to that State as formed by Section 7 of the States Reorganisation Act, 1956 (37 of 1956).

(3) As from the commencement of this Act —

(a) every sitting member of the said Council representing immediately before such commencement a council constituency shall be deemed to have been elected to the said Council by the council constituency in column 2 of the said table —

TABLE

1	2
Mysore (Graduates)	constituency
Mysore South (Graduates)	constituency
Mysore (Teachers)	constituency
Mysore South (Teachers)	constitency
Kolar (Local Authorities)	constituency
Tumkur (Local Authorities)	constituency
Mysore South East (Local Authorities)	constituency
Bangalore (Local Authorities)	constituency
Hassan (Local Authorities)	constituency
Mandya (Local Authorities)	constituency
Mysore South (Local Authorities)	constituency
Mysore (Local Authorities)	constituency
Chickmagalur (Local Authorities)	constituency
Shimoga (Local Authorities)	constituency
Mysore South West (Local Authorities)	constituency
Chitaldrug-cum-Bellary (Local Authorities)	constituency

(b) every sitting member of the said Council elected by the members of the Legislative Assembly of the former State of Mysore, every sitting member of the said Council chosen in pursuance of clause (b) of sub-section (2) of Section 36 of the States Reorganisation Act, 1956 (37 of 1956.), and the sitting member of the said Council specified by the Chairman of the Legislative Council of Madras under sub-rule (7) of rule 4 of the States Reorganisation (Elections to Provisional State Legislatures) Rules, 1956, shall be deemed to have been duly elected by the members of the Legislative Assembly of the present State of Mysore; and

(c) every sitting member of the said Council nominated by the Rajpramukh of the former State of Mysore shall be deemed to have been nominated to the said Council by the Governor of the present State of Mysore.

(4) The three members who, immediately before the 1st November, 1956, were members of the Legislative Council of Bombay and became on that date members of the Legislative Council of Mysore by virtue of sub-rule (7) of rule 4 of the States Reorganisation (Elections to Provisional State Legislatures) Rules, 1956, shall be deemed to have been elected to the Legislative Council of Mysore by the Mysore North West (Local Authorities) constituency.

(5) As soon as may be after the commencement of this Act, elections shall be held to fill such of the seats allotted to the several council constituencies by the Delimitation of Council Constituencies (Mysore) Order, 1951, as modified by this Act and such of the seats to be filled by persons referred to in clause (b) of sub-section (1) as are then vacant, as if those seats had then become vacant.

(6) As soon as may be after such commencement, the vacancies in the seats allotted under clause (c) of sub-section (1) shall be filled by nomination by the Governor.

(7) The said Council shall be deemed to have been first constituted on the date on which the Legislative Council of the former State of Mysore was first constituted.

(8) In order that, as nearly as may be, one-third of the members of the said Council may retire on the [2][13th May, 1958], and on the expiration of every second year thereafter, the Governor of Mysore shall, after consultation with the Election Commission, make by order such provisions as he thinks fit in regard to the terms of office of the sitting members chosen in pursuance of clause (b) of sub-section (2) of Section 36 of the States Reorganisation Act, 1956 (37 of 1956), and of the members to be elected and nominated under sub-sections (5) and (6) of this Section.

(9) Section 36 of the States Reorganisation Act, 1956 (37 of 1956), shall be amended, and shall be deemed always to have been amended, as follows —

(a) in sub-section (2) for the words, brackets and figures" Until the said Council has been reconstituted in accordance with the provisions of sub-sections (3) and (4) of this Section and summoned to meet for the first time", the words" Until otherwise provided by law" shall be substituted; and

(b) sub-sections (3) and (4) shall be omitted.

(10) In this Section, the expression 'the former State of Mysore' means the State of Mysore as it existed immediately before the 1st day of November, 1956.

9. Increase in the strength of the Punjab Legislative Council.

(1) The total number of seats in the Legislative Council of Punjab shall be increased to 51 and of those seats—

(a) the numbers to be filled by persons elected by electorates referred to in sub-clauses (a), (b) and (c) of clause (3) of article 171 shall be 17, 4 and 4 respectively;

(b) the number to be filled by persons elected by the members of the Legislative Assembly of Punjab in accordance with the provisions of sub-clause (d) of the said clause shall be 18; and

(c) the number to be filled by persons nominated by the Governor of Punjab in accordance with the provisions of sub-clause (e) of that clause shall be 8.

(2) As from the commencement of this Act, the Delimitation of Council Constituencies (Punjab) Order, 1951, shall, until other provision is made by law, have effect subject to the modifications directed by the Fifth Schedule, and in the said Order as so modified, any reference to the State of Punjab shall be construed as a reference to that State as formed by Section 11 of the States Reorganisation Act, 1956 (37 of 1956).

(3) As from the commencement of this Act --

(a) every sitting member of the said Council representing immediately before such commencement any local authorities' constituency shall be deemed to have been elected to the said Council by the local authorities' constituency in column 2 of the said table.

TABLE

1	2	
Ambala-cum-Karnal (Local Authorities)	Punjab South (Local Authorities)	constituency constituency
Gurgaon-cum-Rohtak-cum-Hissar (Local Authorites)	Punjab South-cum-Simla (Local Authorites)	constituency constituency
Hoshiarpur-cum-Kangra-cum-Gurdaspur (Local Authorites)	Punjab North (Local Authorites)	constituency constituency
Jullundur-cum-Ferozepur-cum-Punjab North (Local Authorites)	Amritsar-cum-Ludhiana (Local Authorites)	constituency constituency

(b) every sitting member of the said Council representing immediately before such commencement the graduates' constituency or the teachers' constituency shall be deemed to have been elected to the said Council by that constituency as altered by virtue of sub-section (2):

(c) every sitting member of the said Council elected by the members of the Legislative Assembly of the former State of Punjab and every sitting member of the said Council elected under clause (b) of sub-section (2) of Section 37 of the States Reorganisation Act, 1956 (37 of 1956), shall be deemed to have been duly elected by the members of the Legislative Assembly of the present State of Punjab.

(4) As soon as may be after such commencement, elections shall be held to fill —

(a) the additional seats allotted to the several council constituencies by the Delimitation of Council Constituencies (Punjab) Order, 1951, as modified by this Act;

(b) the additional seats to be filled by persons referred to in clause (b) of sub-section (1), as if those seats had become vacant.

(5) The said Council shall be deemed to have been first constituted on the date on which the Legislative Council of the former State of Punjab was first constituted.

(6) In order that, as nearly as may be, one-third of the members of the said Council may retire on the 26th April 1958, and on the expiration of every second year thereafter the Governor of Punjab shall, after consultation with the Election Commission, make by order such provisions as he thinks fit in regard to the terms of office of the sitting members elected under clause (b) of sub-section (2) of Section 37 of the States Reorganisation Act, 1956 (37 of 1956.), and of the members to be elected under sub-section (4) of this Section.

(7) Section 37 of the States Reorganisation Act, 1956 (37 of 1956), shall be amended, and shall be deemed always to have been amended, as follows —

(a) in sub-section (2), for the words, brackets and figures "Until the said Council has been reconstituted in accordance with the provisions of sub-sections (3) and (4) of this Section and of any other law for the time being in force and has been summoned to meet for the first time", the words "Until otherwise provided by law" shall be substituted;

(b) sub-sections (3) and (4) shall be omitted.

(8) In this Section the expression "the former State of Punjab" means the State of Punjab as it existed immediately before the 1st day of November, 1956.

10. Increase in the strength of the Uttar Pradesh Legislative Council.

(1) The total number of seats in the Legislative Council of Uttar Pradesh shall be increased from 72 to 108 and of those seats —

(a) the numbers to be filled by persons elected by the electorates referred to in sub-clauses (a), (b) and (c) of clause (3) of article 171 shall be 39, 9 and 9 respectively;

(b) the number to be filled by persons elected by the members of the Legislative Assembly of Uttar Pradesh in accordance with the provisions of sub-clause (d) of the said clause shall be 39; and

(c) the number to be filled by persons nominated by the Governor of Uttar

Pradesh in accordance with the provisions of sub-clause (e) of that clause shall be 12.

(2) The Delimitation of Council Constituencies (Uttar Pradesh) Order, 1951, shall, until other provision is made by law, have effect subject to the modifications directed by the Sixth Schedule.

(3) As from the commencement of this Act —

(a) every sitting member of the said Council representing immediately before such commencement a graduates' constituency or a teachers' constituency the extent of which is altered by virtue of sub-section (2) shall be deemed to have been elected to the said Council by that constituency as so altered;

(b) every sitting member of the said Council representing immediately before such commencement any local authorities' constituency specified in column 1 of the Table below shall be deemed to have been elected to the said Council by the local authorities' constituency specified against that constituency in column 2 of the said Table.

TABLE

1	2	
Uttar Pradesh North-West	Meerut	constituency
(Local Authorities)	(Local Authorities)	constituency
Uttar Pradesh North-East	Rohilkhand	constituency
(Local Authorities)	(Local Authorities)	constituency
Uttar Pradesh West	Agra	consituency
(Local Authorities)	(Local Authorities)	constituency
Uttar Pradesh Central	Lucknow	constituency
(Local Authorities)	(Local Authorities)	constituency
Uttar Pradesh South	Allahabad	constituency
(Local Authorities)	(Local Authorities)	constituency
Uttar Pradesh East	Varanasi	constituency
(Local Authorities)	(Local Authorities)	constituency

(4) As soon as may be after such commencement, elections shall be held to fill —

(a) the additional seats allotted to the several council constituencies by the said Order as modified by this Act; and

(b) the additional seats to be filled by persons referred to in clause (b) of sub-section (1), as if those seats had become vacant.

(5) In order that, as nearly as may be, one-third of the members of the said Council may retire on the 5th May, 1958, and on the expiration of every second year thereafter, the Governor of Uttar Pradesh shall, after consultation with the Election Commission, make by order such provisions as he thinks fit in regard to the terms of office of the members to be elected under sub-section (4).

11. Increase in the strength of the West Bengal Legislative Council.

(1) The total number of seats in the Legislative Council of West Bengal shall be increased from 51 to 75 and of those seats —

(a) the numbers to be filled by persons elected by the electorates referred to in sub-clauses (a), (b) and (c) of clause (3) of article 171 shall be 27, 6 and 6 respectively;

(b) the number to be filled by persons elected by the members of the Legislative Assembly of West Bengal in accordance with the provisions of sub-clause (d) of the said clause shall be 27; and

(c) the number to be filled by persons nominated by the Governor of West Bengal in accordance with the provisions of sub-clause (e) of that clause shall be 9.

(2) The Delimitation of Council Constituencies (West Bengal) Order, 1951, shall, until other provision is made by law, have effect subject to the modifications directed by the Seventh Schedule.

(3) As from the commencement of this Act —

(a) every sitting member of the said Council representing immediately before such commencement the Calcutta (Graduates) constituency and every such member representing the Calcutta (Teachers) constituency, the extent of which is altered by virtue of sub-section (2) shall be deemed to have been elected to the said Council respectively by the Calcutta (Graduates) constituency and the Calcutta (Teachers) constituency as so altered;

(b) every sitting member of the said Council representing immediately before such commencement any of the council constituencies specified in column 1 of the Table below shall be deemed to have been elected to the said Council by the council constituency specified against that constituency in column 2 of the said Table.

TABLE

1	2	
West Bengal South (Graduates)	West Bengal (Graduates)	constituency constituency
West Bengal West (Graduates)	West Bengal (Graduates)	constituency constituency
West Bengal North (Graduates)	West Bengal (Graduates)	constituency constituency
Burdwan Division (Teachers)	West Bengal (Teachers)	constituency constituency
Presidency Division South (Teachers)	West Bengal (Teachers)	constituency constituency

Presidency Division North (Teachers)	West Bengal (Teachers)	constituency constituency
Darjeeling (Local Authorities)	Bengal North (Local Authorities)	constituency constituency
West Bengal North (Local Authorities)	West Bengal North (Local Authorities)	constituency constituency
Nadia-Murshidabad (Local Authorities)	West Bengal East (Local Authorities)	constituency constituency
Calcutta-24-Parganas (Local Authorities)	West Bengal South (Local Authorities)	constituency constituency
Hooghly-Howrah (Local Authorities)	West Bengal Central (Local Authorities)	constituency constituency
Burdwan Division North (Local Authorities)	Bengal West (Local Authorities)	constituency constituency

(4) As soon as may be after such commencement, elections shall be held to fill—

(a) the additional seats allotted to the several council constituencies by the said Order as modified by this Act; and

(b) the additional seats to be filled by persons referred to in clause (b) of sub-section (1), as if those seats had become vacant.

(5) In order that, as nearly as may be, one-third of the members of the said Council may retire on the 4th June, 1958, and on the expiration of every second year thereafter the Governor of West Bengal shall, after consultation with the Election Commission, make by order such provisions as he thinks fit in regard to the terms of office of the members elected under sub-section (4).

12. [Amendment of Act 43 of 1950] *Rep. by the Repealing and Amending Act, 1960 (58 of 1960), s. 2 and Sch. I.*

13. [Amendment of Act 43 of 1951] *Rep. by s. 2 and Sch. I, ibid.*

❑❑❑

ENDNOTES

1. Omitted by Act 34 of 1985, s. 6 (w. e. f. 1-6-1985).
2. Subs. by Act 58 of 1960, s. 3 and Sch. II, for "26th April, 1958" (retrospectively).

21

The Merged States (Laws) Act, 1949

(Act No. 59 of 1949)[1]

AN ACT to extend certain laws to certain areas administered as parts of Governors' Provinces or as Chief Commissioners' Provinces.

[26TH DECEMBER, 1949]

WHEREAS by orders under section 290A of the Government of India Act, 1935 (26 Geo. 5, c. 2), provision has been made for the administration of certain areas either as if they formed part of an adjoining Governor's Province or as if they were a Chief Commissioner's province;

AND WHEREAS it is expedient to provide that certain laws should be extended to, and by virtue of such extension, be in force in the said areas;

It is hereby enacted as follows:

1. Short title and commencement.

(1) This Act may be called the Merged States (Laws) Act, 1949.

(2) It shall come into force on the 1st day of January, 1950.

2. Definitions. In this Act -

(a) the expression "absorbing Province" and "merged State" have the same meanings as in the State's Merger (Governors' Provinces) Order, 19491 , as amended by the State's Merger (United Provinces) Order, 19492 ; and

(b) the expression "new Provinces" means the Chief Commissioner's Provinces constituted by the State's Merger (Chief Commissioner's Provinces) Order, 1949, as amended by the State's Merger (United Provinces) Order, 1949.

3. Extension of laws.

(1) The Acts, Ordinances and Regulations specified in the Schedule are hereby extended to, and shall be in force in, all the new Provinces.

(2) So much of any of the Acts, Ordinances and Regulations specified in the Schedule as extends to any absorbing Province and relates to matters with respect to which the Dominion Legislature has power to make laws for a Governor's Province is hereby extended to, and shall be in force in, all the Merged States which are now administered as part of that Province.

(3) If any of the said Acts, Ordinances and Regulations as in force in any absorbing Province immediately before the commencement of this Act is subject to any amendments, made by the Legislature of that Province, that Act, Ordinance or Regulation shall be deemed to be extended to, and to be in force in, all the merged States which are now administered as part of that Province, subject to so much of the said amendments as relate to matters with respect to which the Dominion Legislature has power to make laws for a Governor's Province.

4. Interpretation of laws as extended. In any Act, Ordinance or Regulation specified in the Schedule, notwithstanding anything contained in the General Clauses Act, 1897 (10 of 1897) —

(a) any reference, by whatever form of words, to the acceding States shall be construed as not including a reference to any of the merged States or to any of the States (other than the United State of Saurashtra) mentioned in the State's Merger (Chief Commissioners' Provinces) Order 1949, as amended by the States' Merger (United Provinces) Order, 1949;

(b) any reference, by whatever form of words, to Indian British subjects shall be deemed to include a reference to persons who, immediately before the 1st day of August, 1949, were subjects of any of merged states or of any of the States (other than the United State of Saurashtra) mentioned in the State's Merger (Chief Commissioners' Provinces) Order 1949, as amended by the States' Merger (United Provinces) Order, 1949;

(c) any reference, by whatever form of words, to the Provinces generally or to the Chief Commissioner's Provinces generally shall be construed as including a reference to the new Provinces; and

(d) any reference, by whatever form of words, to an absorbing Province shall be construed as including a reference to the merged States which are now administered as part of that Province.

5. Repeal of corresponding laws. If immediately before the commencement of this Act there is in force in any of the new Provinces or merged States an Act, Ordinance, Regulation or other law corresponding to an Act, Ordinance or Regulation specified in the Schedule, whether such Act, Ordinance or Regulation is in force by virtue of an Order under the Extra-Provincial Jurisdiction Act, 1947 (47 of 1947), or by virtue of any other Legislative power, such corresponding law shall upon the commencement of this Act -

(a) in a new Province, stand repealed, and

(b) in a merged State, stand repealed to the extent to which the law relates to matters with respect to which the Dominion Legislature has power to make laws for a Governor's Province.

6. Savings.

(1) The repeal by section 5 of this Act of any corresponding law in force in the new Provinces or merged States immediately before the commencement of this Act shall not affect-

(a) the previous operation of any such law, or

(b) any penalty, forfeiture or punishment incurred in respect of any offence committed against any such law, or

(c) any investigation, legal proceeding or remedy in respect of any such penalty, forfeiture or punishment, and any such investigation, legal proceeding or remedy may be instituted, continued or enforced and any such penalty, forfeiture or punishment may be imposed as if this Act had not been passed.

(2) Subject to the provisions of sub-section (1), anything done or any action taken, including any appointment or delegation made, notification, order, instruction or direction issued, rule, regulation, form, bye-law or scheme framed, certificate, patent, permit or license granted or registration effected, under such corresponding law shall be deemed to have been done or taken under the corresponding provision of the Act, Ordinance or Regulation as now extended to, and in force in, the new Province or merged State and shall continue in force accordingly unless and until superseded by anything done or any action taken under the said Act, Ordinance or Regulation.

7. Powers of Courts and other authorities for purposes of facilitating application of laws. For the purpose of facilitating the application in any of the new Provinces or merged States of any Act, Ordinance or Regulation specified in the Schedule, any Court or other authority may construe any such Act, Ordinance or Regulation with such alterations, not affecting the substance, as may be necessary or proper to adapt it to the matter before the Court or other authority.

LAWS EXTENDED TO THE NEW PROVINCES AND MERGED STATES

Year	Number		Short title
ACTS			
1839	XXXII	..	The Interest Act, 1839, (a)
1841	X	..	The Indian Registration of Ships Act, 1841. (a)
1850	XI	..	The Indian Registration of Ships Act (1841) Amendment Act, 1850. (a)
1850	XVIII	..	The Judicial Officers' Protection Act, 1850.
1850	XIX	..	The Apprentices Act, 1850. (a)
1850	XXI	..	The Caste Disabilities Removal Act, 1850.
1850	XXXIV	..	The State Prisoners Act, 1850.
1850	XXXVII	..	The Public Servants (Inquiries) Act, 1850.
1855	XII	..	The Legal Representatives Suits Act, 1855.

1855	XIII	..	The Indian Fatal Accidents Act, 1855.
1856	IX	..	The Indian Bills of Lading Act, 1856.
1856	XV	..	The Hindu Widows' Re-marriage Act, 1856.
1857	XIII	..	The Opium Act, 1857.
1858	III	..	The State Prisoners Act, 1858.
1860	XXI	..	The Societies Registration Act, 1860.
1860	XLV	..	The Indian Penal Code, 1860
1861	V	..	The Police Act, 1861.
1862	III	..	The Government Seal Act, 1862.
1863	XXIII	..	The Waste-lands (Claims) Act, 1863.
1865	III	..	The Carriers Act, 1865.
1866	XXI	..	The Native Converts' Marriage Dissolution Act, 1866. (a)
1867	XVI	..	The Acting Judges Act, 1867.
1867	XXV	..	The Press and Registration of Books Act, 1867.
1869	IV	..	The Indian Divorce Act, 1869.
1870	VII	..	The Court-Fees Act, 1870.
1871	I	..	The Cattle-Trespass Act, 1871.
1871	XXIII	..	The Pensions Act, 1871.
1871	XXXI	..	The Indian Weights and Measures of Capacity Act, 1871.
1872	I	..	The Indian Evidence Act, 1872.
1872	III	..	The Special Marriage Act, 1872. (a)
1872	IX	..	The Indian Contract Act, 1872.
1872	XV	..	The Indian Christian Marriage Act, 1872.
1873	V	..	The Government Saving Banks Act, 1873.
1873	X	..	The Indian Oaths Act, 1873. (a)
1874	III	..	The Married Women's Property Act, 1874.
1874	IV	..	The Foreign Recruiting Act, 1874.
1875	IX	..	The Indian Majority Act, 1875.
1875	XVIII	..	The Indian Law Reports Act, 1875.
1877	I	..	The Specific Relief Act, 1877. (a)
1878	I	..	The Opium Act, 1878 (a)
1878	VI	..	The Indian Treasure-Trove Act, 1878.
1878	VIII	..	The Sea Customs Act, 1878. (a)
1878	XI	..	The Indian Arms Act, 1878. (a)
1879	XVIII	..	The Legal Practitioners Act, 1879
1880	I	..	The Religious Societies Act, 1880.
1880	XIII	..	The Vaccination Act, 1880.
1881	XI	..	The Municipal Taxation Act, 1881.

1881	XXVI	..	The Negotiable Instruments Act, 1881.
1882	II	..	The Indian Trusts Act, 1882.
1882	IV	..	The Transfer of Property Act, 1882.
1882	VII	..	The Powers of Attorney Act, 1882.
1884	IV	..	The Indian Explosives Act, 1884.
1885	XVIII	..	The Land Acquisition (Mines) Act, 1885.
1886	VI	..	The Births, Deaths, and Marriages Registration Act, 1886.
1886	XI	..	The Indian Tramways Act, 1886.
1887	VII	..	The Suits Valuation Act, 1887.
1887	IX	..	The Provincial Small Cause Courts Act, 1887.
1888	III	..	The Police Act, 1888.
1889	IV	..	The Indian Merchandise Marks Act, 1889. (a)
1890	I	..	The Revenue Recovery Act, 1890.
1890	VI	..	The Charitable Endowments Act, 1890.
1890	VIII	..	The Guardians and Wards Act, 1890.
1890	XI	..	The Prevention of Cruelty to Animals Act, 1890.(a)
1891	XVIII	..	The Bankers' Books Evidence Act, 1891.
1893	IV	..	The Partition Act, 1893.
1894	I	..	The Land Acquisition Act, 1894.
1894	IX	..	The Prisons Act, 1894.
1897	III	..	The Epidemic Diseases Act, 1897.
1897	IV	..	The Indian Fisheries Act, 1897.
1897	X	..	The General Clauses Act, 1897.
1898	III	..	The Lepers Act, 1898. (a)
1898	V	..	The Code of Criminal Procedure, 1898 (a)
1898	VI	..	The Indian Post Office Act, 1898.
1898	IX	..	The Live-stock Importation Act, 1898.
1899	II	..	The Indian Stamp Act, 1899.
1899	IV	..	The Government Buildings Act, 1899.
1900	III	..	The Prisoners Act, 1900.
1901	II	..	The Indian Tolls (Army and Air Force) Act, 1901.
1903	VII	..	The Indian Works of Defence Act, 1903.
1903	XIV	..	The Indian Foreign Marriage Act, 1903, (a)
1903	XV	..	The Indian Extradition Act, 1903, (a)
1904	VII	..	The Ancient Monuments Preservation Act,1904. (a)
1905	IV	..	The Indian Railway Board Act, 1905.
1906	III	..	The Indian Coinage Act, 1906.
1908	V	..	The Code of Civil Procedure, 1908.

1908	VI	.. The Explosive Substances Act, 1908.
1908	IX	.. The Indian Limitation Act, 1908. (a)
1908	XIV	.. The Indian Criminal Law Amendment Act, 1908.
1908	XV	.. The Indian Ports Act, 1908.
1908	XVI	.. The Indian Registration Act, 1908.
1909	IV	.. The Whipping Act, 1909. (a)
1909	VII	.. The Anand Marriage Act, 1909.
1910	IX	.. The Indian Electricity Act, 1910.
1911	II	.. The Indian Patents and Designs Act, 1911. (a)
1911	VIII	.. The Indian Army Act, 1911. (a)
1911	X	.. The Prevention of Seditious Meetings Act, 1911.
1912	IV	.. The Indian Lunacy Act, 1912. (a)
1913	II	.. The Official Trustees Act, 1913.
1913	III	.. The Administrator General's Act, 1913. (a)
1913	VI	.. The Mussalman Wakf Validating Act, 1913.
1913	VII	.. The Indian Companies Act, 1913. (a)
1914	II	.. The Destructive Insects and Pests Act, 1914.
1914	III	.. The Indian Copyright Act, 1914. (a)
1914	IX	.. The Local Authorities Loans Act, 1914.
1916	VII	.. The Indian Medical Degrees Act, 1916.
1916	XV	.. The Hindu Disposition of Property Act, 1916.
1917	V	.. The Destruction of Records Act, 1917.
1917	XVIII	.. The Post Office Cash Certificates Act, 1917.
1918	II	.. The Cinematograph Act, 1918.
1918	XXII	.. The Bronze Coin (Legal Tender) Act, 1918.
1919	I	.. The Local Authorities Pensions and Gratuities Act, 1919.
1919	XII	.. The Poisons Act, 1919.
1920	V	.. The Provincial Insolvency Act, 1920.
1920	X	.. The Indian Securities Act, 1920.
1920	XIV	.. The Charitable and Religious Trusts Act, 1920.
1920	XXIII	.. The Indian Rifles Act, 1920.
1920	XXXIII	.. The Identification of Prisoners Act, 1920.
1920	XXXIX	.. The Indian Elections Offences and Inquiries Act, 1920. (a)
1920	XLVII	.. The Imperial Bank of India Act, 1920. (a)
1921	XVIII	.. The Maintenance Orders Enforcement Act, 1921. (a)
1922	XXII	.. The Police (Incitement to Disaffection) Act, 1922.
1923	IV	.. The Indian Mines Act, 1923. (a)
1923	V	.. The Indian Boilers Act, 1923.

1923	VI	..	The Cantonments (House Accommodation) Act, 1923.
1923	VIII	..	The Workmen's Compensation Act, 1923.
1923	XIV	..	The Indian Cotton Cess Act, 1923.
1923	XIX	..	The Indian Official Secrets Act, 1923.
1923	XXI	..	The Indian Merchant Shipping Act, 1923. (a)
1923	XXIII	..	The Legal Practitioners (Women) Act, 1923.
1923	XLII	..	The Mussalman Wakf Act, 1923.
1924	II	..	The Cantonments Act, 1924.
1924	IV	..	The Central Board of Revenue Act, 1924.
1924	XIX	..	The Land Customs Act, 1924, (a)
1925	IV	..	The Indian Soldiers (Litigation) Act, 1925.
1925	XII	..	The Cotton Ginning and Pressing Factories Act, 1925.
1925	XIX	..	The Provident Fund Act, 1925
1925	XXVI	..	The Indian Carriage of Goods by Sea Act, 1925.
1925	XXXVI	..	The Indian Succession Act, 1925.
1926	III	..	The Government Trading Taxation Act, 1926.
1926	VII	..	The Indian Naturalization Act, 1926. (a)
1926	XII	..	The Contempt of Courts Act, 1926. (a)
1926	XVI	..	The Indian Trade Unions Act, 1926.
1926	XXI	..	The Legal Practitioners (Fees) Act, 1926. (a)
1926	XXXVIII	..	The Indian Bar Councils Act, 1926. (a)
1927	XVI	..	The Indian Forest Act, 1927.
1927	XVII	..	The Indian Lighthouse Act, 1927.
1928	XII	..	The Hindu Inheritance (Removal of Disabilities) Act, 1928.
1929	II	..	The Hindu Law of Inheritance (Amendment) Act, 1929. (a)
1929	XIX	..	The Child Marriage Restraint Act, 1929.
1930	II	..	The Dangerous Drugs Act, 1930.
1930	III	..	The Indian Sale of Goods Act, 1930.
1930	XXIV	..	The Indian Lac Cess Act, 1930.
1930	XXX	..	The Hindu Gains of Learning Act, 1930.
1930	XXXII	..	The Mussalman Wakf Validating Act, 1930.
1931	XVI	..	The Provisional Collection of Taxes Act, 1931.
1931	XXIII	..	The Indian Press (Emergency Powers) Act,1931. (a)
1932	IX	..	The Indian Partnership Act, 1932.
1932	XII	..	The Foreign Relations Act, 1932. (a)
1932	XIV	..	The Indian Air Force Act, 1932. (a)
1932	XX	..	The Port Haj Committees Act, 1932. (a)
1932	XXII	..	The Tea Districts Emigrant Labour Act, 1932.

1932	XXIII	..	The Criminal Law Amendment Act, 1932.
1933	II	..	The Children (Pledging of Labour) Act, 1933.
1933	XXVII	..	The Indian Medical Council Act, 1933. (a)
1934	II	..	The Reserve Bank of India Act, 1934.
1934	VIII	..	The Khaddar (Name Protection) Act, 1934.
1934	XIX	..	The Indian Dock Labourers Act, 1934. (a)
1934	XX	..	The Indian Carriage by Air Act, 1934.
1934	XXII	..	The Indian Aircraft Act, 1934.
1934	XXX	..	The Petroleum Act, 1934.
1934	XXXII	..	The Indian Tariff Act, 1934.
1934	XXXIV	..	The Indian Navy (Discipline) Act, 1934. (a)
1936	III	..	The Parsi Marriage and Divorce Act, 1936.
1936	IV	..	The Payment of Wages Act, 1936.
1937	I	..	The Agricultural Produce (Grading and Marking) Act, 1937.
1937	XVIII	..	The Hindu Women's Rights to Property Act, 1937. (a)
1937	XIX	..	The Arya Marriage Validation Act, 1937.
1937	XXV	..	The Federal Court Act, 1937.
1937	XXVI	..	The Muslim Personal Law (Shariat) Application Act, 1937.
1938	IV	..	The Insurance Act, 1938.
1938	V	..	The Manoeuvres, Field Firing and Artillery Practice Act, 1938.
1938	VIII	..	The Indian Tea Control Act, 1938. (a)
1938	XX	..	The Criminal Law Amendment Act, 1938.
1938	XXIV	..	The Employers' Liability Act, 1938.
1938	XXVI	..	The Employment of Children Act, 1938.
1939	IV	..	The Motor Vehicles Act, 1939. (a)
1939	VIII	..	The Dissolution of Muslim Marriages Act, 1939.
1939	IX	..	The Standards of Weight Act, 1939. (a)
1939	XIX	..	The Coal Mines Safety (Stowing) Act, 1939. (a)
1939		..	The Indian Naval Reserve Forces (Discipline) Act, 1939. (a)
1940	V	..	The Trade Marks Act, 1940. (a)
1940	X	..	The Arbitration Act, 1940.
1940	XXIII	..	The Drugs Act, 1940.
1940	XXVII	..	The Agricultural Produce Cess Act, 1940.
1941	XIX	..	The Mines Maternity Benefit Act, 1941. (a)
1941	XX	..	The Professions Tax Limitation Act, 1941. (a)
1941	XXI	..	The Federal Court Act, 1941.
1941	XXV	..	The Railway (Local Authorities' Taxation) Act, 1941.

1942	VII	.. The Coffee Market Expansion Act, 1942
1942	XVIII	.. The Weekly Holidays Act, 1942.
1942	XIX	.. The Industrial Statistics Act, 1942. (a)
1942	XXVI	.. Federal Court (Supplemental Powers) Act, 1942. (a)
1943	IX	.. The Reciprocity Act, 1943.
1944	I	.. The Central Excises and Salt Act, 1944.
1944	X	.. The Indian Coconut Committee Act, 1944. (a)
1944	XVIII	.. The Public Debt Act, 1944.
1946	IX	.. The Indian Oil Seeds Committee Act, 1946. (a)
1946	XVII	.. The Protective Duties Act, 1946. (a)
1946	XIX	.. The Hindu Married Women's Right to Separate Residence and Maintenance Act, 1946. (a)
1946	XX	.. The Industrial Employment (Standing Orders) Act, 1946.
1946	XXII	.. The Mica Mines Labour Welfare Fund Act, 1946.
1946	XXIV	.. The Essential Supplies (Temporary Powers) Act, 1946. (a)
1946	XXV	.. The Delhi Special Police Establishment Act, 1946.
1946	XXVIII	.. The Hindu Marriage Disabilities Removal Act, 1946.
1947	II	.. The Prevention of Corruption Act 1947. (a)
1947	VII	.. The Foreign Exchange Regulation Act, 1947. (a)
1947	XII	.. The Railways (Transport of Goods) Act, 1947. (a)
1947	XIV	.. The Industrial Disputes Act, 1947.
1947	XV	.. The Armed Forces (Emergency Duties) Act, 1947.
1947	XVI	.. The Trading with the Enemy (Continuance of Emergency Provisions) Act, 1947.
1947	XVIII	.. The Imports and Exports (Control) Act, 1947.
1947	XXIV	.. The Rubber (Production and Marketing) Act, 1947.
1947	XXIX	.. The Capital Issues (Continuance of Control) Act, 1947. (a)
1947	XXXI	.. The Antiquities (Export Control) Act, 1947.
1947	XXXII	.. The Coal Mines Labour Welfare Fund Act, 1947.
1947	XLIII	.. The United Nations (Security Council) Act, 1947.
1947	XLVI	.. The United Nations (Privileges and Immunities) Act, 1947.
1948	I	.. The Federal Court (Enlargement of Jurisdiction) Act, 1948.
1948	VIII	.. The Pharmacy Act, 1948.
1948	IX	.. The Dock Workers (Regulation of Employment) Act, 1948.
1948	XI	.. The Minimum Wages Act, 1948.
1948	XII	.. The Rehabilitation Finance Administration Act,1948.
1948	XV	.. The Industrial Finance Corporation Act, 1948.
1948	XVI	.. The Dentists Act, 1948.
1948	XXII	.. The Indian Power Alcohol Act, 1948.

1948	XXIX	..	The Atomic Energy Act, 1948. (a)
1948	XXXII	..	The Road Transport Corporations Act, 1948. (a)
1948	XXXIV	..	The Employees State Insurance Act, 1948.
1948	XXXVII	..	The Census Act, 1948.
1948	XL	..	The Indian Matrimonial Causes (War Marriages) Act, 1948.
1948	XLVI	..	The Coal Mines Provident Fund and Bonus Schemes Act, 1948.
1948	XLVII	..	The Displaced Persons (Institution of Suits) Act, 1948. (a)
1948	LIII	..	The Mines and Minerals (Regulation and Development) Act, 1948. (a)
1948	LIV	..	The Electricity (Supply) Act, 1948.
1948	LXI	..	The Central Silk Board Act, 1948.
1948	LXIII	..	The Factories Act, 1948.
1949	X	..	The Banking Companies Act, 1949.
1949	XIII	..	The Central Tea Board Act, 1949. (a)
1949	XXI	..	The Hindu Marriages Validity Act, 1949. (a)
1949	XXIII	..	The Influx from Pakistan (Control) Act, 1949. (a)
1949	XXV	..	The Displaced Persons (Legal Proceedings) Act, 1949. (b)
1949	XXX	..	The Public Companies (Limitation of Dividends) Act, 1949. (a)
1949	XXXVIII	..	The Chartered Accountants Act, 1949.
ORDINANCES			
1940	IV	..	The Currency Ordinance, 1940.
1941	XI	..	The Essential Services (Maintenance) Ordinance, 1941.
1942	XLI	..	The Armed Force (Special Powers) Ordinance, 1942.
1944	XXXVIII	..	The Criminal Law Amendment Ordinance, 1944.
1944	XLII	..	The Post Office National Savings Certificate Ordinance, 1944. (a)
1945	XLVII	..	The International Monetary Fund and Bank Ordinance, 1945.
1949	XI	..	The Industrial Tribunals Payment of Bonus (National Savings Certificates) Ordinance, 1949. (b)
REGULATION			
1818	III	..	The Bengal State Prisoners Regulation, 1818.

□□□

ENDNOTES

1. For Statement of Objects and Reasons, see Government of India Gazette, 1949 Part-V P.401 unmodified by ALO 1950 and for Hindi text see RHP (Extra) Dated 5-11-88, p. 2717.
2. See S.O. 25, Gaz. of India, Extra., 1949, page 1317.
2. See S.O 27, ibid., page 2611.
4. See S.O. 26, Gaz. of India, Extra., 1949, page 1343,

22

The Parliament (Prevention of Disqualification) Act, 1959

ACT NO. 10 OF 1959 [4TH APRIL, 1959]

AN ACT to declare that certain offices of profit under the Government shall not disqualify the holders thereof for being chosen as, or for being, members of Parliament.

[4th April, 1959]

Be it enacted by Parliament in the Tenth Year of the Republic of India as follows -

1. Short title. This Act may be called the Parliament (Prevention of Disqualification) Act, 1959.

2. Definitions. In this Act, unless the context otherwise requires -

(a) "compensatory allowance" means any sum of money payable to the holder of an office by way of daily allowance such allowance not exceeding the amount of daily allowance to which a member of Parliament is entitled under [1][the Salary, Allowances and Pension of Members of Parliament Act, 1954 (30 of 1954)] any conveyance allowance, house-rent allowance or travelling allowance for the purpose of enabling him to recoup any expenditure incurred by him in performing the functions of that office;

(b) "statutory body" means any corporation, committee, commission, council, board or other body of persons, whether incorporated or not, established by or under any law for the time being in force;

(c) "non-statutory body" means any body of persons other than a statutory body.

3. Certain offices of profit not to disquality. It is hereby declared that none of the following offices, insofar as it is an office of profit under the Government of India or the

Government of any State, shall disqualify the holder thereof for being chosen as, or for being, a member of Parliament, namely -

(a) any office held by a Minister, Minister of State or Deputy Minister for the Union or for any State, whether ex officio or by name;

(aa) [2][the office of a leader of the Opposition in Parliament;

(ab) [3][the office of Deputy Chairman, Planning Commission.]

[(ac) the office of each leader of a recognised party and a recognised group in either House of Parliament;]

(b) the office of Chief Whip, Deputy Chief Whip or Whip in Parliament or of a Parliamentary Secretary-;

(ba) [4][the office of chairperson of-

(i) the National Commission for Minorities constituted under Section 3 of the National Commission for Minorities Act, 1992 (19 of 1992);

(ii) the National Commission for the Scheduled Castes and Scheduled Tribes constituted under clause (1) of article 338 of the Constitution;

(iii) the National Commission for Women constituted under Section 3 of the National Commission for Women Act, 1990 (20 of 1990)].

(c) the office of a member of any force raised or maintained under the National Cadet Corps Act, 1948 (31 of 1948), the Territorial Army Act, 1948 (56 of 1948), or the Reserve and Auxiliary Air Forces Act, 1952 (62 of 1952);

(d) the office of a member of a Home Guard constituted under any law for the time being in force in any State;

(e) the office of sheriff in the city of Bombay, Calcutta or Madras the office of chairman or member of the syndicate, senate, executive committee, council or court of a university or any other body connected with a university;

(g) the office of a member of any delegation or mission sent outside India by the Government for any special purpose;

(h) the office of chairman or member of a committee whether consisting of one or more members, set up temporarily for the purpose of advising the Government or any other authority in respect of any matter of public importance or for the purpose of making an inquiry into, or collecting statistics in respect of, any such matter, if the holder of such office is not entitled to any remuneration other than compensatory allowance;

(i) 3[the office of chairman, director or member of any statutory or non-statutory body other than any such body as is referred to in clause (h), if the holder of such office is not entitled to any remuneration other than compensatory allowance, but excluding:

(i) the office of chairman of any statutory or nonstatutory body specified in Part I of the Schedule, and

(ii) the office of chairman or secretary of any statutory or non-statutory body specified in Part II of the Schedule;]

(ii) [2][the office of chairman or secretary of any statutory or non-statutory body specified in Part II of the Schedule; and

(iii) the office of deputy chairman of the non-statutory body specified in Part III of the Schedule].

(j) the office of village revenue officer, whether called a lambardar, malguzar, patel, deshmukh or by any other name, whose duty is to collect land revenue and who is remunerated by a share of, or commission on, the amount of land revenue collected by him, but who does not discharged any police functions.

[1]*[EXPLANATION 1]:* For the purposes of this section, the office of [2][Chairman, Deputy Chairman or Secretary] shall include every office of that description by whatever name called.

[3]*[EXPLANATION 2:* In clause (aa), the expression "Leader of the Opposition" shall have the meaning assigned to it in the Salary and Allowances of Leaders of Opposition in Parliament Act, 1977].

[4]*[EXPLANATION 3:* In clause (ac), the expressions "recognised party" and "recognised group" shall have the meanings assigned to them in the Leaders and Chief Whips of Recognised Parties and Groups in Parliament (Facilities) Act, 1998.]

4. Temporary suspension of disqualification in certain cases. If a person being a member of Parliament who immediately before the commencement of this Act held an office of profit declared by any law repealed by this Act not to disqualify the holder thereof for being such member, becomes so disqualified by reason of any of the provisions contained in this Act, such office shall not, if held by such person for any period not extending beyond a period of six months from the commencement of this Act disqualify him for being a member of Parliament.

5. Repels. The Parliament (Prevention of Disqualification) Act, 1950, (19 of 1950) the Parliament Prevention of Disqualification Act, 1951 (68 of 1951), the Prevention of Disqualification Act, 1953 (1 of 1954), and any provision in any other enactment which is inconsistent with this Act are hereby repealed.

❒❒❒

23

The Parliament (Prevention of Disqualification) Amendment Act, 2006

No. 31 of 2006 [18th August, 2006]

AN ACT further to amend the Parliament (Prevention of Disqualification) Act, 1959.

Be it enacted by Parliament in the Fifty-seventh Year of the Republic of India as follows -

1. Short title. This Act may be called the Parliament (Prevention of Disqualification) Amendment Act, 2006.

2. Amendment of Section 3. In Section 3 of the Parliament (Prevention of Disqualification) Act, 1959 (hereinafter referred to as the principal Act) -

(i) after clause (ac), the following clause shall be inserted, namely -

"(ad) the office of the Chairperson of the National Advisory Council constituted by the Government of India in the Cabinet Secretariat *vide* Order No. 631/2/1/2004-Cab., dated the 31st May, 2004;";

(ii) after clause (j) and before Explanation 1, the following clauses shall be inserted and shall be deemed to have been inserted with effect from the 4th day of April, 1959, namely -

"(k) the office of Chairman, Deputy Chairman, Secretary or Member (by whatever name called) in any statutory or non-statutory body specified in the Table;

(l) the office of Chairperson or trustee (by whatever name called) of any Trust, whether public or private, not being a body specified in the Schedule;

(m) the office of Chairman, President, Vice-President or Principal Secretary or Secretary of the Governing Body of any society registered under the Societies Registration Act, 1860 or under any other law relating to registration of societies, not being a body specified in the Schedule.".

3. Insertion of new Table. After the Schedule to the principal Act, the following Table shall be inserted and shall be deemed to have been inserted with effect from the 4th day of April, 1959, namely -

TABLE

[*See* Section 3(k)]

S. No.	Name of body
1.	The Tripura Khadi and Village Industries Board, a body constituted under the Tripura Khadi and Village Industries Act, 1966.
2.	The Uttar Pradesh Development Council.
3.	The Irrigation and Flood Control Commission, Uttar Pradesh.
4.	The Indian Statistical Institute, Calcutta.
5.	The West Bengal Handicrafts Development Corporation Limited.
6.	The West Bengal Small Industries Development Corporation Limited.
7.	The West Bengal Industrial Development Corporation Limited.
8.	The Sriniketan Santiniketan Development Authority, a body constituted under the West Bengal Town and Country (Planning and Development) Act, 1979 (West Bengal Act No. 13 of 1979).
9.	The Haldia Development Authority, a body constituted under the West Bengal Town and Country (Planning and Development) Act, 1979 (West Bengal Act No. 13 of 1979).
10.	The West Bengal Minorities Development and Finance Corporation, a body constituted under the West Bengal Minorities Development and Finance Corporation Act, 1995.
11.	The Hooghly River Bridge Commissioners, constituted under the Hooghly River Bridge Act, 1969 (West Bengal Act No. 36 of 1969).
12.	The Board of Wakf, West Bengal, a body constituted under the Wakf Act, 1995 (43 of 1995).
13.	The State Fisheries Development Corporation Limited, West Bengal.
14.	The West Bengal State Haj Committee, constituted under the Haj Committee Act, 2002 (35 of 2002).
15.	The Asansol Durgapur Development Authority, West Bengal, a body constituted under the West Bengal Town and Country (Planning and Development) Act, 1979 (West Bengal Act No. 13 of 1979).
16.	The West Bengal Pharmaceutical and Phytochemical Development Corporation Limited.

17. The West Bengal Handloom and Powerloom Development Corporation Limited.
18. The West Bengal Khadi and Village Industry Board.
19. The Society for Self-employment for Urban Youth, a society registered under the West Bengal Societies Registration Act, 1961 (West Bengal Act No. 26 of 1961).
20. The Tirumala Tirupathi Devasthanams Board.
21. The Agricultural and Processed Food Products Export Development Authority, an authority constituted under Section 4 of the Agricultural and Processed Food Products Export Development Authority Act, 1985 (2 of 1986).
22. The National Agricultural Co-operative Marketing Federation of India Limited (NAFED).
23. The Indian Farmer Fertilizers Co-operative Limited (IFFCO).
24. The Krishak Bharati Co-operative Limited (KRIBHCO).
25. The National Co-operative Consumers Federation of India Limited (NCCF).
26. The Auroville Foundation established under sub-section (1) of Section 10 of the Auroville Foundation Act, 1988 (54 of 1988).
27. The National Commission of Enterprises in the Unorganised Sector.
28. The Planning Board (Asiatic Society) established under sub-section (1) of Section 8 of the Asiatic Society Act, 1984 (5 of 1984).
29. The Delhi Rural Development Board.
30. The Maulana Azad Education Foundation.
31. The Indira Gandhi National Centre for the Arts.
32. The Dr. Ambedkar Foundation.
33. The Bihar State Board of Religious Trust, a body constituted under the Bihar Hindu Religious Trust Act, 1950 (Bihar Act No. 1 of 1951).
34. The Research and Information System for the Non-Aligned and Other Developing Countries.
35. The Indian Institute of Psychometry.
36. The Uttar Pradesh Film Development Council.
37. The Uttar Pradesh Provincial Co-operative Federation.
38. The Uttar Pradesh Co-operative Federation Limited.
39. The National Co-operative Union of India.
40. The Uttar Pradesh Krishi and Gram Vikas Bank.
41. The Uttar Pradesh Co-operative Bank Limited.
42. The Indian Council for Cultural Relations.
43. The Board of Control - A.N. Sinha Institute of Social Studies, Patna.
44. All India Council for Sports.
45. The Howrah Improvement Trust.
46. The Dalit Sena, 12, Janpath, New Delhi.

47. The Social Justice Trust, 12, Janpath, New Delhi.
48. The Bahujan Foundation (Charitable Trust), Lucknow, Uttar Pradesh.
49. The Bahujan Prerna Charitable Trust, Delhi.
50. The Central Wakf Council, established under Section 9 of the Wakf Act, 1995 (43 of 1995).
51. The Nehru Memorial Museum and Library (NMML).
52. The Jalianwala Bagh Memorial Trust.
53. The Haj Committee of India constituted under Section 3 of the Haj Committee Act, 2002 (35 of 2002).
54. The Mallickghat Phoolbazar Parichalan Committee.
55. The West Bengal Fisheries Corporation Limited.

4. Special provisions as to validation and other matters.

(1) Notwithstanding any judgment or order of any court or tribunal or any order or opinion of any other authority, the offices mentioned in clauses (ad), (k), (l) and (m) of Section 3 of the principal Act shall not disqualify or shall be deemed never to have disqualified the holders thereof for being chosen as, or for being, a member of either House of Parliament as if the principal Act as amended by this Act had been in force at all material times.

(2) Nothing contained in sub-section (1) shall be construed as to entitle any person who has vacated a seat owing to any order or judgment as aforesaid, to claim any re-instatement or any other claim in that behalf.

(3) For the removal of doubts, it is hereby clarified that any petition or reference pending before any court or other authority on the date of commencement of this Act, shall be disposed of in accordance with the provisions of the principal Act, as amended by this Act.

❑❑❑

24

The Parliamentary Proceedings (Protection of Publication) Act, 1956

This Act has been repealed by the Parliamentary Proceedings (Protection of Publication) Repeal Act, 1976 (28 of 1976) s.1 (w.e.f. 8-12-1975).

❑❑❑

25

The Parliamentary Proceedings (Protection of Publication) Act, 1977

ACT NO. 15 OF 1977 18TH APRIL, 1977

Preamble

AN ACT to protect the publication of reports of proceedings of Parliament.

Be it enacted by Parliament in the Twenty-eighth Year of the Republic of India as follows -

1. Short title, extent and commencement.

(1) This Act may be called the Parliamentary Proceedings (Protection of Publication) Act, 1977.

(2) It extends to the whole of India except the State of Jammu and Kashmir.

(3) It shall be deemed to have come into force on the 25th day of March, 1977.

2. Definition. In this Act, "newspaper" means any printed periodical work containing public news or comments on public news, and includes a news agency supplying material for publication in a newspaper.

3. Publication of reports of Parliamentary proceedings privileged.

(1) Save as otherwise provided in sub-section (2), no person shall be liable to any proceedings, civil or criminal, in any court in respect of the publication in a newspaper of a substantially true report of any proceedings of either House of Parliament, unless the publication is proved to have been made with malice.

(2) Nothing in sub-section (1) shall be construed as protecting the publication of any matter, the publication of which is not for the public good.

4. Act also to apply to Parliamentary proceedings broadcast by wireless telegraphy. This Act shall apply in relation to reports or matters broadcast by means of wireless telegraphy as part of any programme or service provided by means of a broadcasting station situate within the territories to which this Act extends as it applies in relation to reports or matters published in a newspaper.

❑❑❑

26

The Part B States (Laws) Act, 1951

ACT NO. III OF 1951 [22ND FEBRUARY, 1951]

AN ACT to provide for the extension of certain laws to Part B States.

Be it enacted by Parliament as follows -

1. * * * *

2. Definition. In this Act, "appointed day" means the date on which this Act comes into force.

3. Extension and amendment of certain Acts and Ordinances. The Acts and Ordinances specified in the Schedule shall be amended in the manner and to the extent therein specified, and the territorial extent of each of the said Acts and Ordinances shall, as from the appointed day an insofar as any of the said Acts or Ordinances or any of the provisions contained therein relates to matters with respect of which Parliament has power to make laws, be as stated in the extent clause thereof as so amended.

4. Construction of references to laws not in force in Part B States. Any reference in any Act or Ordinance specified in the Schedule to a law which is not in force in a Part B State shall, in relation to that State, be construed as a reference to the corresponding law, if any, in force in that State.

5. Construction of references to authorities where new authorities have been constituted. Act reference, by whatever form of words, in any law for the time being in force in a Part B State to any authority competent at the date of the passing of that law of exercise any powers or discharge any functions in that State shall, where a corresponding new authority has been constituted by or under any Act or Ordinance now extended to that State, have effect as if it were a reference to that new authority.

6. Repeals and savings. If immediately before the appointed day, there is in force in any Part B State any law corresponding to any of the Acts or Ordinances now extended to that State, that law shall, save as otherwise expressly provided in the Act, stand repealed:

PROVIDED that the repeal shall not affect —

(a) The previous operation of any law so repealed or anything duly done or suffered thereunder, or

(b) Any right, privilege, obligation or liability acquired, accrued or incurred under any law so repealed, or

(c) Any penalty, forfeiture or punishment incurred in respect of any offence committed against any law so repealed, or

(d) Any investigation, legal proceeding or remedy in respect of any such right, privilege, obligation, liability, penalty, forfeiture or punishment as aforesaid;

And any such investigation, legal proceeding or remedy may be instituted, continued or enforced, and any such penalty, forfeiture or punishment may be imposed as if this Act had not been passed.

PROVIDED FURTHER that, subject to the preceding proviso, anything done or any action taken (including any appointment or delegation made, notification, order, instruction or direction issued, rule, regulation, form, bye-law or scheme framed, certificate obtained, patent, permit or licence granted or registration effected) under any such law shall be deemed to have been done or taken under the corresponding provision of the Act or Ordinance as now extended to that State, and shall continue to be in force accordingly, unless and until superseded by anything done or any action taken under the said Act or Ordinance.

7. Power to remove difficulties.

(1) If any difficulty arises in giving effect in any Part B state to the provisions of any Act or Ordinance now extended to that state, the Central Government may, by order notified in the Official Gazette, make such provisions or give such directions as appear to it to be necessary for the removal of the difficulty.

(2) In particular, and without prejudice to the generality of the foregoing power, any such notified order may-

(a) Specify the corresponding authorities within the meaning of section 5;

(b) Provide for the transfer of any matter pending before the appointed day, to any corresponding court, tribunal or other authority, immediately before the appointed day, to any corresponding court, tribunal or other authority for disposal;

(c) Specify the areas or circumstances in which, or the extent to which or the conditions subject to which, anything done or any action taken (including any of the matters specified in the second proviso to section 6) under any law repealed by that section shall be recognised or given effect to under the corresponding provision of the Act or Ordinance as now extended.

□□□

27

The Partition Act, 1893

Act No. 4 of 1893 [1][9th March, 1893]

AN ACT to amend the Law relating to Partition.

WHEREAS it is expedient to amend the law relating to partition; It is hereby enacted as follows —

1. Title, extent and saving.

(1) This Act may be called the Partition Act, 1893 ;

(2) It extends to the whole of India [1][except the State of Jammu and Kashmir].

(3) But nothing herein contained shall be deemed to affect any local law providing for the partition of immovable property paying revenue to Government.

2. Power to Court to order sale instead of division in partition suits. Whenever in any suit for partition in which, if instituted prior to the commencement of this Act, a decree for partition might have been made, it appears to the Court that, by reason of the nature of the property to which the suit relates, or of the number of the shareholders therein, or of any other special circumstance, a division of the property cannot reasonably or conveniently be made, and that a sale of the property and distribution of the proceeds would be more beneficial for all the shareholders, the Court may, if it thinks fit, on the request of any of such shareholders interested individually or collectively to the extent of one moiety or upwards, direct a sale of the property and a distribution of the proceeds.

3. Procedure when sharer undertakes to buy.

(1) If, in any case in which the Court is requested under the last foregoing section to direct a sale, any other shareholder applies for leave to buy at a valuation the share or shares of the party or parties asking for a sale, the Court shall order a valuation of the share or shares in such manner as it may think fit

and offer to sell the same to such shareholder at the price so ascertained, and may give all necessary and proper directions in that behalf.

(2) If two or more shareholders severally apply for leave to buy as provided in sub-section (1), the Court shall order a sale of the share or shares to the shareholder who offers to pay the highest price above the valuation made by the Court.

(3) If no such shareholder is willing to buy such share or shares at the price so ascertained, the applicant or applicants shall be liable to pay all costs of or incident to the application or applications.

4. Partition suit by transferee of share in dwelling-house.

(1) Where a share of a dwelling- house belonging to an undivided family has been transferred to a person who is not a member of such family and such transferee sues for partition, the Court shall, if any member of the family being a shareholder shall undertake to buy the share of such transferee, make a valuation of such share in such manner as it thinks fit and direct the sale of such share to such shareholder, and may give all necessary and proper directions in that behalf.

(2) If in any case described in sub-section (1) two or more members of the family being such shareholders severally undertake to buy such share, the Court shall follow the procedure prescribed by sub-section (2) of the last foregoing section.

5. Representation of parties under disability. In any suit for partition a request for sale may be made or an undertaking, or application for leave, to buy may be given or made on behalf of any party under disability by any person authorised to act on behalf of such party in such suit, but the Court shall not be bound to comply with any such request, undertaking or application unless it is of opinion that the sale or purchase will be for the benefit of the party under such disability.

6. Reserved bidding and bidding by shareholders.

(1) Every sale under Section 2 shall be subject to a reserved bidding, and the amount of such bidding shall be fixed by the Court in such manner as it may think fit and may be varied from time to time.

(2) On any such sale any of the shareholders shall be at liberty to bid at the sale on such terms as to non-payment of deposit or as to setting off or accounting for the purchase-money or any part thereof instead of paying the same as to the Court may seem reasonable.

(3) If two or more persons, of whom one is a shareholder in the property, respectively advance the same sum at any bidding at such sale, such bidding shall be deemed to be the bidding of the shareholder.

7. Procedure to be followed in case of sales. Save as hereinbefore provided, when any property is directed to be sold under this Act, the following procedure shall, as far as practicable, be adopted, namely —

(a) if the property be sold under a decree or order of the High Court of Calcutta, Madras or Bombay in the exercise of its original jurisdiction, [1][the procedure of such Court in its original civil jurisdiction for the sale of property by the Registrar;

(b) if the property be sold under a decree or order of any other Court, such procedure as the High Court may from time to time by rules prescribe in this behalf, and until such rules are made, the procedure prescribed in the [2][Code of Civil Procedure (14 of 1882) in respect of sales in execution of decrees.

8. Orders for sale to be deemed decrees. Any order for sale made by the Court under Section 2, 3 or 4 shall be deemed to be a decree within the meaning of Section 2 of the [2][Code of Civil Procedure (14 of 1882)].

9. Saving of power to order partly partition and partly sale. In any suit for partition the Court may, if it shall think fit, make a decree for a partition of part of the property to which the suit relates and a sale of the remainder under this Act.

10. Application of Act to pending suits. This Act shall apply to suits instituted before the commencement thereof, in which no scheme for the partition of the property has been finally approved by the Court.

❑❑❑

28

The Pondicherry (Alteration of Name) Act, 2006

No. 44 of 2006 [13th September, 2006]

AN ACT to alter the name of the Union territory of Pondicherry.

Be it enacted by Parliament in the Fifty-seventh Year of the Republic of India as follows -

1. Short title and commencement.

(1) This Act may be called the Pondicherry (Alteration of Name) Act, 2006.

(2) It shall come into force on such date as the Central Government may, by notification in the Official Gazette, appoint.

2. Definitions. In this Act, unless the context otherwise requires-

(a) "appointed day" means the date appointed under sub-section (2) of Section 1 for the coming into force of this Act;

(b) "appropriate Government" means the Central Government, and as respects a law relating to a matter enumerated in the State List or the Concurrent List in the Seventh Schedule to the Constitution insofar as any such matter is applicable in relation to the Union territory of Puducherry, also the administrator of the Union territory of Puducherry;

(c) "law" includes any enactment, Ordinance, regulation, order, bye-law, rule, scheme, notification or other instrument having the force of law in the whole or any part of the Union territory of Pondicherry.

3. Alteration of name of the Union territory of Pondicherry. As from the appointed day, the Union territory of Pondicherry shall be known as the Union territory of Puducherry.

4. Amendment of Part VIII of the Constitution. In Part VIII of the Constitution, for the word "Pondicherry", wherever it occurs, the word "Puducherry" shall be substituted.

5. Amendment of First Schedule to the Constitution. In the First Schedule to the Constitution, under the heading "II. THE UNION TERRITORIES", in entry 6, under the column "Name", for the word "Pondicherry", the word "Puducherry" shall be substituted.

6. Amendment of Fourth Schedule to the Constitution. In the Fourth Schedule to the Constitution, under the heading "TABLE", in entry 30, in the second column, for the word "Pondicherry", the word "Puducherry" shall be substituted.

7. Amendment of Section 2 of Act 20 of 1963. In the Government of Union Territories Act, 1963, in Section 2, in sub-section 1, in clause (h), for the word "Pondicherry", the word "Puducherry" shall be substituted.

8. Power to adapt laws.

(1) For the purpose of giving effect to the alteration of the name of the Union territory of Pondicherry by Section 3, the appropriate Government may, before the expiration of one year from the appointed day, by order, make such adaptations and modifications of any law made before the appointed day, whether by way of repeal or amendment, as may be necessary or expedient, and thereupon every such law shall have effect subject to the adaptations and modifications so made.

(2) Nothing in sub-section (1) shall be deemed to prevent Parliament or Legislative Assembly of the Union territory of Puducherry or other competent authority from repealing or amending any law adapted or modified by the appropriate Government under the said sub-section.

9. Power to construe laws. Notwithstanding that no provision or insufficient provision has been made under Section 8 for the adaptation of a law made before the appointed day, any court, tribunal or authority, required or empowered to enforce such law, may construe the law in such manner, without affecting the substance, as may be necessary or proper in regard to the matter before the court, tribunal or authority.

10. Legal proceedings. Where immediately before the appointed day any legal proceedings are pending to which the administrator of the Union territory of Pondicherry is a party, or the Union of India represented by the said administrator is a party, then, for the purposes of those proceedings, any reference to the administrator of the Union territory of Pondicherry shall be construed as a reference to the administrator of the Union territory of Puducherry.

□□□

29

The President's (Emoluments and Pension) Act, 1951

The Principal Act received the assent of the President on the 13th May, 1951 and published in the Gazette of India on 17th May, 1951

AN ACT to provide 1^(for the emoluments of the President and for) pension to retiring Presidents.

Be it enacted by Parliament as follows -

1. Short title. This Act may be called the President's [1](Emoluments and) Pension Act, 1951.

[1][1A. There shall be paid to the President by way of emoluments [2](one lakh fifty thousand rupees) per mensem.]

2. Pension to retiring Presidents.

(1) There shall be paid to every person who ceases to hold office as President either by the expiration of his term of office or by resignation of his office, a pension of [2](at the rate of fifty per cent of the emoluments of the President per month) for the remainder of his life.

[3]*PROVIDED that if any person before assuming the office of President, has held the office of the Vice-President, such person shall not be entitled to any pension and other benefits under the provisions of the Vice-President's Pension Act, 1997.*

(2) Subject to any rules that may be made in this behalf, every such person shall, for the remainder of his life, be entitled to –

[4]{(a) to the use of a furnished residence (including its maintenance), without payment of rent, two telephones (one for internet and broadband connectivity), one mobile phone with national roaming facility and a

motor-car, free of charge or to such car allowance as may be specified in the rules;

(b) to secretarial staff consisting of a Private Secretary, one Additional Private Secretary, one Personal Assistant, two Peons, and office expenses up to sixty thousand rupees per annum;}

[5][(c) to medical attendance and treatment free of charge;]

[6](d) to travel anywhere in India accompanied by one person by the highest class by air, rail or steamer.

EXPLANATION: For the purpose of this sub-section "residence" shall have the meaning assigned to it in the Salaries and Allowances of Ministers Act, 1952.

[7][(2A) Subject to any rules that may be made in this behalf, the spouse of every such person shall, for the remainder of life be entitled to medical attendance and treatment, free of charge.

(3) Where any person is re-elected to the office of President, such person or the spouse of such person shall not be entitled to any benefit under this Section for the period during which such person again holds that office.]

[8][2A. The spouse of a person who dies –

(a) while holding the office of President, or

(b) after ceasing to hold office as president either by the expiration of his term of office or by resignation of his office, shall be paid a family pension at the rate of fifty per cent of pension as is admissible to a retiring President, for the remainder of her life.

3. Subject to any rules that may be made in this behalf, the spouse of a person who dies. While holding the office of President shall, for the remainder of life be entitled to medical attendance and treatment, free of charge.

3A. Subject to any rules that may be made in this behalf, the spouse of a person who dies –

(a) while holding the office of President, or

[9]{(b) after ceasing to hold office as President, either on the expiration of his term of office or by resignation of his office, shall be entitled -

(i) to the use of furnished residence (including its maintenance) without payment of licence fee;

(ii) to secretarial staff consisting of a Private Secretary and a Peon and office expenses as per actuals, the total expenditure on which shall not exceed twelve thousand rupees per annum;

(iii) to a telephone and a motor-car, free of charge or such car allowance for the remainder of his life, as may be specified in the rules;

(iv) to travel anywhere in India, in a calendar year to twelve single journeys, by the highest class, by air, rail or steamer, accompanied by a companion or a relative.}]

4. Pensions to be charged on the Consolidated Fund of India. Any sum payable under this Act shall be charged on the Consolidated Fund of India.

5. (1) The Central government may, by notification in the Official Gazette, make rules for carrying out the purposes of this Act.

(2) Every rule made by the Central Government under this Act shall be laid as soon as may be after it is made, before each House of Parliament, while it is in session, for a total period of thirty days which may be comprised in one session or in two or more successive sessions, and if, before the expiry of the successive sessions aforesaid, both Houses agree in making any modification in the rule or both Houses agree that the rule should not be made, the rule shall thereafter have effect only in such modified form or be of no effect, as the case may be; so, however, that any such modification or annulment shall be without prejudice to the validity of anything previously done under that rule.

[9]{**6. Power to remove difficulties.**

(1) If any difficulty arises in giving effect to the provisions of this Act, as amended by the President's Emoluments and Pension (Amendment) Act, 2008, the Central Government may, by order, do anything not inconsistent with such provisions for the purpose of removing the difficulty:

PROVIDED that no such order shall be made after the expiration of two years from the date on which this Act comes into force.

(2) Every order made under sub-section (1) shall be laid before each House of Parliament.}

❑❑❑

ENDNOTES

1. Inserted *vide* the President's Pension (Amendment) Act, 1985 (77 of 1985). Made effective from 26-12-1985.
2. Substituted *vide* the President's Emoluments and Pension Act, 2008 (28 of 2008). Made effective from 1-1-2006.
3. Inserted *vide* President's Emoluments and Pension (Amendment) Act, 1998 (25 of 1998).
4. Substituted *vide* the President's Emoluments and Pension Act, 2008 (28 of 2008). Made effective from 30.12.2008.
5. Substituted *vide* the President's Emoluments and Pension Act, 1990 (16of 1990). Made effective from 29-6-1990.
6. Added *vide* the President's Emoluments and Pension (Amendment) Act, 1993 (71 of 1993). Made effective from 27-12-1993.
7. Added *vide* the President's Pension (Amendment) Act, 1976.
8. Inserted *vide* President's Emoluments and Pension (Amendment) Act, 2000 (14 of 2000). Made effective from 11-8-2000.
9. Substituted *vide* the President's Emoluments and Pension Act, 2008 (28 of 2008). Made effective from 30.12.2008.

30

The Presidential and Vice-Presidential Elections Act, 1952

AN ACT to regulate certain matters relating to or connected with elections to the offices of President and Vice-President of India.

Be it enacted by Parliament as follows:-

PART - I : PRELIMINARY

1. Short title. This Act may be called the Presidential and Vice-Presidential Elections Act, 1952.

2. Definitions. In this Act, unless the context otherwise requires -

(a) "article" means an article of the Constitution;

(b) "election" means a Presidential election or Vice-Presidential election ;

(c) "Election Commission" means the Election Commission appointed by the President under article 324;

(d) "elector", in relation to a Presidential election, means a member of the electoral college referred to in article 54, and in relation to a Vice-Presidential election, means [1][a member of the electoral college referred to in article 66];

(e) "prescribed" means prescribed by rules made, under this Act ;

(f) "Presidential election" means an election to fill the office of the President of India;

[2]["(ff) "public holiday" means any day which is a public holiday for the purposes of Section 25 of the Negotiable Instruments Act, 1881;"]

(g) "Returning Officer" includes an Assistant Returning Officer performing any function which he is [competent][3] to perform under sub-section (2) of Section 3;

(h) "Vice-Presidential election" means an election to fill the office of the Vice-President of India.

PART - II : CONDUCT OF PRESIDENTIAL AND VICE-PRESIDENTIAL ELECTIONS

3. Returning officer and his assistants.

(1) For the purposes of each election the Election Commission shall, in consultation with the Central Government, appoint a Extended to and brought into force in Dadra and Nagar Haveli (w.e.f. 1.7.1965) by Reg. 6 of 1963, s. 2 & Sch. I. Returning Officer who shall have his office in New Delhi and may also appoint one or more Assistant Returning Officers.

(2) Subject to rules made under this Act, every Assistant Returning Officer shall be competent to perform all or any of the functions of the Returning Officer.

4. Appointment of dates for nominations, etc.

[4][(1) The Election Commission shall, by notification in the Official Gazette, appoint for every election-

(a) the last date for making nominations, which shall be the fourteenth day after the date of publication of the notification under this sub-section, or, if that day is a public holiday, the next succeeding day which is not a public holiday;

(b) the date for the scrutiny of nominations, which shall be the day immediately following the last date for making nominations or, if that day is a public holiday, the next succeeding day which is not a public holiday;

(c) the last date for the withdrawal of candidatures, which shall be the second day after the date for the scrutiny of nominations or, if that day is a public holiday, the next succeeding day which is not a public holiday;

(d) the date on which a poll shall, if necessary, be taken, which shall be a date not earlier than the fifteenth day after the last date for the withdrawal of the candidatures.]

(2) In the case of the first Presidential and Vice-Presidential elections, the notifications under sub-section (1) shall be issued as soon, as may be after both Houses of Parliament have been constituted.

(3) In the case of an election to fill a vacancy caused by the expiration of the term of office of the President or Vice-President, the notification under sub-section (1) shall be issued on, or as soon as conveniently may be after, the sixtieth day before the expiration of the term of office of the outgoing President or Vice-President, as the case may be, and the dates shall be so appointed under the said subsection that the election will be completed at such time as will enable the President or the Vice-President thereby elected to enter upon his office on the day following the expiration of the term of office of the outgoing President or Vice-President, as the case may be.

(4) In the case of an election to fill a vacancy in the office of President or Vice-President occurring by reason of his death, resignation or removal or otherwise, the notification under sub-section (1) shall be issued as soon as may be after the occurrence of such vacancy.

5. Public notice of election. [5][On the issue of a notification under sub-section (1) of Section 4, the, returning officer for the election shall give public notice of the intended election in such form and in such manner as may be prescribed, inviting nominations of candidates for such election and specifying the place at which the nomination papers are to be delivered.

5A. Nomination of candidates. Any person may be nominated as a candidate for election to the office of President or Vice-President if he is qualified to be elected to that office under the Constitution.

5B. Presentation of nomination papers and requirements for a valid nomination.

(1) On or before the date appointed under clause (a) of sub-section (1) of Section 4, each candidate shall, either in person or by any of his proposers or seconders, between the hours of eleven O' clock in the forenoon and three oclock in the afternoon, deliver to the returning officer at the place specified in this behalf in the public notice issued under Section 5 a nomination paper completed in the prescribed form and subscribed by the candidate as assenting to the nomination, and

(a) in the case of Presidential election, also by at least 2fifty electors as proposers and at least ten electors seconders;

(b) in the case of Vice-Presidential election, also by at least 3twenty electors as proposers and at least twenty electors as seconders:

PROVIDED that no nomination paper shall be presented to the returning officer on a day which is a public holiday.

(2) Each nomination paper shall be accompanied by a certified copy of the entry relating to the candidate in the electoral roll for the parliamentary constituency in which the candidate is registered as an elector.

(3) The returning officer shall not accept any nomination paper which is presented on any day before eleven O' clock in the forenoon and after three oclock in the afternoon.

(4) Any nomination paper which is not received before three O' clock in the afternoon on the last date appointed under clause (a) of sub-section (1) of Section 4 or to which the certified copy referred to in sub-section (2) of this section is not attached shall be rejected and a brief note relating to such rejection shall be recorded on the nomination paper itself.

(5) No elector shall subscribe, whether as proposer or as seconder, more than one nomination paper at the same election and, if he does, his signature shall be inoperative on any paper other than the one first delivered.

(6) Nothing in this section shall prevent any candidate from being nominated by more than one nomination paper for the same election:

PROVIDED that not more than four nomination papers shall be presented by or on behalf of any candidate or accepted by the returning officer.

5C. Deposit.

(1) A candidate shall not be deemed to be duly nominated for election unless he deposits or causes to be deposited a sum of fifteen thousand rupees:

PROVIDED that where a candidate has been nominated by more than one nomination paper for the same election, not more than one deposit shall be required of him under this sub-section.

(2) The sum required to be deposited under sub-section (1) shall not, be deemed to have been deposited under that sub-section unless at the time of presentation of the nomination paper under sub-section (1) of Section 5B, the candidate has either deposited or caused to be deposited that sum with the returning officer in cash or enclosed with the nomination paper a receipt showing that the said sum has been deposited by him or on his behalf in the Reserve Bank of India or in a Government Treasury.

5D. Notice of nominations and the time and place for their scrutiny. On the presentation of a nomination paper, the returning officer shall -

(a) sign thereon a certificate stating the date and time of presentation of the nomination paper and enter thereon its serial number;

(b) inform the person or persons presenting the nomination paper of the date, time and place fixed for the scrutiny of nominations; and

(c) cause to be affixed in some conspicuous place in his office a copy of the nomination paper as certified and numbered under clause (a).

5E. Scrutiny of nominations.

(1) On the date fixed for the scrutiny of nominations under sub-section (1) of Section 4, the candidates, one proposer or one seconder of each candidate and one other person duly authorised in writing by each candidate, but no other person, shall be entitled to be present at the time of scrutiny of nominations and the returning officer shall give them all reasonable facilities for examining the nomination papers of all candidates which have not been rejected under sub-section (4) of Section 5B.

(2) For the removal of doubts, it is hereby declared that it small not be necessary to scrutinise on the date fixed for the scrutiny of nominations the nomination papers already rejected under sub-section (4) of Section 5B.

(3) The returning officer shall then examine the nomination papers and shall decide all objections which may be made to any nomination paper and may, either on such objection or on his own notion, after such summary inquiry, if any, as he thinks necessary, reject any nomination on any of the following grounds:-

(a) that, on the date fixed for the scrutiny of nominations, the candidate is not eligible for election as President or Vice-President, as the case may be, under the Constitution; or

(b) that any of the proposers or seconders is not qualified to subscribe a nomination paper under sub-section (1) of Section 5B; or

(c) that the nomination paper is not subscribed by the required number of proposers or seconders; or

(d) that the signature of the candidate or any of the proposers or seconders is not genuine or has been obtained by fraud; or

(e) that there has been a failure to comply with any of he provision of Section 5B or Section 5C.

(4) Nothing contained in clauses (b) to (e) of sub-section (3) shall be deemed to authorise the rejection of the nomination of any candidate on the ground of any irregularity in respect of a nomination paper, if the candidate has been duly nominated by means of another nomination paper in respect of which no irregularity has been committed.

(5) The returning officer shall not reject any nomination paper on the ground of any defect which is not of a substantial character.

(6) The returning officer shall hold the scrutiny on the date appointed in this behalf under clause (b) of sub-section (1) of Section 4 and shall not allow any adjournment of the proceedings except when such proceedings are interrupted or obstructed by riot or open violence or by causes beyond his control :

PROVIDED that in case an objections is raised by the returning officer or is made by any other person the candidate concerned may be allowed time to rebut it not later than the next day but one following the date fixed for scrutiny, and the returning officer shall record his decision on the date to which the proceedings have been adjourned.

(7) The returning officer shall endorse on each nomination paper his decision accepting or rejecting the same and if the nomination paper is rejected, shall record in writing a brief statement of his reasons for such rejection.

(8) For the purposes of this section, a certified copy of an entry in the electoral roll for the time being in force shall be conclusive evidence of the fact that the person referred to in that entry is an elector for that constituency, unless it is proved, that he, is subject to any of the disqualifications mentioned in Section 16.of the Representation of the People Act, 1950.]

6. Withdrawal of candidature.

(1) Any candidate may withdraw his candidature by a notice in writing in the prescribed form subscribed by him and delivered before three O' clock in the afternoon on the date fixed under clause (c) of sub-section (1) of Section 4, to the Returning Officer either by such candidate in person or [6][by any one of his proposers or seconders] who has been authorised in this behalf in writing by such candidate.

(2) No person who has given notice withdrawal of his candidature under sub-section (1) shall be allowed to cancel the notice.

[7][(3) The Returning Officer shall, on being satisfied as to the genuineness of a notice of withdrawal and the identity of the person delivering it under sub-

section (1), cause the notice to be affixed in some conspicuous place in his office.]

7. Death of candidate before poll. If a candidate, whose nomination has been made and is found to be in order on scrutiny, dies after the time fixed for nomination and a report of his death is received by the Returning Officer before the commencement of the poll, the Returning Officer shall, upon being satisfied of the fact of the death of the candidate, countermand the poll and report the fact, to the Election Commission, and all proceedings with reference to the election shall be commenced anew in all respects as if for a new election:

PROVIDED that no further nomination shall be necessary in the case of a candidate whose nomination was valid at the time of the countermanding of the poll:

PROVIDED FURTHER that no person who has under sub-section (1) of Section 6 given a notice of withdrawal of his candidature before the countermanding of the poll shall be ineligible for being nominated as a candidate for the election after such countermanding.

8. Procedure in contested and uncontested elections. If after the expiry of the period within which candidatures may be withdrawn under sub-section (1) of Section 6 -

(a) there is only one candidate who has been validly nominated and has not withdrawn his candidature in the manner and within the time specified in that subsection, the Returning Officer shall forthwith declare such candidate to be duly elected to the office of President or Vice-President, as the case may be;

(b) the number of candidates who have been duly nominated but have not so withdrawn their candidatures exceeds one, the Returning Officer shall forthwith publish in such form and manner as may be prescribed a list containing the names in alphabetical order and addresses of candidates as given in the nomination papers, together with such other particulars as may be prescribed, and a poll shall be taken;

(c) there is no candidate who has been duly nominated and has not so withdrawn his candidature, the Returning Officer shall report the fact to the Election Commission and thereafter all the proceedings in relation to the election shall be commenced afresh and for that purpose the Election Commission shall cancel the notification issued under sub-section (1) of Section 4 in respect of such election and issue another notification under that subsection appointing the dates referred to in that sub-section for the purposes of such fresh election.

9. Manner of voting at elections. At every election where a poll is taken, votes shall be given by ballot in such manner as may be prescribed, and no votes shall be received by proxy.

10. Counting of votes. At every election where a poll is taken, votes shall be counted by, or under the supervision of, the Returning Officer, and each candidate and one representative of each candidate authorised in writing by the candidate, shall have a right to be present at the time of counting.

11. Declaration of results. When the counting of the votes has been completed, the Returning Officer shall forthwith declare the result of the election in the manner provided by this Act or the rules made thereunder.

12. Report of the result. As soon as may be after the result of an election has been declared, the Returning Officer shall report the result to the Central Government and the Election Commission, and the Central Government shall cause to be published in the Official Gazette the declaration containing the name of the person elected to the office of President or Vice-President, as the case may be.

[8][PART - III : DISPUTES REGARDING ELECTIONS

13. Definitions. In this Part, unless the context otherwise requires -

(a) "candidate" means a person who has been or claims to have been duly nominated as a candidate at an election;

(b) "costs" means all costs, charges and expenses of, or incidental to, a trial of an election petition;

(c) "returned candidate" means a candidate whose name has been published under Section 12 as duly elected.

14. Authority to try election petitions.

(1) No election shall be called in question except by presenting an election petition to the authority specified in sub-section (2).

(2) The authority having jurisdiction to try an election petition shall be the Supreme Court.

(3) Every election petition shall be presented to such authority in accordance with the provisions of this Part and of the rules made by the Supreme Court under article 145.

14A. Presentation of petition.

(1) An election petition calling in question an election may be presented on one or more of the grounds specified in subsection (1) of Section 18 and Section 19, to the Supreme Court by any candidate at such election, or-

   (i) in the case of Presidential election, by twenty or more electors joined together as petitioners;

   (ii) in the case of Vice-Presidential election, by ten or more electors joined together as petitioners.

(2) Any such petition may be presented at any time after the date of publication of the declaration containing the name of the returned candidate at the election under Section 12, but not later than thirty days from the date of such publication.

15. Form of petitions, etc., and procedure. Subject to the provisions of this Part, rules made [whether before or after the commencement of the Presidential and Vice-Presidential Elections (Amendment) Act, 1977] by the Supreme Court under article 145 may regulate the form of election petitions, the manner in which they are to be presented, the persons who are to be made parties thereto, the procedure to be adopted in connection therewith and the circumstances in which petitions are to abate, or may be withdrawn, and in which new petitioners may be substituted, and may require security to be given for costs.

16. Relief that may be claimed by the petitioner. A petitioner may claim either of the following declarations:-

(a) that the election of the returned candidate is void;

17. Orders of the Supreme Court.

(1) At the conclusion of the trial of the election petition, the Supreme Court shall make an order-

(a) dismissing the election petition; or

(b) declaring the election of the returned candidate to be void; or

(c) declaring the election of the returned candidate to be void and the petitioner or any other candidate to have been duly elected.

(2) At the time of making an order under sub-section (1), the Supreme Court shall also make an order fixing the total amount of costs payable and specifying the persons by and to whom costs shall be paid.

18. Grounds for declaring the election of a returned candidate to be void.

(1) If the Supreme Court is of opinion -

(a) that the offence of bribery or undue influence at the election has been committed by the returned candidate or by any person with the consent of the returned candidate; or

(b) that the result of the election has been materially affected-

(i) by the improper reception or refusal of a vote, or

(ii) by any non-compliance with the provisions of the Constitution or of this Act or of any rules or orders made under this Act; or

(iii) by reason of the fact that the nomination of any candidate (other than the successful candidate), who has not withdrawn his candidature, has been wrongly accepted; or

(c) that the nomination of any candidate has been wrongly rejected or the nomination of the successful candidate has been wrongly accepted; the Supreme Court shall declare the election of the returned candidate to be void.

(2) For the purposes of this section, the offences of bribery and undue influence at an election have the same meaning as in Chapter IXA of the Indian Penal Code.

19. Grounds for which a candidate other than the returned candidate may be declared to have been elected. If any person who has lodged an election petition has, in addition to calling in question the election of the returned candidate, claimed a declaration that he himself or any other candidate has been duly elected and the Supreme Court is of opinion that in fact the petitioner or such other candidate received a majority of the valid votes, the Supreme Court shall, after declaring the election of the returned candidate to be void, declare the petitioner or such other candidate, as the case may be, to have been duly elected:

PROVIDED that the petitioner or such other candidate shall not be declared to be duly elected if it is proved that the election of such candidate would have been void if he had been the returned candidate and a petition had been presented calling in question his election.

20. Transmission of orders to the Central Government and its publication. The Supreme Court shall, after announcing the orders made under Section 17, send a copy thereof to the Central Government, and on receipt of such copy the Central Government shall forthwith cause the order to be published in the Official Gazette.

PART - IV : MISCELLANEOUS

[9][**20A. Return or forfeiture of candidates deposit.**

(1) The deposit made under Section 5C shall either be returned to the person making it or his legal representative or be forfeited to the Central Government in accordance with the provisions of this section.

(2) Except in cases hereafter mentioned in this section, the deposit shall be returned as soon as practicable after the result of the election is declared.

(3) If the candidate is not shown in the list referred to in clause (b) of Section 8, or if he dies before the commencement of the poll, the deposit shall be returned as soon as practicable after the publication of the list or after his death as the case may be.

(4) Subject to the provisions of sub-section (3), the deposit shall be forfeited if at the election where the poll has been taken, the candidate is not elected, and the number of valid votes polled by such, candidate does not exceed one-sixth of the number of votes necessary to secure the return of a candidate at such election.]

21. Power to make rules.

(1) The Central Government may, after consulting the Election Commission, by notification in the Official Gazette, make [10]rules for carrying out the purposes of this Act.

(2) In particular, and without prejudice to the generality of the foregoing power, such rules may provide for all or any of the following matters, namely:-

(a) the maintenance of a list of members of the electoral college referred to in article 54 with their addresses corrected up to date for the purposes of Presidential elections ;

(b) the maintenance of a list of [11][members of the electoral college referred to in article 66] with their addresses corrected up to date for the purposes of Vice-Presidential elections ;

(c) the powers and duties of a Returning Officer and the performance by any officer appointed to assist the Returning Officer of any function of the Returning Officer;

[11][(cc) the form and manner in which public notice under Section 5 shall be given by the returning officer;]

(d) the form and manner in which nominations may be made and the procedure to be followed in respect of the presentation of nomination papers;

(e) the scrutiny of nominations and, in particular, the manner in which such scrutiny shall be conducted and the conditions and circumstances under which any person may be present or may enter objections thereat;

(f) the publication of a list of valid nominations;

[12][(g) the place and hours of polling, the manner in which votes are to be given both generally and in the case of illiterate voters or voters not conversant with the language in which ballot papers are printed or voters under physical or other disability and the procedure as to voting to be followed at elections;]

(h) the scrutiny and counting of votes including cases in which a re-count of the votes may be made before the declaration of the result of the election;

(i) the safe custody of ballot boxes, ballot papers and other election papers, the period for which such papers shall be preserved and the inspection and production of such papers ;

(j) any other matter required to be prescribed by this Act.

[12][(3) Every rule made under this Act shall be laid, as soon as may be after it is made, before each House of Parliament, while it is in session, for a total period of thirty days which may be comprised in one session or in two or more successive sessions, and if, before the expiry of the session immediately following the session or the successive sessions aforesaid, both Houses agree in making any modification in the rule or both Houses agree that the rule should not be made, the rule shall thereafter have effect only in such modified form, or be of no effect, as the case may be; so, however, that any such modification or annulment shall be without prejudice to the validity of anything previously done under that rule.]

22. Maintenance of secrecy of voting.

(1) Every officer, clerk or other person who performs any duty in connection with the recording or counting of votes at an election shall maintain, and aid in maintaining, the secrecy of the voting and shall not (except for some purpose authorised by or under any law) communicate to any person any information calculated to violate such secrecy.

(2) Any person who contravenes the provisions of sub-section (1) shall be punishable with imprisonment for a term which may extend to three months, or with fine, or with both.

23. Jurisdiction of Civil Courts barred. Save as provided in Part III, no Civil Court shall have jurisdiction to question the legality of any action taken or of any decision given by the Returning Officer or by any other person appointed under this Act in connection with an election.

ENDNOTES

1. Subs. & ins. by Act 5 of 1974, S. 2.
2. Ins. by s. 2, *ibid.*
3. Subs. by s. 2 *ibid* for "authorised".
4. Subs. by Act 5. of 1974, S. 3 for sub-section (1).
5. Subs. by Act 35 of 1997, s. 3 (w.e.f. 29-8-1997).
6. Subs. by Act 5 of 1974, s.5, for certain words.
7. Subs. by s. 5, *ibid,* for sub-section (3).
8. Subs. by Act 20 of 1977, s.2.118 (b) that the election of the returned candidate is void and that he himself or any other candidate has been duly elected.
9. Ins. by Act 5 of 1974, S. 8.
10. For Presidential and Vice-Presidential Rules, 1952, see Gazette of India, Extraordinary, Pt. II, Sec. 3 (ii), p. 429.
11. Subs. by Act 5 of 1974, s.p.
12. Subs. & ins. by Act 5 of 1974, S, 9.

31

The Presidential and Vice-Presidential Elections Rules, 1974

CHAPTER I : PRELIMINARY

1. Short title and commencement.

(1) These rules][1] may be called the Presidential and Vice-Presidential Elections Rules, 1974.

(2) They shall come into force at once.

2. Interpretation.

(1) In these rules, unless the context otherwise requires.—

(a) "Act" means the Presidential and Vice-Presidential Elections Act, 1952;

(b) "article" means an article of the Constitution of India;

(c) "Form" means a Form appended to these rules;

(d) "section" means a section of the Act.

(2) The General Clauses Act, 1897 (10 of 1897), shall apply for the interpretation of these rules as it applies for the interpretation of an Act of Parliament.

CHAPTER - II : NOMINATION OF CANDIDATES

3. Public notice of intended election. The public notice of an intended election referred to in Section 5 shall be in Form 1 and shall be published by the Returning Officer by such means, in such language or languages and in such places as the Election Commission may direct.

4. Nomination paper. Every nomination paper presented under sub-section (1) of Section 5B shall be completed in Form 2 or Form 3, as may be appropriate.

5. Notice of withdrawal of candidature.

(1) A notice of withdrawal of candidature under sub-section (1) of Section 6 shall be in Form 4.

(2) On receipt of such notice, the Returning Officer shall note thereon the date on which and the hour at which it was delivered, and cause a copy thereof, together with the note, to be affixed in some conspicuous place in his office.

6. Preparation and publication of the list of contesting candidates. In every case in which a poll is to be taken under clause (b) of Section 8, the Returning Officer shall, immediately after the expiry of the period within which candidature may be withdrawn under sub-section (1) of Section 6—

(a) prepare in Form 5 a list of contesting candidates (that is to say, candidates who have been duly nominated but have not withdrawn their candidatures within the time specified in that behalf), containing the names in alphabetical order as given in the nomination papers together with their addresses;

(b) cause the list to be published in the Gazette of India and in such other manner as the Election Commission may direct; and

(c) cause a copy of the list to be affixed in some conspicuous place in his office.

CHAPTER - III : THE POLL

7. Fixing place and time of polling for Presidential election. At every Presidential election where a poll is to be taken, the Election Commission shall—

(a) fix a place of polling in the Parliament House in New Delhi, and also in the premises in each State in which the Legislative Assembly, if any, of that State meets for the transaction of business;

(b) specify with reference to each such place of polling the group of electors who will be entitled to vote, and the hours during which the poll will be taken, at such place; and

(c) give due publicity to the places so fixed and the groups of electors and the hours so specified.

8. Fixing place and time of polling for Vice-Presidential election. At every Vice-Presidential election where a poll is to be taken, the Election Commission shall—

(a) fix a place of polling in the Parliament House in New Delhi;

(b) specify the hours during which the poll will be taken; and

(c) give due publicity to the place so fixed and the hours so specified.

9. Presiding and polling officers.

(1) The Returning Officer or such Assistant Returning Officer as may be specified in this behalf by the Election Commission shall conduct the poll at each place of polling. Every such officer is hereinafter referred to as the presiding officer.

(2) The presiding officer may appoint such polling officer or officers as he thinks necessary to assist him in taking the poll, but he shall not so appoint any

person who has been employed by, or on behalf of, or has been working for, a candidate in or about the election.

10. Design and form of ballot papers.

(1) Every ballot paper shall have a counterfoil attached thereto and the said ballot paper and the counterfoil shall be in such form, and the particulars therein shall be in such language or languages, as the Election Commission may direct.

(2) The names of the candidates shall be printed on the ballot paper in the same order as in the list of contesting candidates published under Rule 6.

(3) Every presiding officer shall be supplied with a sufficient number of ballot papers by the Election Commission.

11. Ballot boxes. Every ballot box used at the poll shall be of a design previously approved by the Election Commission.

12. Procedure before the commencement of poll.

(1) The presiding officer shall, immediately before the commencement of the poll, allow inspection of the ballot box to be used at the poll to such candidates and authorized representatives of candidates as may be present at the place of polling.

(2) The presiding officer shall then secure and seal the box in such manner that the slit for the insertion of ballot papers remains open, and shall also allow such candidates and authorized representatives of candidates as may be present to affix their own seals, if they so desire.

13. Admission to the place of polling.

(1) The presiding officer shall exclude from the place of polling all persons except—

(a) the polling officers and other public servants on duty;

(b) the candidates, and one representative authorized in writing by each candidate;

(c) the electors;

(d) persons authorized by the Election Commission; and

(e) such other persons as the presiding officer may from time to time admit for the purpose of assisting him in taking the poll.

(2) The presiding officer shall close the place of polling at the hour fixed under clause (b) of Rule 7 or, as the case may be, under clause (b) of Rule 8 for the close of the poll and shall not admit therein any elector after that hour:

PROVIDED that all electors present at the place before it is so closed shall be entitled to have their votes recorded.

14. Procedure for giving ballot papers.

(1) The polling officer shall be furnished with an authentic list or part thereof of the electors entitled to vote at the place of polling.

(2) Immediately before a ballot paper is delivered to an elector, a mark shall be placed against his name in that list, and the number of the elector as shown in that list shall be entered on the counterfoil of the ballot paper.

(3) The elector shall sign his name in the list in token of receipt of the ballot paper, whereupon, but not earlier, the ballot paper shall be delivered to him.

15. Supply of fresh ballot paper in certain circumstances.

(1) An elector who has inadvertently dealt with his ballot paper in such a manner that it cannot be conveniently used as a ballot paper may, on delivering it to the presiding officer and on satisfying him of the inadvertence, obtain another ballot paper in place of the ballot paper so delivered, and the latter shall, together with its counterfoil, be marked as cancelled by the presiding officer.

(2) Any ballot papers so cancelled shall be kept in a separate envelope set apart for the purpose.

16. Return of unused ballot papers by electors. If an elector after obtaining any ballot paper for the purpose of recording his vote decides not to use the same, he shall return the ballot paper to the presiding officer, who shall mark it 'Returned and Cancelled' and keep it in a separate envelope set apart for the purpose.

17. Manner of recording votes.

(1) Every elector shall have as many preferences as there are candidates but no ballot paper shall be considered invalid solely on the ground that all such preferences are not marked.

(2) An elector in giving his vote—

- (a) shall place on his ballot paper the figure 1 in the space opposite the name of the candidate whom he chooses for his first preference; and
- (b) may, in addition, mark as many subsequent preferences as he wishes by placing on his ballot paper the figures 2, 3, 4 and so on, in the spaces opposite the names of other candidates, in order of preference.

  EXPLANATION. The figures referred to in clauses (a) and (b) of this sub-rule may be marked in the international form of Indian numerals or in the Roman form or in the form used in any Indian language but shall not be indicated in words.

(3) The presiding officer shall, if requested by an elector, explain to him the instructions contained on the ballot paper for the recording of votes.

18. Maintenance of secrecy of voting by electors within place of polling and voting procedure.

(1) Every elector to whom a ballot paper has been delivered under Rule 14 shall maintain secrecy of voting within the place of polling and for that purpose observe the voting procedure hereinafter laid down.

(2) An elector on receiving the ballot paper shall forthwith—

- (a) proceed to one of the voting compartments;
- (b) record his vote in accordance with sub-rule (2) of Rule 17;
- (c) fold the ballot paper so as to conceal his vote;
- (d) insert the folded ballot paper into the ballot box; and
- (e) quit the place of polling.

(3) Every elector shall vote without undue delay.

(4) No elector shall be allowed to enter a voting compartment when another elector is inside it.

19. Recording of votes of illiterate or disabled elector.

(1) If an elector is unable to read the ballot paper or to record his vote thereon in accordance with Rule 17 by reason of illiteracy or blindness or, by not being conversant with the language in which the ballot papers are printed or, by reason of any physical or other disability, the presiding officer shall record the vote on the ballot paper in accordance with the wishes of the elector.

(2) The elector shall then himself or with the assistance of the presiding officer fold up the ballot paper so as to conceal his vote and insert it into the ballot box.

(3) While acting under this rule, the presiding officer shall observe as much secrecy as is feasible and shall keep a brief record of each such instance but shall not indicate therein the manner in which any vote has been cast.

20. Account of ballot papers.

(1) The presiding officer shall at the close of the poll prepare a ballot paper account in Form 6 and enclose it in a separate cover with the words "Ballot Paper Account" superscribed thereon.

(2) The presiding officer shall permit the authorized representative of a candidate, who so desires, to take a true copy of the entries in the ballot paper account and shall attest it as true copy.

21. Sealing up of ballot boxes and papers after the close of poll.

(1) As soon as practicable after the close of poll the presiding officer shall, in the presence of such candidates and authorized representatives of candidates as may be present, close and seal up the slit as well as the ballot box.

(2) He shall also make up into separate packets —

(a) the copy of the list of electors marked in accordance with Rule 14:

(b) the counterfoils of ballot papers;

(c) the ballot papers cancelled under Rules 15 and 16; and

(d) the unused ballot papers.

and seal each such packet with his own seal and the seals of those candidates and authorized representatives of candidates who may desire to affix their seal thereon.

22. Transfer of ballot papers from ballot boxes in certain cases.

(1) Notwithstanding anything contained in Rule 21, the Election Commission may, at a Presidential election, direct the presiding officer at any place of polling other than the Parliament House in New Delhi to follow after the close of the poll the procedure laid down in this rule instead of the procedure laid down in sub-rule (1) of Rule 21.

(2) Where a direction has been issued under sub-rule (1), the presiding officer shall, as soon as practicable after the close of the poll, open the ballot box in

the presence of such candidates and authorized representatives of candidates as may be present and transfer all the ballot papers contained in it without examining or counting them into a separate cover and record on such cover—

(i) the name of the place of polling; and

(ii) the date of the poll.

(3) After such transfer he shall allow the candidates and their authorized representatives who may be present, to inspect the ballot box and demonstrate to them that it is empty.

(4) He shall then seal the cover with his own seal and the seals of those candidates and authorized representatives of candidates who may desire to affix their seals thereon.

(5) The cover so sealed shall, for the purposes of Rules 23, 25, 32 and 33, be deemed to be the ballot box used at that place of polling and the provisions of those rules shall apply accordingly.

23. Despatch and custody of ballot boxes and papers.

(1) At a Presidential election, the presiding officer at every place of polling other than the Parliament House in New Delhi shall forthwith cause the sealed ballot box and packets and all other papers used at the poll to be sent to the Returning Officer in accordance with such general or special instructions as may be issued in that behalf by the Election Commission.

(2) The Returning Officer shall make adequate arrangements for the safe custody of all sealed ballot boxes and packets and other papers used at the poll, until the commencement of the counting of votes.

24. Adjournment of poll in emergencies.

(1) If the proceedings at any place of polling are interrupted or obstructed by riot or open violence, or if it is not possible to take the poll at any such place on account of a natural calamity or other sufficient cause, the presiding officer shall announce an adjournment of the poll to a date to be notified later, and immediately report the circumstances to the Election Commission and, unless he is the Returning Officer, also to the Returning Officer.

(2) Whenever a poll is adjourned under sub-rule (1), the Election Commission shall, as soon as may be, fix the day on which, the place at which, and the hours during which the adjourned poll shall be taken, and shall notify the said details to all concerned in such manner as it may think fit.

(3) On the date on which such adjourned poll is taken, the electors who have already voted at the poll before its adjournment will not be entitled to vote, but only the remaining electors who were entitled to vote at the place of polling before its adjournment may vote.

25. Fresh poll in case of destruction, etc., of ballot boxes.

(1) If at an election, any ballot box is unlawfully taken away from the custody of the presiding officer or the Returning Officer or is in any way tampered with, destroyed or lost, the poll taken at the place of polling where that ballot box was

used shall be deemed to have been vitiated; and the Returning Officer shall, as soon as practicable, report the matter to the matter to the Election Commission, which shall appoint a day for the taking of a fresh poll at that place and fix the hours during which it will be taken.

(2) In every such case as aforesaid, the provisions of these rules shall apply to the fresh poll as they apply to the original poll.

26. Voting by electors under preventive detention.

(1) Notwithstanding anything in the fore going provisions of this Chapter, an elector may, if he is subjected to preventive detention under any law for the time being in force, give his vote by postal ballot.

(2) The Election Commission shall send by registered post to the officer-in-charge of the jail or other place where the elector is detained the appropriate ballot paper, together with a form of declaration of identity and attestation of signature and necessary envelopes specially prepared for the purpose and a letter of instructions, so as to reach that officer in good time before the date fixed for polling.

(3) On the date of polling the said officer shall deliver the ballot paper and other necessary papers to the elector, allow him all reasonable facilities and sufficient time, not exceeding two hours, for recording his vote in accordance with the instructions of the Election Commission, and if and when the elector has so recorded his vote, send the ballot paper and other connected papers in a sealed cover, either by registered post or through a special messenger, to the Returning Officer so as to reach him before the time fixed for the counting of votes under Rule 27.

(4) It shall be the duty of every Government to intimate to the Election Commission at the appropriate time the names of electors, if any, who are subjected to preventive detention by or under the authority of that Government, together with the necessary particulars as to their places of detention.

CHAPTER - IV : COUNTING OF VOTES AND DECLARATION OF RESULTS

27. Place and time for counting of votes. The counting of votes shall take place at the office of the Returning Officer in New Delhi on such day and at such day and at such time as the Election Commission may appoint in this behalf; and the Election Commission shall give notice to all the candidates of the date and time so appointed.

28. Admission to the place fixed for counting. The Returning Officer shall exclude from the place fixed for counting of votes all persons except-

(a) such persons as he may appoint to assist him in the counting;

(b) the candidates and one representative at time a authorized in writing by each candidate;

(c) public servants on duty in connection with the election; and

(d) persons authorized by the Election Commission.

29. Maintenance of secrecy of voting. Before the counting begins, the Returning Officer shall read out the provisions of Section 22 to the persons present.

30. Statement showing the number of votes of each elector at the Presidential election. For the purposes of every Presidential election, the Election Commission shall furnish the Returning Officer with a statement showing the number of votes which every elector has under the provisions of clause (2) of article 55 ; and every ballot paper put in by an elector at that election shall be deemed to represent as many votes as that elector is shown as shaving in that statement.

31. Ballot papers when invalid.

(1) A ballot paper shall be invalid on which—

(a) the figure 1 is not marked; or

(b) the figure 1 is marked opposite the name of more than one candidate or is so marked as to render it doubtful to which candidate it is intended to apply; or

(c) the figure 1 and some other figure are marked opposite the name of the same candidate; or

(d) any mark is made by which the elector may afterwards be identified.

EXPLANATION. The figures referred to in clauses (a), (b) and (c) of this sub-rule may be marked in the international form of Indian numerals or in the Roman form or in the form used in any Indian language, but shall not be indicated in words.

(2) A ballot paper shall also be invalid if, being a postal ballot paper, the signature of the elector is not duly attested.

32. Procedure upon opening each ballot box. After each ballot box and also each sealed cover (if any) received under sub-rule (3) of Rule 26, has been opened, the Returning Officer shall—

(a) count the number of ballot papers taken out there from and complete Part II of the Ballot Paper Account in Form 6;

(b) scrutinize the ballot papers and separate those which in his opinion are valid from those which in his opinion are invalid, endorsing on the latter the word 'rejected' and the ground of rejection; and

(c) arrange all the valid ballot papers in parcels according to the first preferences recorded for each candidate:

PROVIDED that if, at a Presidential election, the ballot box used at a place of polling contains ballot papers of electors who, at their request are specially permitted by the Election Commission in pursuance of Rule 7 to cast their votes at the said place of polling, such ballot papers shall, after the counting and recording in Form 6 is completed, be separated and added to the other ballot papers of the same kind used by electors in the same category and shall thereafter be scrutinized.

33. Determination of result. After all the ballot boxes and sealed covers (if any) have been opened and the ballot papers have been scrutinized and arranged, the Returning

Officer shall proceed to determine the result of the voting in accordance with the instructions contained in the Schedule to these rules.

34. Recounting. The Returning Officer may, either on his own initiative or at the instance of any candidate or of the authorized representative of a candidate in the absence of that candidate, recount votes, whether once or more than once, when the Returning Officer is not satisfied as to the accuracy of a previous count:

PROVIDED that nothing herein contained shall make it obligatory on the Returning Officer to recount the same votes more than once.

35. Declaration of result.

(1) When the counting is complete and the result of the voting has been determined, the Returning Officer shall forthwith—

(a) announce the result to those present;

(b) report the result to the Central Government and the Election Commission under Section 12;

(c) prepare and certify a return of the election in Form 7; and

(d) seal up in separate packets the valid ballot papers and the rejected ballot papers and record on each such packet a description of its contents.

(2) The Returning Officer shall, as soon as may be thereafter, forward the certified return to the Election Commission.

CHAPTER - V : MISCELLANEOUS

36. Custody of ballot boxes and election papers. All ballot boxes used at the election and the packets of ballot papers and all other papers relating to the election shall, after the election, be kept in such custody as the Election Commission may direct.

37. Production and inspection of election papers.

(1) The packets of ballot papers, whether valid or rejected, and their counterfoils and the packets containing the lists of electors marked in accordance with Rule 14 shall not be opened, nor shall their contents be inspected by, or produced before, any person or authority, except under the order of the Supreme Court or other competent court.

(2) All other papers relating to the election shall be open to public inspection subject to such conditions and to the payment of such fee, if any, as the Election Commission may direct.

38. Disposal of election papers. The packets and other papers referred to in Rule 37 shall be retained for a period of two years from the date of declaration of the result of the election, and shall thereafter be destroyed unless a direction to the contrary is given by the Supreme Court or other competent court or by the Election Commission.

39. Copies of return of election. Copies of the certified return of the election referred to in Rule 35 shall be furnished by the Election Commission on payment of a fee of one rupee per copy.

40. List of electors. The Election Commission shall maintain a list of members of the electoral college referred to in article 54 and a list of members of the electoral college referred to in article 66, with their addresses corrected up to date for the purposes, respectively, of Presidential election and Vice-Presidential election.

41. Repeal. The Presidential and Vice-Presidential Election Rules, 1952, are hereby repealed.

FORM 1

(*See* Rule 3)

PUBLIC NOTICE OF ELECTION TO THE OFFICE OF PRESIDENT/*VICE-PRESIDENT OF INDIA

WHEREAS a notification under sub-section (1) of Section 4 of the Presidential and Vice-Presidential Elections Act, 1952, for the holding of an election to fill the office of President/Vice-President of India has been issued by the Election Commission, I........................, the Returning Officer for such election, do hereby give notice that –

(i) nomination papers may be delivered by a candidate or any one of his proposers or seconders to the undersigned at his office in .... New Delhi, or if he is unavoidably absent, to ....at the said office between 11 a.m. and 3 p.m. on any day (other than a public holiday) not later than the ....;

(ii) each nomination paper shall be accompanied by a certified copy of the entry relating to the candidate in the electoral roll for the Parliamentary constituency in which the is registered as an elector;

(iii) every candidate shall deposit or cause to be deposited a sum of [rupees fifteen thousand][2] only. This amount may be deposited in cash with the Returning Officer at the time of presentation of the nomination paper or deposited earlier in the Reserve Bank of India or in a Government Treasury and in the latter case a receipt showing that the said deposit of the sum has been so made is required to be enclosed with the nomination paper;

(iv) forms of nomination papers may be obtained from the above said office at the times aforesaid;

(v) the nomination papers, other than those rejected under sub-section (4) of Section 5B of the Act, will be taken up for scrutiny at ....(place) on........................(date) at ....(hours);

(vi) the notice of withdrawal of candidates may be delivered by a candidate, or any one of his proposers or seconders who has been authorized in this behalf in writing by the candidate, to the undersigned at the place specified in paragraph (i) above before three o'clock in the afternoon of ....(date);

(vii) in the event of the election being contested, the poll will be taken on ....(date) between hours of ....and.............at the places of polling fixed under the Rules.

Place........................ (Signature).................

Dated the................. (Returning Officer)

(Designation)...............

*Strike off if inapplicable.

FORM 2

(*See* Rule 4)

NOMINATION PAPER ELECTION TO THE OFFICE OF THE PRESIDENT OF INDIA

We hereby nominate...
(Full name and address of the candidate)
as a candidate for election to the office of the President of India.

We have verified, and do hereby declare, that the said candidate has completed the age of 35 years and is registered in the electoral roll for the Parliamentary constituency of.......................................in the State of ....

A certified copy of the entry in that electoral roll relating to the said candidate is attached.

We further declare that we are members of the electoral college referred to in article 54 of the Constitution being elected members of the House of the People or Council of States or the Legislative Assembly as indicated hereunder and we append our signatures below in token of subscribing to this nomination:-

Particulars of the proposers and their signatures

Sl. No.	**Full name**	**Whether elected member of the House of The People/Council of States/Legislative Assembly**	**State/Union territory (in the case of member elected to the House of the People or Council of States from A Union territory) in/ from which elected.**	**Signature**	**Date**
1	2	3	4	5	6
1.					
2.					
3.					
4.					
5.					
6.					
7.					
8.					
9.					
10.					
11.					
12.					
13.					
14.					
15.					
*etc.					

[*There should be at least fifty electors as proposers.][2]

Particulars of the seconders and their signatures

Sl. No.	**Full name**	**Whether elected member of the House of the People/Council of States/Legislative Assembly**	**State/Union territory (in the case of member elected to the House of the People or Council of States from a Union territory) in/ from which elected.**	**Signature**	**Date**
1	**2**	**3**	**4**	**5**	**6.**
1.					
2.					
3.					
4.					
5.					
6.					
7.					
8.					
9.					
10.					
11.					
12.					
13.					
14.					
15.					
*etc.					

[*There should be at least fifty electors as proposers.][2]

I assent to this nomination.

Signature of candidate

Date....................

(To be filled by the Returning Officer)

Serial Number of nomination paper...

This nomination paper was delivered to me at my office at..............(hour) on..........(date) by the candidate/proposer..................(name)/seconder............(name) with enclosures as indicated below purporting to be—

(1)

(2)

Date..............

....

Returning Officer.

[Decision of the Returning Officer (if any) under sub-section (4) of Section 5B

I have rejected this nomination paper under sub-section (4) of Section 5B of the Presidential and Vice-Presidential Elections Act, 1952 for the reasons given below—

Date............ Returning Officer]

Decision of the Returning Officer accepting or rejecting the nomination paper

I have examined this nomination paper in accordance with Section 5E of the Presidential and Vice-Presidential Elections Act, 1952 and decide as follows:—

Date............ Returning Officer]

(Perforation)...

Receipt for Nomination Paper and Notice of Scrutiny

(To be handed over to the person presenting the nomination paper)

Serial Number of the nomination paper..

The nomination paper of...................(name), a candidate for election to the office of the President of India, was delivered to me at my office at............(hour) on..............(date) by the candidate/proposer................(name)/seconder....................(name).

All nomination papers, other than those rejected under sub-section (4) of Section 5B of the Presidential and Vice-Presidential Elections Act, 1952, will be taken up for scrutiny at..............................(hour) on.....................(date) at..........(place.).

[2. The nomination paper of this candidate has been rejected by me under sub-section (4) of Section 5B of the Presidential and Vice-Presidential Elections Act, 1952 for the reasons given below:—]

Date.............................. Returning Officer

[ ] Score out if not applicable.

FORM 3

(*See* Rule 4)

NOMINATION PAPER

ELECTION TO THE OFFICE OF THE VICE-PRESIDENT OF INDIA

We, the undersigned Members of the electoral college referred to in article 66 of the Constitution being Members of Parliament hereby nominate.................................... ....(full name and address of candidate) as a candidate for election to the office of the Vice-President of India.

We have verified, and do hereby declare, that the said candidate has completed the age of 35 years and is registered in the electoral roll for the Parliamentary constituency of ....in the State of ....

A certified copy of the entry in that electoral roll relating to the said candidate is attached. We furnish our full particulars as indicated hereunder and append our signatures below in token of subscribing to this nomination.

Particulars of the proposers and their signatures

Sl. No.	Full name	Whether member of the House of the People/Council of States.	State/Union territory from which elected.	Signature	Date
1	2	3	4	5	6
1.					
2.					
3.					
4.					
5.					
6.					
7.					
8.					
9.					
10.					
*etc.					

[*There should be at least fifty electors as proposers.][2]

Particulars of the seconders and their signatures

Sl. No.	Full name	Whether member of the House of the People/Council of States.	State/Union territory from which elected.	Signature	Date
1	2	3	4	5	6
1.					
2.					
3.					
4.					
5.					
6.					

7.					
8.					
9.					
10.					
*etc.					

[*There should be at least fifty electors as proposers.][2]

I assent to this nomination.

Signature of candidate.

(To be filled by the Returning Officer)

Serial Number of nomination paper............................

This nomination was delivered to me at my office at...............................(hour) on.............................(date) by the candidate/proposer................................(name)/ seconder.....................(name) with enclosures as indicated below purporting to be—

(1)

(2)

Date................ Returning Officer

[Decision of the Returning Officer (if any) under sub-section (4) of Section 5B

I have rejected this nomination paper under sub-section (4) of Section 5B of the Presidential and Vice-Presidential Elections Act, 1952, for the reasons given below:—

Date.............. Returning Officer

Decision of the Returning Officer accepting or rejecting the nomination paper.

I have examined this nomination paper in accordance with Section 5E of the Presidential and Vice-Presidential Elections Act, 1952 and decide as follows:-

Date.............. Returning Officer

(Perforation)..

Receipt for nomination paper and notice of scrutiny

(To be handed over to the person presenting the nomination paper)

Serial Number of the nomination paper..

The nomination of ....(name), a candidate for election to the office of the Vice-President of India was delivered to me at my office at..........................(hour) on............................(date) by the candidate/proposer..................................(name)/ seconder..........................(name).

All nomination papers other than those rejected under sub-section (4) of Section 5B of the Presidential and Vice-Presidential Elections Act, 1952, will be taken up for scrutiny at .... (hour) on .... (date) at .... (place).

[2. The nomination paper of this candidate has been rejected by me under sub-section (4) of Section 5B of the Presidential and Vice-Presidential Elections Act, 1952, for the reasons given below:—]

Date................ Returning Officer

[ ] Score out if not applicabale.

FORM 4

[*See* Rule5(1)]

NOTICE OF WITHDRAWL

To,

The Returning Officer for the election to the office of President/Vice-President of India.

I,.....................................(name) of............(address) a candidate at the above-mentioned election do hereby give notice that I withdraw my candidature.

Place.................

Date.....................   Signature of candidate

NOTE: The notice of withdrawal is required to be delivered under Section 6(1) of the Presidential and Vice-Presidential Elections Act, 1952, by the candidate in person or by any one of his proposers or seconders who has been authorized in this behalf in writing by such candidate.

FORM 5

(*See* Rule 6)

ELECTION TO THE OFFICE OF PRESIDENT/VICE-PRESIDENT OF INDIA

List of contesting Candidate

Sl. No.	**Name of candidate**	**Address of candidate**
1.		
2.		
3.		
4.		
etc.		

Place ....

Date ....   Returning Officer

FORM 6

[*See* Rule 20]

Part I - BALLOT PAPER ACCOUNT

ELECTION TO THE OFFICE OF PRESIDENT/VICE-PRESIDENT OF INDIA

Name of the place of polling.....................................

	Serial Numbers From	Serial Numbers To	Total Numbers
1. Ballot papers received			
2. Ballot papers unused			
3. Ballot papers issued to voters			
4. Ballot papers cancelled.			

Date — Signature of Presiding Officer

PART II- RESULT OF COUNTING

[*See* Rule 32]

(1) Total number of ballot papers found in the ballot box (boxes) used at the place of polling...............................

(2) Discrepancy if any between the total number as shown against item (1) in this Part and the total number of ballot papers issued to voters as shown in item 3 of Part I minus the number of ballot papers cancelled as shown in item 4 of Part I.

Date — Signature of the Returning Officer

FORM 7

[*See* Rule 35(1)(c)]

RETURN OF ELECTION TO THE OFFICEOFTHE PRESIDENT/VICE-PRESIDENT OF INDIA

Serial No	Name of candidate	Votes secured at first count	Vote credited at first exclusion	Total of columns 3 and 4	Votes credited at second exclusion	Total of columns 5 and 6	Votes credited at third exclusion	Total of columns 7 and 8	Votes credited at fourth exclusion	Total of columns 9 and 10
1	2	3	4	5	6	7	8	9	10	11
Exhausted votes										
TOTAL										

Total No. of valid ballot papers..................representing ....votes.

Total number of invalid ballot papers.............representing ....votes.

I declare that

(Name)..

(Address)..

has been duly elected to the office of the President/Vice-President of India.

Place......................

Date........................ Returning Officer

THE SCHEDULE
[*See* Rule 33]
INSTRUCTIONS FOR THE DETERMINATION OF RESULT

1. In this Schedule—

(1) the expression "continuing candidate" means any candidate not elected and not excluded from the poll at any given time.

(2) the expression "first preference" means the figure 1 set opposite the name any candidate, the expression "second preference" similarly means the figure 2,the expression "third preference" the figure 3, and so on;

(3) the expression "next available preference" means the second or subsequent preference recorded in consecutive numerical order for a continuing candidate, preferences for candidates already excluded being ignored;

(4) the expression "unexhausted paper" means a ballot paper on which a further preference is recorded for a continuing candidate;

(5) the expression "exhausted paper" means a ballot paper on which no further preference is recorded for a continuing candidate, provided that a paper shall be deemed to be exhausted in any case in which—

(a) the names of two or more candidates whether continuing or not are marked with the same figure, and are next in order of preference; or

(b) the name of the candidate next in order of preference, whether continuing or not, is marked by a figure not following consecutively after some other figure on the ballot paper or by two or more figures.

2. Every ballot paper represents at each count———

(a) in a Presidential election, the number of votes as determined under Rule 30; and

(b) in a Vice-Presidential election, one vote.

3. Ascertain the number of first preference votes secured by each candidate and credit him with that number.

4. Add up the numbers so credited to all the candidates, divide the total by two, and add one to the quotient disregarding any remainder. The resulting number is the quota sufficient to secure the turn of a candidate at the election.

5. If at the end of the first or any subsequent count, the total number of votes credited to any candidate is equal to, or greater than, the quota, or there is only one continuing candidate, that candidate is declared elected.

6. If at the end of any count, no candidate can be declared elected,-

(a) exclude the candidate who up to that stage has been credited with the lowest number of votes.

(b) examine all the ballot papers in his parcel and sub-parcels, arrange the unexhausted papers in sub-parcels according to the next available preferences recorded thereon for the continuing candidates, count the number of votes in each such sub-parcel and credit it to the candidate for whom such preference is recorded, transfer the sub-parcel to that candidate, and make as separate sub-parcel of all the exhausted papers; and

(c) see whether any of the continuing candidates has, after such transfer and credit, secure the quota.

If, when a candidate has to be excluded under clause (a) above, two or more candidates have been credited with the same number of votes and stand lowest on the poll, exclude that candidate who had secured the lowest number of first preference votes, and if that number also was the same in the case of two or more or more candidates, decide by lot which of them shall be excluded.

All the sub-parcels of exhausted papers referred to in clause (b) above shall be set apart as finally dealt with and the votes recorded thereon shall not thereafter be taken into account.

❑❑❑

ENDNOTES

1. These rules were published with the Ministry of Law, Justice and Company Affairs, (Legislative Department) Notification No.S.O. 305 (E) dated 21st May, 1974. See Gazette of India, Extraordinary. Part II, Section 3(ii).
2. Subs. by S.O.431(E), dated 6th June,1997 (w.e.f. 6-6-1997).

32

The Representation of the People (Amendment) Ordinance, 2002

ACT NO. 4 OF 2002

Promulgated by the President in the Fifty-third Year of the Republic of India.

An Ordinance further to amend the Representation of the People Act, 1951.

WHEREAS Parliament is not in session and the President is satisfied that circumstances exist which render it necessary for him to take immediate action.

NOW, THEREFORE, in exercise of the powers conferred by clause (1) of article 123 of the Constitution, the President is pleased to promulgate the following Ordinance:-

1. (1) This Ordinance may be called the Representation of the People (Amendment) Ordinance, 2002.

(2) Save as otherwise provided in this Ordinance, the provisions of this Ordinance shall come into force at once.

2. After Section 33 of the Representation of the People Act, 1951 (hereinafter referred to as the principal Act), the following section shall be inserted, namely -

"**33A.** (1) A candidate shall, apart from any information which he is required to furnish, under this Act or the rules made thereunder, in his nomination paper delivered under sub-section (1) of Section 33, also furnish the information as to whether-

(i) he is accused of any offence punishable with imprisonment for two years or more in a pending case in which a charge has been framed by the court of competent jurisdiction;

(ii) he has been convicted of an offence [other than any offence referred to in sub-section (1) or sub-section (2), or covered in sub-section (3), of Section 8] and sentenced to imprisonment for one year or more.

(2) The candidate or his proposer, as the case may be, shall, at the time of delivering to the returning officer the nomination paper under sub-section (1) of Section 33, also deliver to him an affidavit sworn by the candidate in a prescribed form verifying the information specified in sub-section (1).

(3) The returning officer shall, as soon as may be after the furnishing of information to him under sub-section (1), display the aforesaid information by affixing a copy of the affidavit, delivered under sub-section (1), at a conspicuous place at his office for the information of the electors relating to a constituency for which the nomination paper is delivered."

3. After Section 33A of the principal Act as so inserted, the following section shall be inserted and shall be deemed to have been inserted with effect from the 2nd day of May, 2002, namely:-

"**33B.** Notwithstanding anything contained in any judgment, decree or order of any court or any direction, order or any other instruction issued by the Election Commission, no candidate shall be liable to disclose or furnish any such information, in respect of his election, which is not required to be disclosed or furnished under this Act or the rules made thereunder."

4. In Part V of the principal Act, after Chapter VII, the following Chapter shall be inserted, namely:-

CHAPTER - VIIA : DECLARATION OF ASSETS AND LIABILITIES

75A. (1) Every elected candidate for a House of Parliament or the Legislature of a State shall, with in ninety days from the date on which he makes and subscribes an oath or affirmation, according to the form set out for the purpose in the Third Schedule to the Constitution, for taking his seat in either House of Parliament or in the Legislative Assembly of a State or the Legislative Council of a State, as the case may be, furnish the information, relating to-

(i) the movable and immovable property of which he is the owner or a beneficiary;

(ii) his liabilities to any public financial institution; and

(iii) his liabilities to the Central Government or the State Government, to the Chairman of the Council of States or the Speaker of the House of the People or the Chairman of the Legislative Council of a State or the Speaker of the Legislative Assembly of a State, as the case may be.

(2) The information under sub-section (1) shall be furnished in such form and in such manner as may be prescribed in the rules made under sub-section (3).

(3) The Chairman of the Council of States or the Speaker of the House of the People or the Chairman of the Legislative Council of a State or the Speaker of the Legislative Assembly of a State, as the case may be, may make rules for the purposes of sub-section (2).

(4) The rules made by the Chairman of the Council of States or the Speaker of the House of the People or, as the case may be, by the Chairman of the Legislative

Council of a State or the Speaker of the Legislative Assembly of a State under sub-section (3) shall be laid, as soon as may be after they are made, before the Council of States or the House of the People or the Legislative Council or the Legislative Assembly, as the case may be, for a total period of thirty days which may be comprised in one session or in two or more successive sessions and shall take effect upon the expiry of the said period of thirty days unless they are sooner approved with or without modifications or disapproved by the Council of States or the House of the People or the Legislative Council or the Legislative Assembly and where they are so approved, they shall take effect on such approval in the form in which they were laid or in such modified form, as the case may be, and where they are so disapproved, they shall be of no effect.

(5) The Chairman of the Council of States or the Speaker of the House of the People or, as the case may be, the Chairman of the Legislative Council of a State or the Speaker of the Legislative Assembly of a State may direct that any wilful contravention of the rules made under sub-section (3) by an elected candidate referred to in sub-section (1) may be dealt with in the same manner as a breach of privilege of the Council of States or the House of the People or the Legislative Council or the Legislative Assembly, as the case may be.

EXPLANATION: For the purposes of this section,-

(i) "immovable property" means the land and includes any building or other structure attached to the land or permanently fastened to anything which is attached to the land;

(ii) "movable property" means any other property which is not the immovable property and includes corporeal and incorporeal property of every description;

(iii) "public financial institution" means a public financial institution within the meaning of Section 4A of the Companies Act, 1956 and includes bank; and

(iv) "bank" referred to in clause (iii) means –

(a) "State Bank of India" constituted under Section 3 of the State Bank of India Act, 1955;

(b) "subsidiary bank" having the meaning assigned to it in clause (k) of Section 2 of the State Bank of India (Subsidiary Banks) Act, 1959;

(c) "Regional Rural Bank" established under Section 3 of the Regional Rural Banks Act, 1976;

(d) "corresponding new bank" having the meaning assigned to it in clause (da) of Section 5 of the Banking Regulation Act, 1949; and

(e) "co-operative bank" having the meaning assigned to it in clause (cci) of Section 5 of the Banking Regulation Act, 1949 as modified by sub-clause (i) of clause of (c) of Section 56 of that Act.

5. After Section 125 of the principal Act, the following section shall be inserted, namely:-

"125A. A candidate who himself or through his proposer, with intent to be elected in an election,

(i) fails to furnish information relating to sub-section (I) of Section 33A; or

(ii) gives false information which he knows or has reason to believe to be false; or

(iii) conceals any information, in his nomination paper delivered under sub-section (1) of Section 33 or in his affidavit which is required to be delivered under sub-section (2) of Section 33A, as the case may be, shall, notwithstanding anything contained in any other law for the time being in force, be punishable with imprisonment for a term which may extend to six months, or with fine, or with both."

6. In Section 169 of the principal Act, in sub-section (2), clause (a) shall be renumbered as clause (aa) thereof, and before clause (aa) as so renumbered, the following clause shall be inserted, namely:-

"(a) the form of affidavit under sub-section (2) of Section 33A;"

❑❑❑

33

The Representation of the People (Miscellaneous Provisions) Act, 1956

Act No. 88 of 1956 [28th December, 1956]

AN ACT to provide for the removal of disqualifications for membership of, and voting at elections to, Parliament and State Legislatures, and for certain miscellaneous matters in connection with such elections.

Be it enacted by Parliament in the Seventh Year of the Republic of India as follows:-

1. Short title.

(1) This Act may be called the Representation of the People (Miscellaneous Provisions) Act, 1956.

2. Removal of disqualifications.

(1) Every disqualification for membership of Parliament or of the Legislature of a State incurred by any person under the Representation of the People Act, 1951 (43 of 1951) (hereinafter referred to as the principal Act) before the commencement of the Representation of the People (Second Amendment) Act, 1956, (27 of 1956) for failure to lodge a return of election expenses as required by clause (c) of Section 7 of the principal Act is hereby removed.

(2) Every disqualification for membership of Parliament or of the Legislature of a State or for voting at an election incurred by any person under the principal Act before the commencement of the Representation of the People (Second Amendment) Act, 1956, for any illegal practice or for any corrupt practice, other than the corrupt practice of bribery or undue influence is hereby removed.

3. [Amendment of Section 7 of Act 43 of 1951. *Rep. by the Repealing and Amending Act, 1960 (58 of 1960), s. 2 and Sch. I.*

4. [Special provision for nomination in case of prisoners in Portuguese territory]. *Rep. by s. 2 and Sch. 1, ibid.*

5. Prevention of dispualification for membership of Parliament in certain cases. It is hereby declared that the office of member of the Council of Advisers associated with the Chief Commissioner of Manipur or with the Chief Commissioner of Tripura shall not disqualify the holder thereof for being chosen as, or for being, a member of Parliament.

❑❑❑

34

The Representation of the People (Second Amendment) Act, 1996

ACT NO. 29 OF 1996 [13TH SEPTEMBER, 1996]

AN ACT further to amend the Representation of the People Act, 1950.

Be it enacted by Parliament in the Forty- seventh Year of the Republic of India as follows -

1. Short title. This Act may be called the Representation of the People (Second Amendment) Act, 1996 .

2. Amendment of Act, 43 of 1950. In the Fourth Schedule to the Representation of the People Act, 1950 -

(a) under the heading "KARNATAKA", for the entries 1 to 5, the following entries shall be substituted, namely -

1. City Municipal Corporations.
2. City Municipal Councils.
3. Town Municipal Councils.
4. Town Panchayats.
5. Zilla Panchayats.
6. Taluk Panchayats.
7. Grama Panchayats.
8. Cantonment Boards.".

(b) under the heading "UTTAR PRADESH", for the entries 1 to 6, the following entries shall be substituted, namely -

1. Municipal Corporations.
2. Municipal Councils.
3. Zila Panchayats.
4. Nagar Panchayats.
5. Kshettra Panchayats.
6. Cantonment Boards.

❑❑❑

35

The Representation of the People (Second Amendment) Act, 2003

ACT No. 2 OF 2004 [1ST JANUARY, 2004]

AN ACT further to amend the Representation of the People Act, 1950 and the Representation of the People Act, 1951.

Be it enacted by Parliament in the Fifty- fourth Year of the Republic of India as follows:-

CHAPTER - I : PRELIMINARY

1. Short title and commencement.

(1) This Act may be called the Representation of the People (Second Amendment) Act, 2003.

(2) It shall be deemed to have come into force on the 29th day of October, 2003 .

CHAPTER - II : AMENDMENT OF THE REPRESENTATION OF THE PEOPLE ACT, 1950

2. Amendment of Section 13AA of Act 43 of 1950. In Section 13AA of the Representation of the People Act, 1950, in sub-section 1, the words "other than a Union territory", shall be omitted.

CHAPTER - III : AMENDMENT OF THE REPRESENTATION OF THE PEOPLE ACT, 1951

3. Amendment of Sections 26 and 78 of Act 43 of 1951. In the Representation of the People Act, 1951 -

(a) in Section 26, sub-section (5) shall be omitted;

(b) in Section 78, sub-section (2) shall be omitted.

4. Repeal and saving.

(1) The Representation of the People (Amendment) Ordinance, 2003 (Ord. 5 of 2003) is hereby repealed.

(2) Notwithstanding such repeal, anything done or any action taken under the Representation of the People Act, 1950 (43 of 1950) and the Representation of the People Act, 1951 (43 of 1951) as amended by the said Ordinance, shall be deemed to have been done or taken under the said Acts, as amended by this Act.

❑❑❑

36

The Representation of the People (Third Amendment) Act, 2002

ACT NO. 72 OF 2002 [28TH DECEMBER, 2002]

AN ACT further to amend the Representation of the People Act, 1951.

Be it enacted by Parliament in the Fifty-third Year of the Republic of India as follows:-

1. Short title and commencement.

(1) This Act may be called the Representation of the People (Third Amendment) Act, 2002.

(2) Save as otherwise provided in this Act, the provisions of this Act shall be deemed to have come into force on the 24th August, 2002.

2. Insertion of new Section 33A. After Section 33 of the Representation of the People Act, 1951 (43 of 1951) (hereinafter referred to as the principal Act), the following section shall be inserted, namely:-

33A. Right to information.

(1) A candidate shall, apart from any information which he is required to furnish, under this Act or the rules made thereunder, in his nomination paper delivered under sub-section (1) of Section 33, also furnish the informatio as to whether-

(i) he is accused of any offence punishable with imprisonment for two years or more in a pending case in which a charge has been framed by the court of competent jurisdiction;

(ii) he has been convicted of an offence [other than any offence referred to in sub-section (1) or sub-section (2), or covered in sub-section (3), of Section 8] and sentenced to imprisonment for one year or more.

(2) The candidate or his proposer, as the case may be, shall, at the time of delivering to the returning officer the nomination paper under sub-section (1) of Section 33, also deliver to him an affidavit sworn specified in sub-section (1) by the candidate in a prescribed form verifying the information.

(3) The returning officer shall, as soon as may be after the furnishing of information to him under sub-section (1), display the aforesaid information by affixing a copy of the affidavit, delivered under sub-section (2), at a conspicuous place at his o fice for the information of the electors relating to a constituency for which the nomination paper is delivered".

3. Insertion of new Section 33B. After Section 33A of the principal Act as so inserted, the following section shall be inserted and shall be deemed to have been inserted with effect from the 2nd day of May, 2002, namely -

33B. Candidate to furnish information only under the Act and the rules. Notwithstanding anything contained in any judgment, decree or order of any court or any direction, order or any other instruction issued by the Election Commission, no candidate shall be liable to disclose or furnish any such information, in respect of his election, which is not required to be disclosed or furnished under this Act or the rules made thereunder".

4. Insertion of new Chapter VIIA. In Part V of the principal Act, after Chapter VII, the following Chapter shall be inserted, namely -'

CHAPTER - VIIA : DECLARATION OF ASSETS AND LIABILITIES

75A. Declaration of assets and liabilities.

(1) Every elected candidate for a House of Parliament shall, within ninety days from the date on which he makes and subscribes an oath or affirmation, according to the form set out for the purpose in the Third Schedule to the Constitution, for taking his seat in either House of Parliament, furnish the information, relating to-

  (i) the movable and immovable property of which he, his spouse and his dependant children are jointly or severally owners or beneficiaries;

  (ii) his liabilities to any public financial institution; and

  (iii) his liabilities to the Central Government or the State Government, to the Chairman of the Council of States or the Speaker of the House of the People, as the case may be.

(2) The information under sub-section (1) shall be furnished in such form and in such manner as may be prescribed in the rules made under sub-section (3).

(3) The Chairman of the Council of States or the Speaker of the House of the People, as the case may be, may make rules for the purposes of sub-section (2).

(4) The rules made by the Chairman of the Council of States or the Speaker of the House of the People, under sub-section (3) shall be laid, as soon as may be after they are made, before the Council of States or the House of the People, as

the case may be, for a total period of thirty days which may be comprised in one session or in two or more successive sessions and shall take effect upon the expiry of the said period of thirty days unless they are sooner approved with or without modifications or disapproved by the Council of States or the House of the People and where they are so approved, they shall take effect on such approval in the form in which they were laid or in such modified form, as the case may be, and where they are so disapproved, they shall be of no effect.

(5) The Chairman of the Council of States or the Speaker of the House of the People, as the case may be, may direct that any wilful contravention of the rules made under sub-section (3) by an elected candidate for a House of Parliament referred to in sub-section (1) may be dealt with in the same manner as a breach of privilege of the Council of States or the House of the People, as the case may be.

EXPLANATION. For the purposes of this section -

(i) "immovable property" means the land and includes any building or other structure attached to the land or permanently fastened to anything which is attached to the land;

(ii) "movable property" means any other property which is not the immovable property and includes corporeal and incorporeal property of every description;

(iii) "public financial institution" means a public financial institution within the meaning of Section 4A of the Companies Act, 1956 (1 of 1956) and includes bank;

(iv) "bank" referred to in clause (iii) means-

(a) State Bank of India constituted under Section 3 of the State Bank of India Act, 1955 (23 of 1955);

(b) subsidiary bank having the meaning assigned to it in clause (k) of Section 2 of the State Bank of India (Subsidiary Banks) Act, 1959 (38 of 1959);

(c) Regional Rural Bank established under Section 3 of the Regional Rural Banks Act, 1976 (21 of 1976);

(d) corresponding new bank having the meaning assigned to it in clause (da) of Section 5 of the Banking Regulation Act, 1949 (10 of 1949); and

(e) co-operative bank having the meaning assigned to it in clause (cci) of Section 5 of the Banking Regulation Act, 1949 (10 of 1949) as modified by sub-clause (i) of clause (c) of Section 56 of that Act; and

(v) "dependant children" means sons and daughters who have no separate means of earning and are wholly dependant on the elected candidate referred to in sub-section (1) for their livelihood'.

5. Insertion of new Section 125A. After Section 125 of the principal Act, the following section shall be inserted, namely -

"**125A. Penalty for filing false affidavit, etc.** A candidate who himself or through his proposer, with intent to be elected in an election,-

(i) fails to furnish information relating to sub-section (1) of Section 33A; or

(ii) gives false information which he knows or has reason to believe to be false; or

(iii) conceals any information, in his nomination paper delivered under sub-section (1) of Section 33 or in his affidavit which is required to be delivered under sub-section (2) of Section 33A, as the case may be, shall, notwithstanding anything contained in any other law for the time being in force, be punishable with imprisonment for a term which may extend to six months, or with fine, or with both".

6. Amendment of Section 169. In Section 169 of the principal Act, in sub-section (2), clause (a) shall be renumbered as clause (aa) thereof, and before clause (aa) as so renumbered, the following clause shall be inserted, namely - "(a) the form of affidavit under sub-section (2) of Section 33A".

7. Repeal and saving.

(1) The Representation of the People (Amendment) Ordinance, 2002 (Ord. 4 of 2002) is hereby repealed.

(2) Notwithstanding such repeal, anything done or any action taken under the principal Act, as amended by the said Ordinance, shall be deemed to have been done or taken under the principal Act, as amended by this Act.

❏❏❏

37

The Representation of the People Act, 1950

(Act 43 of 1950) [12th May, 1950]

AN ACT to provide the allocation of seats in, and the delimitation of constituencies for the purpose of election to, the House of the People and the Legislatures of States, the qualifications of voters at such elections, the preparation of electoral rolls, [1][the manner of filling seats in the Council of States to be filled by representatives of [2][Union territories]], and matters connected therewith.

Be it enacted by Parliament as follows —

PART - I : PRELIMINARY

1. Short title. This Act may be called the Representation of the People Act, 1950.

2. Definitions. [3]In this Act, unless the context otherwise requires —

(a) "article" means an article of the Constitution;

(b) "Assembly constituency" means a constituency provided [4][by law] for the purpose of elections to the Legislative Assembly of a State;

(c) "Council constituency" means a constituency provided [5][by law] for the purpose of elections to the Legislative Council of a State;

[6](d) "Election Commission" means the Election Commission appointed by the President under article 324;

(e) "order" means an order published in the Official Gazette;

(f) "Parliamentary constituency" means a constituency provided [7][by law] for the purpose of elections to the House of the People;

[8](g) "person" does not include a body of persons;

(h) "prescribed" means prescribed by rules made under this Act;

[9][(i) "State" includes a Union territory;]

(j) "State Government", in relation to a Union territory, means the administrator thereof].

[10]*****

PART - II : ALLOCATION OF SEATS AND DELIMITATION OF CONSTITUENCIES

The House of the People

[11][**3. Allocation of seats in the House of the People**. The allocation of seats to the States in the House of the People and the number of seats, if any, to be reserved for the Scheduled Castes and for the Scheduled Tribes of each State shall be as shown in the First Schedule.

4. Filling of seats in the House of the People and parliamentary constituencies. —
[12]* * * *

[13][(2) All the seats in the House of the People allotted to the States under Section 3 shall be seats to be filled by persons chosen by direct election from parliamentary constituencies in the States].

(3) Every parliamentary constituency referred to in sub-section (2) shall be a single-member constituency.

(4) Every State to which only one seat is allotted under Section 3 shall form one parliamentary constituency.

[14][(5) Save as provided in sub-section (4), the extent of all parliamentary constituencies except the parliamentary constituencies in the Union territory of Arunachal Pradesh shall be as determined by the orders of the Delimitation Commission made under the provisions of the Delimitation Act, 1972 (76 of 1972) and the extent of the parliamentary constituencies in the Union territory of Arunachal Pradesh shall be as determined by the order of the Election Commission under the provisions of the Government of Union Territories Act, 1963 (20 of 1963)]].

5. [Parliamentary constituencies]. *Rep. by the Representation of the People (Amendment) Act, 1956 (2 of 1956), s. 4.*

6. [Delimitation of parliamentary constituencies]. *Rep. by the Adaptation of Laws (No. 2) Order, 1956.*

The State Legislative Assemblies

[15][**7. Total number of seats in Legislative Assemblies and Assembly Constituencies**.

(1) [16][Subject to the provisions of [17][sub-sections (1A), (1B) and (1C)], the total number of seats] in the Legislative Assembly of each State specified in the Second Schedule, to be filled by persons chosen by direct election from Assembly Constituencies, and the number of seats, if any, to be reserved for the Scheduled Castes and for the Scheduled Tribes of the State, shall be as shown in that Schedule:

PROVIDED that for the period referred to in clause (2) of article 371A, the total number of seats allotted to the Legislative Assembly of the State of Nagaland shall be [18][fifty-two], of which —

(a) [19][twelve seats] shall be allocated to the Tuensang district and shall be filled by persons chosen by the members of the regional council, referred to in that article, from amongst themselves in such manner as the Governor, after consulting that Council may, by notification in the Official Gazette, specify, and

(PART II — Acts of Parliament)

(b) the remaining forty seats shall be filled by persons chosen by direct election from assembly constituencies in the rest of the State.

[20][(1A) Notwithstanding anything contained in sub-section (1), the total number of seats in the Legislative Assembly of the State of Sikkim, to be constituted at any time after the commencement of the Representation of the People (Amendment) Act, 1980 (8 of 1980), to be filled by persons chosen by direct election from assembly constituencies shall be thirty-two, of which—

(a) twelve seats shall be reserved for Sikkimese of Bhutia-Lepcha origin;

(b) two seats shall be reserved for the Scheduled Castes of that State; and

(c) one seat shall be reserved for the Sanghas referred to in Section 25A.

EXPLANATION. In this sub-section "Bhutia" includes Chumbipa, Dopthapa, Dukpa, Kagatey, Sherpa, Tibetan, Tromopa and Yolmo].

[21][(1B) Notwithstanding anything contained in sub-section (1), in the Legislative Assemblies of the States of Arunachal Pradesh, Meghalaya, Mizoram and Nagaland, to be constituted at any time after the commencement of the Representation of the People (Third Amendment) Act, 1987 (40 of 1987) —

(a) thirty-nine seats shall be reserved for the Scheduled Tribes in the Legislative Assembly of the State of Arunachal Pradesh;

(b) fifty-five seats shall be reserved for the Scheduled Tribes in the Legislative Assembly of the State of Meghalaya;

(c) thirty-nine seats shall be reserved for the Scheduled Tribes in the Legislative Assembly of the State of Mizoram; and

(d) fifty-nine seats shall be reserved for the Scheduled Tribes in the Legislative Assembly of the State of Nagaland].

[22][(1C) Notwithstanding anything contained in sub-section (1), twenty seats shall be reserved for the Scheduled Tribes in the Legislative Assembly of the State of Tripura to be constituted at any time after the commencement of the Representation of the People (Amendment) Act, 1992 (38 of 1992)].

(2) Every assembly constituency referred to [23][in sub-section (1) or sub-section (1A)] shall be a single-member constituency.

[24][(3) [25][The extent of each assembly constituency in all the States and Union territories except the assembly constituencies in the State of Sikkim and] in the Union territory of Arunachal Pradesh shall be as determined by the orders of the Delimitation Commission made under the provisions of the Delimitation Act, 1972 (76 of 1972); [20][the extent of each assembly constituency in the State of Sikkim shall be as provided for in the Delimitation of Parliamentary and Assembly Constituencies Order, 1976, as amended by Section 4 of the Representation of the People (Amendment) Act, 1980 (8 of 1980)] and the extent of each assembly constituency in the Union territory of Arunachal Pradesh shall be as determined by the order of the Election Commission made under the provisions of the Government of Union Territories Act, 1963 (20 of 1963)].

[26][**7A. Total number of seats in the Legislative Assembly of Sikkim and Assembly constituencies.**

(1) Notwithstanding anything contained in Section 7, in the Legislative Assembly of the State of Sikkim [deemed under the Constitution (Thirty-sixth Amendment) Act, 1975 to be the Legislative Assembly of that State duly constituted], the total number of seats to be filled by persons chosen by direct election from Assembly constituencies shall be 32.

(PART II — Acts of Parliament)

(2) Every Assembly constituency referred to in sub-section (1) shall be a single-member constituency.

(3) In the Legislative Assembly so deemed to be duly constituted, the extent of each constituency and the reservation of seats shall be as provided for immediately before the commencement of the Constitution (Thirty-sixth Amendment) Act, 1975].

The Delimiation of Parliamentary and Assembly Constituencies Order

8. Consolidation of delimitation orders.

(1) As soon as may be, after all the orders referred to in sub-section (5) of Section 4 or in sub-section (3) of Section 7 relating to the delimitation of parliamentary and assembly constituencies have been made by the Delimitation Commission or, as the case may be, the Election Commission and published in the Official Gazette, the Election Commission shall, after making such amendments as appear to it to be necessary for bringing up-to-date the description of the extent of the parliamentary and assembly constituencies as given in such orders, consolidate all such orders into one single order to be known as [27][the Delimitation of Parliamentary and Assembly Constituencies Order, 1976] and shall send authentic copies of that Order to the Central Government and to the Government of each State having a Legislative Assembly; and thereupon that Order shall supersede all the orders referred to in sub-section (5) of Section 4 or in sub-section (3) of Section 7 and shall have the force of law and shall not be called in question in any court.

(2) As soon as may be, after the said Order is received by the Central Government or by the Government of a State, that Government shall cause it to be laid before the House of the People or, as the case may be, the Legislative Assembly of the State.

[28][(3) The consolidation under sub-section (1) of the orders referred to in sub-section (5) of Section 4, or as the case may be, sub-section (3) of Section 7 shall not, as provided in sub-section (5) of Section 10 of the Delimitation Act, 1972 (76 of 1972), affect the representation in, and the territorial constituencies of, the House of the People or the Legislative Assembly of the State existing on the date of publication in the Gazette of India of any such order or orders as may be relevant].

9. Power of Election Commission to maintain Delimitation Order up-to-date.

(1) The Election Commission may, from time to time, by notification published in the Gazette of India and in the Official Gazette of the State concerned

(a) correct any printing mistake in [29][the Delimitation of Parliamentary and Assembly Constituencies Order, 1966, or, as the case may be, the Delimitation of Parliamentary and Assembly Constituencies Order, 1976] or any error arising therein from inadvertent slip or omission;

[30][(aa) make such amendments in the Delimitation of Parliamentary and assembly Constituencies Order, 1976 as appear to it to be necessary or expedient for consolidating with that Order any notification or order relating to delimitation of parliamentary or assembly constituencies (including reservation of seats for the Scheduled Castes or the Scheduled Tribes in such constituencies) issued under any Central Act;]

(b) where the boundaries or name of any district or any territorial division mentioned in the Order are or is altered, make such amendments as appear to it to be necessary or expedient for bringing the Order up-to-date.

(2) Every notification under this Section shall be laid, as soon as may be after it is issued, before the House of the People and the Legislative Assembly of the State concerned].

[31][**9A. Power of Election Commission to determine the constituencies to be reserved for Scheduled Tribes in certain States.**

(1) As soon as may be after the coming into force of the Representation of the People (Second Amendment) Act, 1987 (38 of 1987), the Election Commission shall, having regard to the provisions of the Constitution and the principle specified in clause (d) of sub-section (1) of Section 9 of the Delimitation Act, 1972 (76 of 1972), determine the assembly constituencies in the States of Meghalaya, Mizoram and Nagaland in which seats shall be reserved for the Scheduled Tribes.

(2) The Election Commission shall —

(a) publish its proposals under sub-section (1) with respect to any State in the Official Gazette and also in such other manner as it thinks fit;

(b) specify a date on or after which the proposals will be further considered by it;

(c) consider all objections and suggestions which may have been received by it before the date so specified;

(d) hold, for the purpose of such consideration, if it thinks fit so to do, one or more public sittings at such place or places in such State as it thinks fit;

(e) after considering all objections and suggestions which may have been received by it before the date so specified, determine, by order, the assembly constituency or constituencies in the State in which seats shall be reserved for the Scheduled Tribes and cause such order to be published in the Official Gazette; and, upon such publication, the order shall have the full force of law and shall not be called in question in any court and the Delimitation of Parliamentary and Assembly Constituencies Order, 1976, or, as the case may be, the Mizoram (Delimitation of Assembly Constituencies) Order, 1986 shall be deemed to have been amended accordingly.

(3) Every order made under sub-section (2) shall, as soon as may be after it is published under that sub-section, be laid before the Legislative Assembly of the State concerned.

EXPLANATION. For the purposes of this Section, "assembly constituency" means,—

(a) in relation to the States of Meghalaya and Nagaland, the assembly constituencies in those States as specified in the Delimitation of Parliamentary and Assembly Constituencies Order, 1976; and

(b) in relation to the State of Mizoram, the assembly constituencies as specified in the Mizoram (Delimitation of Assembly Constituencies) Order, 1986].

[32][**9B. Power of Election Commission to determine certain constituencies to be reserved for Scheduled Tribes in the State of Tripura.**

(1) As soon as may be after the coming into force of the Representation of the People (Amendment) Act, 1992 (38 of 1992),the Election Commission shall, having regard to the provisions of the Constitution and the principle specified in clause (d) of sub-section (1) of Section 9 of the Delimitation Act, 1972 (76 of 1972), determine the three assembly constituencies in the State of Tripura in which the three additional seats for Scheduled Tribes, as increased by sub-section (lC) of Section 7, shall be reserved.

(2) The Election Commission shall —

(a) publish its proposals under sub-section (1) in the Official Gazette and also in such other manner as it thinks fit;

(b) specify a date on or after which the proposals will be further considered by it;

(c) consider all objections and suggestions which may have been received by it before the date so specified;

(d) hold, for the purpose of such consideration, if it thinks fit so to do, one or more public sittings at such place or places in the State as it thinks fit;

(e) after considering all objections and suggestions which may have been received by it before the date so specified determine, by order, the three assembly constituencies in the State in which the said three additional seats shall be reserved for the Scheduled Tribes and cause such order to be published in the Official Gazette; and upon such publication, the order shall have the full force of law and shall not be called in question in any court and the Delimitation of Parliamentary and Assembly Constituencies Order, 1976, shall be deemed to have been amended accordingly.

(3) Every order made under sub-section (2) shall, as soon as may be after it is published under that sub-section, be laid before the Legislative Assembly of the State of Tripura].

The State Legislative Councils

10. Allocation of seats in the Legislative Councils.

(1) The allocation of seats in the Legislative Councils of the States having such Councils shall be as shown in the Third Schedule.

(2) In the Legislative Council of each State specified in the first column of the Third Schedule, there shall be the number of seats specified in the second column thereof opposite to that State, and of those seats —

(a) the numbers specified in the third, fourth and fifth columns shall be the number of seats to be filled by persons elected, respectively, by the electorates referred to in sub-clauses (a), (b) and (c) of clause (3) of article 171;

(b) the number specified in the sixth column shall be the number of seats to be filled by persons elected by the members of the Legislative Assembly of the State from amongst persons who are not members of that Assembly; and

(c) the number specified in the seventh column shall be the number of seats to be filled by persons nominated by the Governor [33]* * * of the State in accordance with the provisions of clause (5) of article 171.

11. Delimitation of Council Constituencies. As soon as may be after the commencement of this Act, the President shall, by order, determine-

(a) the constituencies into which each State having a Legislative Council shall be divided for the purpose of elections to that Council under each of the sub-clauses (a), (b) and (c) of clause (3) of article 171;

(b) the extent of each constituency; and

(c) the number of seats allotted to each constituency.

Provisions as to orders delimiting constituencies

12. Power to alter or amend orders.

[34][(1)] The President may, from time to time, after consulting the Election Commission, by order, alter or amend any order made by him under [35]* * * Section 11.

[36][(2) An order under sub-section (1) may contain provisions for the allocation of any member representing any council constituency immediately before the making of the order to any constituency delimited anew or altered by the order and for such other incidental and consequential matters as the President may deem necessary].

13. Procedure as to orders delimiting constituencies. [37]* * * * *

(3) Every order made under [38]* * * Section 11 or Section 12 shall be laid before Parliament as soon as may be after it is made, and shall be subject to such modifications as Parliament may make on a motion made within twenty days from the date on which the order is so laid.

[39][PART IIA OFFICERS

13A. Chief electoral officers.

(1) There shall be for each State a chief electoral officer who shall be such officer of Government as the Election Commission may, in consultation with that Government, designate or nominate in this behalf.

(2) Subject to the superintendence, direction and control of the Election Commission, the chief electoral officer shall supervise the preparation, revision and correction of all electoral rolls in the State under this Act.

[40][**13AA. District election officers.**

(1) For each district in a State, [41][***], the Election Commission shall, in consultation with the Government of the State, designate or nominate a district election officer who shall be an officer of Government:

PROVIDED that the Election Commission may designate or nominate more than one such officer for a district if the Election Commission is satisfied that the functions of the office cannot be performed satisfactorily by one officer.

(2) Where more than one district election officer are designated or nominated for a district under the proviso to sub-section (1), the Election Commission shall in the order designating or nominating the district election officers also specify the area in respect of which each such officer shall exercise jurisdiction.

(3) Subject to the superintendence, direction and control of the chief electoral officer, the district election officer shall coordinate and supervise all work in the district or in the area within his jurisdiction in connection with the preparation and revision of the electoral rolls for all parliamentary, assembly and council constituencies within the district.

(4) The district election officer shall also perform such other functions as may be entrusted to him by the Election Commission and the chief electoral officer].

13B. Electoral registration officers.

(1) The electoral roll [42][[43][for each parliamentary constituency in the State of Jammu and Kashmir or in a Union territory not having a Legislative Assembly], each assembly constituency and each Council constituency] shall be prepared and revised by an electoral registration officer who shall be such officer of Government or of a local authority as the Election Commission may, in consultation with the Government of the State in which the constituency is situated, designate or nominate in this behalf.

(2) An electoral registration officer may, subject to any prescribed restrictions, employ such persons as he thinks fit for the preparation and revision of the electoral roll for the constituency.

13C. Assistant electoral registration officers.

(1) The Election Commission may appoint one or more persons as assistant electoral registration officers to assist any electoral registration officer in the performance of his functions.

(2) Every assistant electoral registration officer shall, subject to the control of the electoral registration officer, be competent to perform all or any of the functions of the electoral registration officer.

[44][**13CC. Chief Electoral Officers, District Election Officers, etc., deemed to be on deputation to Election Commission**. The officers referred to in this Part and any other officer or staff employed in connection with the preparation, revision and correction of the electoral rolls for, and the conduct of, all elections shall be deemed to be on deputation to the Election Commission for the period during which they are so employed and such officers and staff shall, during that period, be subject to the control, superintendence and discipline of the Election Commission].

PART IIB : ELECTORAL ROLLS FOR PARLIAMENTARY CONSTITUENCIES

[45][**13D. Electoral rolls for parliamentary constituencies.**

(1) The electoral roll for every parliamentary constituency, other than a parliamentary constituency in the State of Jammu and Kashmir or in a Union territory not having a Legislative Assembly, shall consist of the electoral rolls for all the assembly constituencies comprised within that parliamentary constituency; and it shall not be necessary to prepare or revise separately the electoral roll for any such parliamentary constituency:

PROVIDED that for the period referred to in clause (2) of article 371A, it shall be necessary to prepare and revise separately the electoral roll for that part of the parliamentary constituency of Nagaland which comprises the Tuensang district and the provisions of Part III shall apply in relation to the preparation and revision of the electoral roll of the said part as they apply in relation to an assembly constituency.

(2) The provisions of Part III shall apply in relation to every parliamentary constituency in the State of Jammu and Kashmir or in a Union territory not

having a Legislative Assembly as they apply in relation to an assembly constituency].

PART - III : [46][ELECTORAL ROLLS FOR ASSEMBLY [47]* * * CONSTITUENCIES]

[48][**14. Definitions.** In this Part, unless the context otherwise requires —

(a) "constituency" means an Assembly constituency [47]* * * ;

(b) "qualifying date", in relation to the preparation or revision of every electoral roll under this Part, means [49][the 1st day of January] of the year in which it is so prepared or revised:]

[50][PROVIDED that "qualifying date", in relation to the preparation or revision of every electoral roll under this Part in the year 1989, shall be the 1st day of April, 1989].

15. Electoral roll for every constituency. For every constituency there shall be an electoral roll which shall be prepared in accordance with the provisions of this Act under the superintendence, direction and control of the Election Commission.

16. Disqualifications for registration in an electioral roll.

(1) A person shall be disqualified for registration in an electoral roll if he—

(a) is not a citizen of India; or

(b) is of unsound mind and stands so declared by a competent court; or

(c) is for the time being disqualified from voting under the provisions of any law relating to corrupt [51]* * *practices and other offences in connection with elections.

(2) The name of any person who becomes so disqualified after registration shall forthwith be struck off the electoral roll in which it is included:

[52][PROVIDED that the name of any person struck off the electoral roll of a constituency by reason of a disqualification under clause (c) of sub-section (1) shall forthwith be re-instated in that roll if such disqualification is, during the period such roll is in force, removed under any law authorising such removal].

17. No person to be registered in more than one constituency. No person shall be entitled to be registered in the electoral roll for more than one constituency [53]* * *.

18. No Person to be registered more than once in any constituency. No person shall be entitled to be registered in the electoral roll for any constituency more than once.

[54][**19. Conditions of registration.** Subject to the foregoing provisions of this Part, every person who —

(a) is not less than [55][eighteen years] of age on the qualifying date, and

(b) is ordinarily resident in a constituency,

shall be entitled to be registered in the electoral roll for that constituency].

20. Meaning of "ordinarily resident".

[56][(1) A person shall not be deemed to be ordinarily resident in a constituency on the ground only that he owns, or is in possession of, a dwelling house therein.

(1A) A person absenting himself temporarily from his place of ordinary residence shall not by reason thereof cease to be ordinarily resident therein.

(1B) A member of Parliament or of the Legislature of a State shall not during the term of his office cease to be ordinarily resident in the constituency in the electoral roll of which he is registered as an elector at the time of his election as such member, by reason of his absence from that constituency in connection with his duties as such member].

(2) A person who is a patient in any establishment maintained wholly or mainly for the reception and treatment of persons suffering from mental illness or mental defectiveness, or who is detained in prison or other legal custody at any place, shall not by reason thereof be deemed to be ordinarily resident therein.

[57][(3) Any person having a service qualification shall be deemed to be ordinarily resident on any date in the constituency in which, but for his having such service qualification, he would have been ordinarily resident on that date].

(4) Any person holding any office in India declared[58] by the President in consultation with the Election Commission to be an office to which the provisions of this sub-section apply, [59]* * * shall be deemed to be ordinarily resident [60]*** on any date in the constituency in which, but for the holding of any such office [61]* * *, he would have been ordinarily resident [62]* * * on that date.

(5) The statement of any such person as is referred to in sub-section (3) or sub-section (4) made in the prescribed form and verified in the prescribed manner, that [63][but for his having the service qualification] or but for his holding any such office [64]* * * as is referred to in sub-section (4) he would have been ordinarily resident in a specified place [65]* * * on any date, shall, in the absence of evidence to the contrary, be [63][accepted as correct].

(6) The wife of any such person as is referred to in sub-section (3) or sub-section (4) shall if she be ordinarily residing with such person [66]* * * be deemed to be ordinarily resident on [67]*** in the constituency specified by such person under sub-section (5).

[68][(7) If in any case a question arises as to where a person is ordinarily resident at any relevant time, the question shall be determined with reference to all the facts of the case and to such rules as may be made in this behalf by the Central Government in consultation with the Election Commission].

(8) In sub-sections (3) and (5) "service qualification" means—

(a) being a member of the armed forces of the Union; or

(b) being a member of a force to which the provisions of the Army Act, 1950 (46 of 1950), have been made applicable whether with or without modifications; or

(c) being a member of an armed police force of a State, who is serving outside that State; or

(d) being a person who is employed under the Government of India, in a post outside India.

[69][**21. Preparation and revision of electoral rolls.**

(1) The electoral roll for each constituency shall be prepared in the prescribed manner by reference to the qualifying date and shall come into force immediately upon its final publication in accordance with the rules made under this Act.

[70][(2) The said electoral roll—

(a) shall, unless otherwise directed by the Election Commission for reasons to be recorded in writing, be revised in the prescribed manner by reference to the qualifying date—

(i) before each general election to the House of the People or to the Legislative Assembly of a State; and

(ii) before each bye-election to fill a casual vacancy in a seat allotted to the constituency; and

(b) shall be revised in any year in the prescribed manner by reference to the qualifying date if such revision has been directed by the Election Commission:

PROVIDED that if the electoral roll is not revised as aforesaid, the validity or continued operation of the said electoral roll shall not thereby be affected].

(3) Notwithstanding anything contained in sub-section (2), the Election Commission may at any time, for reasons to be recorded, direct a special revision of the electoral roll for any constituency or part of a constituency in such manner as it may think fit:

PROVIDED that subject to the other provisions of this Act, the electoral roll for the constituency, as in force at the time of the issue of any such direction, shall continue to be in force until the completion of the special revision so directed.

[71][**22. Correction of entries in electoral rolls.** If the electoral registration officer for a constituency, on application made to him or on his own motion, is satisfied after such inquiry as he thinks fit, that any entry in the electoral roll of the constituency-

(a) is erroneous or defective in any particular,

(b) should be transposed to another place in the roll on the ground that the person concerned has changed his place of ordinary residence within the constituency, or

(c) should be deleted on the ground that the person concerned is dead or has ceased to be ordinarily resident in the constituency or is otherwise not entitled to be registered in that roll, the electoral registration officer shall, subject to such general or special directions, if any, as may be given by the Election Commission in this behalf, amend, transpose or delete the entry:

PROVIDED that before taking any action on any ground under clause (a) or clause (b) or any action under clause (c) on the ground that the person concerned has ceased to be ordinarily resident in the constituency or that he is otherwise not entitled to be registered in the electoral roll of that constituency, the electoral registration officer shall give the person concerned a reasonable opportunity of being heard in respect of the action proposed to be taken in relation to him].

[72][**23. Inclusion of names in electoral rolls.**

(1) Any person whose name is not included in the electoral roll of a constituency may apply to the electoral registration officer for the inclusion of his name in that roll.

(2) The electoral registration officer shall, if satisfied that the applicant is entitled to be registered in the electoral roll, direct his name to be included therein:

PROVIDED that if the applicant is registered in the electoral roll of any other constituency, the electoral registration officer shall inform the electoral registration officer of that other constituency and that officer shall, on receipt of the information, strike off the applicant's name from that roll.

(3) No amendment, transposition or deletion of any entry shall be made under Section 22 and no direction for the inclusion of a name in the electoral roll of a constituency shall be given under this Section, after the last date for making nominations for an election in that constituency or in the parliamentary constituency within which that constituency is comprised and before the completion of that election].

[73][**24. Appeals**. An appeal shall lie within such time and in such manner as may be prescribed—

(a) to the chief electoral officer, from any order of the electoral registration officer under Section 22 or Section 23 [74]* * *.

[75]* * * * *

25. Fee for applications and appeals. Every applications under Section 22 or Section 23 and every appeal under Section 24 shall be accompanied by the prescribed fee which shall, in no case, be refunded].

[76][**25A. Conditions of registration as elector in Sangha constituency in Sikkim.** Notwithstanding anything contained in Sections 15 and 19, for the Sangha constituency in the State of Sikkim, only the Sanghas belonging to monasteries, recognised for the purpose of the elections held in Sikkim in April, 1974, for forming the Assembly for Sikkim, shall be entitled to be registered in the electoral roll, and the said electoral roll shall, subject to the provisions of Sections 21 to 25, be prepared or revised in such manner as may be directed by the Election Commission, in consultation with the Government of Sikkim].

PART - IV : [77][ELECTORAL ROLLS FOR COUNCIL CONSTITUENCIES]

26. [Preparation of electoral rolls for Assembly constituencies]. *Rep. by the Representation of the People (Amendment) Act, 1956 (2 of 1956), s. 17.*

27. Preparation of electoral roll for Council constituencies.

(1) In this Section, "local authorities' constituency", "graduates' constituency" and "teachers' constituency" mean a constituency for the purpose of elections to a Legislative Council under sub-clause (a), sub-clause (b) and sub-clause (c), respectively, of clause (3) of article 171.

[78][(2) For the purpose of elections to the Legislative Council of a State in any local authorities' constituency—

(a) the electorate shall consist of members of such local authorities exercising jurisdiction in any place or area within the limits of that constituency as are specified in relation to that State in the Fourth Schedule;

(b) every member of each such local authority within a local authorities' constituency shall be entitled to be registered in the electoral roll for that constituency;

(c) the electoral registration officer for every local authorities' constituency shall maintain in his office in the prescribed manner and form the electoral roll for that constituency corrected up-to-date;

(d) in order to enable the electoral registration officer to maintain the electoral roll corrected up-to-date, the chief executive officer of every local authority (by whatever designation such officer may be known) shall immediately inform the electoral registration officer about every change in the membership of that local authority; and the electoral registration officer shall, on receipt of the information, strike off from the electoral roll the names of persons who have ceased to be, and include therein the names of persons who have become, members of that local authority; and

(e) the provisions of Sections 15, 16, 18, 22 and 23 shall apply in relation to local authorities' constituencies as they apply in relation to assembly constituencies].

(3) For the purpose of elections to the Legislative Council of a State in the graduates' constituencies and the teachers' constituencies, the State Government concerned may, with the concurrence of the Election Commission, by notification in the Official Gazette, specify—

(a) the qualifications which shall be deemed to be equivalent to that of a graduate of a university in the territory of India, and

(b) the educational institutions within the State not lower in standard than that of a secondary school.

[79][(4) The provisions of Sections 15, 16, 18, 21, 22 and 23 shall apply in relation to graduates' constituencies and teachers' constituencies as they apply in relation to assembly constituencies].

(5) Subject to the foregoing provisions of this Section, —

[80]* * * * *

[81][(a)] every person who [82][is] ordinarily resident in a graduates' constituency and has, for at least three years [83] [before the qualifying date], been either a graduate of a University in the territory of India or in possession of any of the qualifications specified under clause (a) of sub-section (3) by the State Government concerned, shall be entitled to be registered in the electoral roll for that constituency; and

[84][(b)] every person who [82][is] ordinarily resident in a teachers' constituency, and has, within the six years immediately [83][before the qualifying date]

for a total period of at least three years, been engaged in teaching in any of the educational institutions specified under clause (b) of sub-section (3) by the State Government concerned shall be entitled to be registered in the electoral roll for that constituency.

[85][(6) For the purposes of sub-sections (4) and (5) the qualifying date shall be the 1st day of November of the year in which the preparation or revision of the electoral roll is commenced].

[86][PART - IVA : MANNER OF FILLING SEATES IN THE COUNCIL OF STATES TO BE FILLED BY REPRESENTATIVES OF [87][UNION TERRITORIES]

27A. Constitution of electoral colleges for the filling of seats in the Council of States allotted to Union territories.

(1) [88][For the purpose of filling any seat] or seats in the Council of States allotted to any [87][Union territory] [89]* * * in the Fourth Schedule to the Constitution there shall be an electoral college for [90][each such territory] [91] * * *.

[92]*

[93]*

[94][(3) The electoral college for the Union territory of Delhi shall consist of the elected members of the Legislative Assembly constituted for that territory under the Government of National Capital Territory of Delhi Act, 1991 (1 of 1992)].

[95][(4) [96][The electoral college for the Union territory of [97]*** Pondicherry] shall consist of the elected members of the Legislative Assembly constituted for that territory under the Government of Union Territories Act, 1963 (20 of 1963)].

[98] *****

[99] *****

27B. [Electoral College constituencies]. *Rep. by the Territorial Councils Act, 1956 (103 of 1956), s. 65.*

27C. [Delimitation of Electoral College constituencies]. *Rep. by s. 65, ibid.*

27D. [Power to alter or amend orders]. *Rep. by s. 65, ibid.*

27E. [Procedure as to orders delimiting constituencies]. *Rep. by the Representation of the People (Amendment) Act, 1956 (2 of 1956), s. 21.*

27F. [Electoral rolls for Council of States constituencies]. *Rep. by s. 22, ibid.*

27G. Termination of membership of electoral college for certain disqualifications — If a person who is a member of an electoral college becomes subject to any disqualification for membership of Parliament under the provisions of any law relating to corrupt and illegal practices and other offences in connection with elections to Parliament, he shall thereupon cease to be such member of the electoral college.

27H. Manner of filling of seats in the Council of States allotted to Union territories — [100]* * * The seat or seats in the Council of States allotted to any [101][Union territory] [102]* * * in the Fourth Schedule to the Constitution shall be filled by a person or persons elected by the members of the electoral college for [103][that territory] [104]* * * in accordance with the system of proportional representation by means of the single transferable vote:

> [105]*[PROVIDED that the person who immediately before the commencement of the Constitution (Seventh Amendment) Act, 1956, is filling the seat allotted to the Part C States of Manipur and Tripura shall, as from such commencement, be deemed to have been duly elected to fill the seat allotted to the Union territory of Tripura].*

27-I. [Special provisions for the filling of the seats in the Council of States allotted to the States of Ajmer and Coorg and the States of Manipur and Tripura]. Rep. by the Adaptation of Laws (No. 2) Order, 1956.

27J. Powers of electoral colleges to elect notwithstanding vacancies therein. No election by the members of an electoral college [106]*** under this Act shall be called in question on the ground merely of the existence of any vacancy in the membership of such college [106]* * *.

27K. [Electoral colleges for certain States for which Legislative Assemblies have been constituted]. *Rep. by the Adaptation of Laws (No. 2) Order, 1956].*

PART - V : GENERAL

28. Power to make rules.

(1) The Central Government may, after consulting the Election Commission, by notification in the Official Gazette, make rules[107] for carrying out the purposes of this Act.

(2) In particular and without prejudice to the generality of the foregoing power, such rules may provide for all or any of the following matters, namely:—

[108][(a) the determination of ordinary residence under sub-section (7) of Section 20; (aa) the particulars to be entered in the electoral rolls;]

(b) the preliminary publication of electoral rolls [109]* * *;

(c) the manner in which and the time within which claims and objections as to entries in electoral rolls may be preferred;

[110]*****(d)

(e) the manner in which notices of claims or objections shall be published;

(f) the place, date and time at which claims or objections shall be heard and the manner in which claims or objections shall be heard and disposed of;

(g) the final publication of electoral rolls;

[111][(h) the revision and correction of electoral roll and inclusion of names therein;] (i) any other matter required to be prescribed by this Act.

[112][(3) Every rule made by the Central Government under this Act shall be laid, as soon as may be after it is made, before each House of Parliament, while it is in session, for a total period of thirty days which may be comprised in one session or in two or more successive sessions, and if, before the expiry of the session immediately following the session or the successive sessions aforesaid, both Houses agree in making any modification in the rule or both Houses agree

that the rule should not be made, the rule shall thereafter have effect only in such modified form or be of no effect, as the case may be; so, however, that any such modification or annulment shall be without prejudice to be validity of anything previously done under that rule].

[113][**29. Staff of local authorities to be made available**. Every local authority in a State shall, when so requested by the chief electoral officer of the State, make available to any electoral registration officer such staff as may be necessary for the performance of any duties in connection with the preparation and revision of electoral rolls].

30. Jurisdiction of civil courts barred. No civil court shall have jurisdiction—

(a) to entertain or adjudicate upon any question whether any person is or is not entitled to be registered in an electoral roll for a constituency; or

(b) to question the legality of any action taken by or under the authority of an electoral registration officer, or of any decision given by any authority appointed under this Act for the revision of any such roll.

[114][[115][**31. Making false declarations**. If any person makes in connection with—

(a) the preparation, revision or correction of an electoral roll, or

(b) the inclusion or exclusion of any entry in or from an electoral roll,

a statement or declaration in writing which is false and which he either knows or believes to be false or does not believe to be true, he shall be punishable with imprisonment for a term which may extend to one year, or with fine, or with both].

32. Breach of official duty in connection with the preparation, etc., of electoral rolls.

(1) If any electoral registration officer, assistant electoral registration officer or other person required by or under this Act to perform any official duty in connection with the preparation, revision or correction of an electoral roll or the inclusion or exclusion of any entry in or from that roll, is without reasonable cause, guilty of any act or omission in breach of such official duty, he shall be punishable [116][with imprisonment for a term which shall not be less than three months but which may extend to two years and with fine].

(2) No suit or other legal proceeding shall lie against any such officer or other person for damages in respect of any such act or omission as aforesaid.

(3) No court shall take cognizance of any offence punishable under sub-section (1) unless there is a complaint made by order of, or under authority from, the Election Commission or the Chief Electoral Officer of the State concerned].

[THE FIRST SCHEDULE
[*See* Section 3]
ALLOCATION OF SEATS IN THE HOUSE OF THE PEOPLE

Name of the State / Union territory	Number of seats in the House as constituted on 1-1-1973			Number of seats in the House as subsequently constituted		
	Total	Reserved for the Scheduled Castes	Reserved for the Scheduled Tribes	Total	Reserved for the Scheduled Castes	Reserved for the Scheduled Tribes
1	2	3	4	5	6	7
I. STATES :						
1. Andhra Pradesh	41	6	2	42	6	2
2. Assam	14	1	2	14	1	2
3. Bihar	53	7	5	54	8	5
4. Gujarat	24	2	3	26	2	4
5. Haryana	9	2		10	2	
6. HimachalPradesh	4	1		4	1	
7. Jammu & Kashmir	6			6		
8. Karnataka	27	4		28	4	
9. Kerala	19	2		20	2	
10. Madhya Pradesh	37	5	8	40	5	8
11.Maharashtra	45	3	3	48	3	3
12. Manipur	2		1	2		1
13. Meghalaya	2		2	2		
14. Nagaland	1			1		
15. Orissa	20	3	5	21	3	5
16. Punjab	13	3		13	3	
17. Rajasthan	23	4	3	25	4	3
18. Sikkim				1		
19. TamilNadu	39	7		39	7	
20. Tripura	2		1	2		1
21. Uttar Pradesh	85	18		85	18	
22. West Bengal	40	8	2	42	8	2
II. UNION TERRITORIES						
1. Andaman and Nicobar Islands	1	..	..	1	..	..
2. Arunachal Pradesh	1	..	1	[2]	..	..
3. Chandigarh	1	..	..	1	..	..
4. Dadra and Nagar Haveli	1	..	1	1	..	1
5. Delhi	7	1	..	7	1	..
6. Goa, Daman and Diu	2	..	..	[3]	..	..
7. Lakshadweep	1	..	1	1	..	1
8. Mizoram	1	..	1	1	..	[1]
9. Pondicherry	1	..	..	1	..	..
Total	**522**	**77**	**41**	**542**	**78**	**38**

THE SECOND SCHEDULE
[*See* Sections 7 and 7A]
TOTAL NUMBER OF SEATS IN THE LEGISLATIVE ASSEMBLIES

Name of the State / Union territory	Number of seats in the Legislative Assembly as constituted on 1-1-1973			Number of seats in the Legislative Assembly as subsequently constituted		
	Total	Reserved for the Scheduled Castes	Reserved for the Scheduled Tribes	Total	Reserved for the Scheduled Castes	Reserved for the Scheduled Tribes
1	2	3	4	5	6	
I. STATES :						
1. Andhra Pradesh	287	40	11	294	39	11
2. Assam	114	8	10	126	8	16
3. Bihar	318	45	29	324	46	28
4. Gujarat	168	11	22	182	12	25
5. Haryana	81	15	..	90	17	..
6. Himachal Pradesh	68	16	3	68	15	3
7. Jammu & Kashmir*						
8. Karnataka	216	29	2	224	29	2
9. Kerala	133	11	2	140	12	2
10. Madhya Pradesh	296	39	61	320	42	64
11. Maharashtra	270	15	16	288	17	17
12. Manipur	60	1	19	60	1	19
13. Meghalaya	60	..	50	60	..	..
14. Nagaland	52	..	..	60	..	..
15. Orissa	140	22	34	147	22	34
16. Punjab	104	23	..	117	29	..
17. Rajasthan	184	31	21	200	32	24
18. Sikkim	..	..	..	32	1	1**
19. Tamil Nadu	234	42	2	234	42	2
20. Tripura	60	6	19	60	7	17
21. Uttar Pradesh	425	89	..	425	89	1
22. West Bengal	280	55	16	294	59	17

* *Under the Constitution of Jammu and Kashmir, the number of seats in the Legislative Assembly of that State excluding the 24 seats earmarked for Pakistan occupied territory is 76 out of which 6 seats have been reserved for the Scheduled Castes in pursuance of the Jammu and Kashmir Representation of the People Act, 1957.*

***Reserved 1 seat for Sanghas and 12 seats for Bhutia Lapcha origin.*

1	2	3	4	5	6	7
II. UNION TERRITORIES :						
1. Arunachal Pradesh	..	..	..	40	..	..
2. Goa, Daman and Diu	30	..	..	40	..	..
3. Mizoram	30	..	..	40	..	..
4. Pondicherry	30	5	..	30	5	..

[THE THIRD SCHEDULE [*See* Section 10]
ALLOCATION OF SEATS IN THE LEGISLATIVE COUNCILS

Number to be elected or nominated under article 171(3)

	Number to be elected or nominated under article 171 (3)					
Name of State	**Total number of seats**	**Sub-clause (a)**	**Sub-clause (b)**	**Sub-clause (c)**	**Sub-clause (d)**	**Sub-clause (e)**
1	**2**	**3**	**4**	**5**	**6**	**7**
1. [***]	*	*	*	*	*	*
2. Bihar	96	34	8	8	34	12
[***]	*	*	*	*	*	*
[3.] Madhya Pradesh	90	31	8	8	31	12
4. [***]	*	*	*	*	*	*
[5.Maharashtra	78	22	7	7	30	12
6. [Karnataka.]	[75	25	7	7	25	11
[***]	*	*	*	*	*	*
8. Uttar Pradesh	108	39	9	9	39	12
[***]	*	*	*	*	*	*

THE FOURTH SCHEDULE
[*See* Section 27 (2)]
LOCAL AUTHORITIES FOR PURPOSES OF ELECTIONS TO LEGISLATIVE COUNCILS

[117]* * * * *

1. Nagar Parishads.
2. Cantonment Boards.
3. Nagar Panchayats.
4. Zila Parishads.
5. Pānchayat Samitis.
6. Nagar Nigams (Corporations).
7. Gram Panchayats].

[118][BIHAR

[119]* * * * *

[121][1. Municipalities.
2. Janapada Sabhas.
3. Mandal Panchayats.
4. Cantonment Boards.
5. Notified Area Committees.
6. Town Area Committees]].

[120][MADHYA PRADESH

[122]* * * * *

[123][MAHARASHTRA

[124]1. Municipalities.

2. Contonment Boards.

[125]* * * * *

4. Zilla Parishad]].

[127][1. City Municipal Corporations.

2. City Municipal Councils.

3. Town Municipal Councils.

4. Town Panchayats.

5. Zilla Panchayats.

6. Taluk Panchayats.

7. Grama Panchayats.

8. Cantonment Boards]].

[120][[126][KARNATAKA]

[128]* * * * *

UTTAR PRADESH

[129][1. Municipal Corporations.

2. Municipal Councils.

3. Zila Panchayats.

4. Nagar Panchayats.

5. Kshettra Panchayats.

6. Cantonment Boards].

[130]* * * * *

[131]* * * * *

[THE FIFTH SCHEDULE]

Rep. by the Government of Union Territories Act, 1963 (20 of 1963), s. 57 and the Second Schedule.

[THE SIXTH SCHEDULE]

Rep. by the Representation of the People (Amendment) Act, 1956 (2 of 1956), s. 27.

[THE SEVENTH SCHEDULE]

Rep. by s. 27, ibid.

ENDNOTES

1. Ins. by Act 73 of 1950, s. 2.
2. Subs. by the Adaptation of Laws (No. 2) Order, 1956, for "Part C States".
3. The brackets and figure "(1)" omitted by Act 103 of 1956, s. 65.
4. Subs. by Act 2 of 1956, s. 2, for "by order made under Section 9".
5. Subs. by the Adaptation of Laws (No. 2) Order, 1956, for "by order made under Section 11".
6. Cl. (cc) ins. by Act 73 of 1950, s. 3 and omitted by Act 103 of 1956, s. 65.
7. Subs. by Act 2 of 1956, s. 2, for "by Section 6 or by order made thereunder".
8. Cl. (ff) ins. by Act 67 of 1951, s. 2 was omitted by the North-Eastern Areas (Reorganisation) (Adaptation of Laws on Union Subjects) Order, 1974, s. 3 and Sch. (w.e.f. 21-1-1972).
9. Subs. by s. 3 and Sch., *ibid.*, for the former cl. (i) (w.e.f. 21-1-1972).
10. Sub-section (2) omitted by the Adaptation of Laws (No. 2) Order, 1956.
11. Subs. by Act 47 of 1966, s. 2, for ss. 3 and 4 (w.e.f. 14-12-1966).
12. Sub-section (1) omitted by Act 29 of 1975, s. 11 (w.e.f. 15-8-1975).
13. Subs. by s. 11, *ibid.*, for sub-section (2) (w.e.f. 15-8-1975).
14. Subs. by Act 88 of 1976, s. 2, for sub-section (5).
15. Subs. by Act 47 of 1966, s. 4, for s. 7 (w.e.f. 14-12-1966). Original ss. 8 and 9 were rep. by Act 2 of 1956, s. 5 and the Adaptation of Laws (No. 2) Order, 1956, respectively.
16. Subs. by Act 8 of 1980, s. 2, for certain words (w.e.f. 1-9-1979).
17. Subs. by Act 38 of 1992, s. 2, for "sub-sections (1A) and (1B)" (w.e.f. 5-12-1992).
18. Subs. by Act 61 of 1968, s. 4, for "forty-six".
19. Subs. by s. 4, *ibid.*, for "six seats".
20. Ins. by Act 8 of 1980, s. 2 (w.e.f. 1-9-1979).
21. Ins. by Act 40 of 1987, s. 2 (w.e.f. 22-9-1987).
22. Ins. by Act 38 of 1992, s. 2 (w.e.f. 5-12-1992).
23. Subs. by Act 8 of 1980, s. 2, for "in sub-section (1)" (w.e.f. 1-9-1979).
24. Subs. by Act 88 of 1976, s. 3, for sub-section (3).
25. Subs. by Act 8 of 1980, s. 2, for certain words (w.e.f. 1-9-1979).
26. Ins. by Act 10 of 1976, s. 2 and Sch. (w.e.f. 9-9-1975).
27. Subs. by Act 88 of 1976, s. 4, for certain words (w.e.f. 2-9-1976).
28. Ins. by s. 4, *ibid.* (w.e.f. 2-9-1976).
29. Subs.by s. 5, *ibid.*, for certain words.
30. Ins. by Act 21 of 1989, s. 2.
31. Ins. by Act 38 of 1987, s. 2 (w.e.f. 21-9-1987).
32. Ins. by Act 38 of 1992, s. 3 (w.e.f. 5-12-1992).
33. The words "or Rajpramukh, as the case may be" omitted by the Adaptation of Laws (No. 2) Order, 1956.
34. S. 12 re-numbered as sub-section (1) of that Section by Act 20 of 1960, s. 2.
35. The words and figures "section 6, Section 9, or" omitted by Act 2 of 1956, s. 7.
36. Ins. by Act 20 of 1960, s. 2.
37. Sub-sections (1) and (2) omitted by Act 2 of 1956, s. 8.

38. The words and figures "section 6, Section 9," omitted by s. 8, *ibid.*
39. Ins. by s. 9, *ibid.*
40. Ins. by Act 47 of 1966, s. 5 (w.e.f. 14-12-1966).
41. The words "other than a Union territory," omitted by Act, 2 of 2004, s. 2 (a).
42. Subs. by Act 103 of 1956, s. 65, for certain words.
43. Subs. by Act 47 of 1966, s. 6, for certain words (w.e.f.14-12-1966).
44. Ins. by Act 1 of 1989, s. 2 (w.e.f. 15-3-1989).
45. Subs. by Act 47 of 1966, s. 7, for s. 13D (w.e.f. 14-12-1966).
46. Subs. by Act 2 of 1956, s. 10, for the heading "REGISTRATION OF PARLIAMENTARY ELECTORS".
47. Certain words omitted by Act 103 of 1956, s. 65.
48. Subs. by Act 2 of 1956, s. 11, for s. 14.
49. Subs. by Act 58 of 1958, s. 5, for "the 1st day of March" (w.e.f. 1-1-1959).
50. Ins. by Act 21 of 1989, s. 3 (w.e.f. 28-3-1989).
51. The words "and illegal" ins. by Act 73 of 1950, s. 4 and omitted by Act 58 of 1960, s. 3 and Sch. II.
52. Ins. by Act 73 of 1950, s. 4.
53. The words "in the same State" ins. by Act 2 of 1956, s. 12 and omitted by Act 58 of 1958, s. 6.
54. Subs. by Act 58 of 1958, s. 7, for s. 19.
55. Subs. by Act 21 of 1989, s. 4, for "twenty-one years" (w.e.f. 28-3-1989).
56 Subs. by Act 58 of 1958, s. 8, for sub-section (1).
57. Subs. by Act 47 of 1966, s. 8, for sub-section (3) (w.e.f. 14-12-1966).
58. The following offices have been declared by the President by Notification No. S.O. 959, dated the 18th April, 1960 :
    1. The President of India.
    2. The Vice-President of India.
    3. Governors of States.
    4. Cabinet Ministers of the Union or of any State.
    5. The Deputy Chairman and Members of the Planning Commission.
    6. The Ministers of State of the Union or of any State.
    7. Deputy Ministers of the Union or of any State.
    8. The Speaker of the House of the People or of any Legislative Assembly.
    9. The Chairman of any State Legislative Council.
    10. Lieutenant Governors of Union territories.
    11. The Deputy Speaker of the House of the People or of any State Legislative Assembly.
    12. The Deputy Chairman of the Council of States or of any State Legislative Council.
    13. Parliamentary Secretaries of the Union or of any State.
59. Certain words omitted by Act 47 of 1966, s. 8 (w.e.f. 14-12-1966).
60. The words "during any period or" omitted by Act 2 of 1956, s. 14.
61. The words "or employment" omitted by Act 47 of 1966, s. 8 (w.e.f. 14-12-1966).
62. The words "during that period or" omitted by Act 2 of 1956, s. 14.
63. Subs. by Act 47 of 1966, s. 8, for certain words (w.e.f. 14-12-1966).

64. Certain words omitted by s. 8, *ibid.* (w.e.f. 14-12-1966).
65. The words "during any period or" omitted by Act 2 of 1956, s. 14.
66. The words "during any period" omitted by s. 14, *ibid.*
67. The words "during that period" omitted by s. 14, *ibid.*
68. Sub-section (7) omitted by Act 2 of 1956, s. 14 and ins. by Act 47 of 1966, s. 8 (w.e.f. 14-12-1966).
69. Subs. by Act 2 of 1956, s. 15, for ss. 21 to 25.
70. Subs. by Act 47 of 1966, s. 9, for sub-section (2) (w.e.f. 14-12-1966).
71. Subs. by Act 58 of 1958, s. 9, for s. 22.
72. Subs. by Act 47 of 1966, s. 10, for s. 23 (w.e.f. 14-12-1966).
73. Ins. by Act 40 of 1961, s. 3 (w.e.f. 20-9-1961). S. 24 ins. by Act 60 of 1956, s. 2 and was omitted by Act 58 of 1958, s. 10.
74. The word "and" omitted by Act 47 of 1966, s. 11 (w.e.f. 14-12-1966).
75. Cl.(b) omitted by s.11, *ibid.* (w.e.f. 14-12-1966).
76. Ins. by Act 10 of 1976, s. 2 and Sch. (w.e.f. 9-9-1975).
77. Subs. by Act 2 of 1956, s. 16, for the former heading.
78. Subs. by s. 18, *ibid.*, for sub-section (2).
79. Subs. by Act 2 of 1956, s. 18, for sub-section (4).
80. Cl. (a) omitted by s. 18, *ibid.*
81. Cl. (b) re-lettered as cl. (a) by s. 18, *ibid.*
82. Subs. by Act 40 of 1961, s. 4, for " on the qualifying date was" (w.e.f. 20-9-1961).
83. Subs. by s. 4, *ibid.*, for "before that date" (w.e.f. 20-9-1961).
84. Cl. (c) re-lettered as cl. (b) by Act 2 of 1956, s. 18.
85. Subs. by Act 40 of 1960, s. 4, *ibid.*, for sub-section (6) (w.e.f. 20-9-1961).
86. Part IVA ins. by Act 73 of 1950, s. 8.
87. Subs. by the Adaptation of Laws (No. 2) Order, 1956, for "Part C States".
88. Subs. by Act 29 of 1975, s. 11 (w.e.f. 15-8-1975).
89. The words "or group of such States" omitted by the Adaptation of Laws (No. 2) Order, 1956.
90. Subs., *ibid.*, for "each such State".
91. The words "or group of States" and proviso omitted by Act 2 of 1956. s. 19.
92. Proviso omitted by s.19, *ibid.*
93. Sub-section (2) omitted by Act 20 of 1963, s. 57 and Sch. II (w.e.f. 1-7-1963).
94. Subs. by Act 1 of 1992, s. 55, for sub-section (3) (w.e.f. 2-10-1993).
95. Subs. by Act 20 of 1963, s. 57 and Sch. II, for sub-section (4).
96. Subs. by Act 69 of 1986, s. 7, for certain words (w.e.f. 20-2-1987).
97. The word "Mizoram" omitted by Act 34 of 1986, s. 7 (w.e.f. 20-2-1987).
98. Sub-section (5) omitted by Act 29 of 1975, s. 11 (w.e.f. 15-8-1975).
99. Sub-section (6) omitted by Act 32 of 1954, s. 7.
100. Certain words omitted by the Adaptation of Laws (No. 2) Order, 1956.
101. Subs., *ibid.*, for "Part C State".
102. The words "or group of such States" omitted, *ibid.*
103. Subs., *ibid.*, for "such State".

104. The words "or group of States" omitted by Act 2 of 1956, s. 23.
105. Ins. by the Adaptation of Laws (No. 2) Order, 1956.
106. Certain words omitted by Act 49 of 1951, s. 44 and Sch. V.
107. See the Registration of Electors Rules, 1960, in Vol. II, infra.
108. Subs. by Act 47 of 1966, s. 12, for cl. (a) (w.e.f. 14-12-1966).
109. Certain words omitted by Act 73 of 1950, s. 9.
110. Cl. (d) omitted by Act 20 of 1960, s. 3.
111. Subs. by Act 2 of 1956, s. 24, for cl. (h).
112. Subs. by Act 88 of 1976, s. 6, for sub-section (3).
113. Subs. by Act 2 of 1956, s. 25, for s. 29.
114. Ins. by Act 58 of 1958, s. 11.
115. Subs. by Act 20 of 1960, s. 4, for s. 31.
116. Subs. by Act 21 of 1996, s. 2, for certain words (w.e.f. 1-8-1996).
117. The heading "Andhra Pradesh" and the entries relating thereto omitted by Act 34 of 1985, s. 5 (w.e.f. 1-6-1985).
118. Subs. by Act 6 of 2003, s. 2., "for "BIHAR" (w.e.f. 6-1-2003).
119. The heading "Bombay" (that is, Maharashtra) and the entries relating thereto omitted by Act 40 of 1961, s. 6 (w.e.f. 20-9-1961).
120. Ins. by the Adaptation of Laws (No. 2) Order, 1956.
121. Subs. by Act 37 of 1957, s. 12, for the former entries.
122. The heading "Tamil Nadu" and the entries relating thereto omitted by the Tamil Nadu Legislative Council (Abolition) Act, 1986, s. 5 (w.e.f. 1-11-1986).
123. Ins. by Act 40 of 1961, s. 6 (w.e.f. 20-9-1961).
124. Subs. by Act 2 of 1963, s. 2, for the former entries.
125. Entry "3. Town Committees." omitted by Act 21 of 1989, s. 5.
126. Subs. by the Mysore State (Alteration of Name) (Adaptation of Laws on Union Subjects) Order, 1974, s. 3 and Sch., for "Mysore" (w.e.f. 1-11-1973).
127. Subs. by Act 29 of 1996, s. 2, for "the entries 1 to 5".
128. Entry relating to Punjab omitted by Act 46 of 1969, s. 5 (w.e.f. 7-1-1970).
129. Subs. by Act 29 of 1996, s.2, for the entries 1 to 6.
130. The heading "West Bangal" and the entries relating thereto omitted by Act 20 of 1969, s.5 (w.e.f. 1-8-1969).
131. The heading "Mysore" and the entries relating thereto omitted by the Adaptation of Laws (No. 2) Order, 1956.

38

The Representation of The People Act, 1951

ACT NO. 43 OF 1951 [17TH JULY, 1951]

AN ACT to provide for the conduct of elections of the Houses of Parliament and to the House or Houses of the Legislature of each State, the qualifications and disqualifications for membership of those Houses, the corrupt [1]* * * practices and other offences at or in connection with such elections and the decision of doubts and disputes arising out of or in connection with such elections.

Be it enacted by Parliament as follows:—

PART - I : PRELIMINARY

1. Short title. This Act may be called the Representation of the People Act, 1951.

2. Interpretation.

(1) In this Act, unless the context otherwise requires —

(a) each of the expressions defined in Section 2 or sub-section (1) of Section 27 of the Representation of the People Act 1950 (43 of 1950), but not defined in this Act, shall have the same meaning as in that Act;

(b) "appropriate authority" means, in relation to an election to the House of the People or the Council of States [2]* * *, the Central Government, and in relation to an election to the Legislative Assembly or the Legislative Council of a State, the State Government;

[3][(bb) "chief electoral officer" means the officer appointed under Section 13A of the Representation of the People Act, 1950 (43 of 1950)];

(c) "corrupt practice" means any of the practices specified in Section 123 [4]* * *;

[5][(cc) "district election officer" means the officer designated or nominated under Section 13AA of the Representation of the People Act, 1950 (43 of 1950)];

(d) "election" means an election to fill a seat or seats in either House of Parliament or in the House or either House of the Legislature of a State other than the State of Jammu and Kashmir [6]* * * ;

[7][(e) "elector" in relation to a constituency means a person whose name is entered in the electoral roll of that constituency for the time being in force and who is not subject to any of the disqualifications mentioned in Section 16 of the Representation of the People Act, 1950 (43 of 1950)];

[PART - II : ACTS OF PARLIAMENT]

[8][(f) "political party" means an association or a body of individual citizens of India registered with the Election Commission as a political party under Section 29A];

(g) "prescribed" means prescribed by rules made under this Act;

[9][(h) "public holiday" means any day which is a public holiday for the purposes of Section 25 of the Negotiable Instruments Act, 1881 (26 of 1881)];

[10]* * * * *

[11]* * * * *

[12][(i) "sign", in relation to a person who is unable to write his name, means authenticate in such manner as may be prescribed.

[13]* * * * *

[14]* * * * *

(2) For the purposes of this Act, [15]* * * a Parliamentary constituency, an Assembly constituency, a Council constituency, a local authorities' constituency, a graduates' constituency and a teachers' constituency shall each be treated as a constituency of a different class.

(3) Any requirement under this Act that a notification, order, rule, declaration, notice or list issued or made by any authority shall be published in the Official Gazette, shall, unless otherwise expressly provided in this Act, be construed as a requirement that the notification, order, rule, declaration, notice or list shall—

(a) where it is issued or made by the Central Government, be published in the Gazette of India;

(b) where it is issued or made by a State Government, be published in the Official Gazette of the State; and

(c) where it is issued or made by any other authority, be published in the Gazette of India if it relates to an election to, or membership of, either House of Parliament 8* * * and in the Official Gazette of the State if it relates to an election to, or membership of, the House or either House of the Legislature of a State.

(4) Where, under any of the provisions of this Act, anything is to be prescribed, different provisions may be made for different cases or classes of cases.

[16]* * * * *

[17][(5)] Any reference in this Act to a law which is not in force in the State of Jammu and Kashmir shall, in relation to that State, be construed as a reference to the corresponding law, if any, in force in that State.]

[16]* * * * *

PART - II : [18][QUALIFICATIONS AND DISQUALIFICATIONS]

CHAPTER - I : QUALIFICATIONS FOR MEMBERSHIP OF PARLIAMENT

[19][**3. Qualification for membership of the Council of States.** A person shall not be qualified to be chosen as a representative of any State [20]* * * or Union territory in the Council of States unless he is an elector for a Parliamentary constituency [21][in India].]

4. Qualifications for membership of the House of the People. A person shall not be qualified to be chosen to fill a seat in the House of the People [22]* * *, unless—

(a) in the case of a seat reserved for the Scheduled Castes in any State, he is a member of any of the Scheduled Castes, whether of that State or of any other State, and is an elector for any Parliamentary constituency;

(b) in the case of a seat reserved for the Scheduled Tribes in any State (other than those in the autonomous districts of Assam), he is a member of any of the Scheduled Tribes, whether of that State or of any other State (excluding the tribal areas of Assam), and is an elector for any Parliamentary constituency;

(c) in the case of a seat reserved for the Scheduled Tribes in the autonomous districts of Assam, he is a member of any of those Scheduled Tribes and is an elector for the Parliamentary constituency in which such seat is reserved or for any other Parliamentary constituency comprising any such autonomous district;

[23]* * *

[24][(cc) in the case of the seat reserved for the Scheduled Tribes in the Union territory of [25][Lakshadweep], he is a member of any of those Scheduled Tribes and is an elector for the Parliamentary constituency of that Union territory; [26]* * *]

[27][(ccc) in the case of the seat allotted to the State of Sikkim, he is an elector for the Parliamentary constituency for Sikkim];

(d) in the case of any other seat, he is an elector for any Parliamentary constituency.

CHAPTER - II : QUALIFICATIONS FOR MEMBERSHIP OF STATE LEGISLATURES

5. Qualifications for membership of a Legislative Assembly. A person shall not be qualified to be chosen to fill a seat in the Legislative Assembly of a State unless—

(a) in the case of a seat reserved for the Scheduled Castes or for the Scheduled Tribes of that State, he is a member of any of those castes or of those tribes, as the case may be, and is an elector for any Assembly constituency in that State;

(b) in the case of a seat reserved for an autonomous district of Assam, [28]* * * he is a member of a [29][Scheduled Tribe of any autonomous district] and is an elector for the Assembly constituency in which such seat or any other seat is reserved for that district; and

(c) in the case of any other seat, he is an elector for any Assembly constituency in that State:

[30]*[PROVIDED that for the period referred to in clause (2) of article 371A, a person shall not be qualified to be chosen to fill any seat allocated to the Tuensang district in the Legislative Assembly of Nagaland unless he is a member of the regional council referred to in that article.]*

[31][**5A. Qualifications for membership of Legislative Assembly of Sikkim.**

[32][(1)] Notwithstanding anything contained in Section 5, a person shall not be qualified to be chosen to fill a seat in the Legislative Assembly of Sikkim (deemed to be the Legislative Assembly of that State duly constituted under the Constitution) unless —

(a) in the case of a seat reserved for Sikkimese of Bhutia-Lepcha origin, he is a person either of Bhutia or Lepcha origin and is an elector for any Assembly constituency in the State other than the constituency reserved for the Sanghas;

(b) in the case of a seat reserved for Sikkimese of Nepal origin, he is a person of Nepali origin and is an elector for any Assembly constituency in the State;

(c) in the case of a seat reserved for Scheduled Castes, he is a member of any of the castes specified in the Representation of Sikkim Subjects Act, 1974 and is an elector for any Assembly constituency in the State; and

(d) in the case of a seat reserved for Sanghas, he is an elector of the Sangha constituency.]

[33][(2) Notwithstanding anything contained in Section 5, a person shall not be qualified to be chosen to fill a seat in the Legislative Assembly of the State of Sikkim, to be constituted at any time after the commencement of the Representation of the People (Amendment) Act, 1980 (8 of 1980), unless—

(a) in the case of a seat reserved for Sikkimese of Bhutia-Lepcha origin, he is a person either of Bhutia or Lepcha origin and is an elector for any assembly constituency in the State other than the constituency reserved for the Sanghas;

(b) in the case of a seat reserved for the Scheduled Castes, he is a member of any of those castes in the State of Sikkim and is an elector for any assembly constituency in the State;

(c) in the case of a seat reserved for Sanghas, he is an elector of the Sangha constituency; and

(d) in the case of any other seat, he is an elector for any assembly constituency in the State.

EXPLANATION: In this sub-section "Bhutia" includes Chumbipa, Dopthapa, Dukpa, Kagatey, Sherpa, Tibetan, Tromopa and Yolmo.]

6. Qualification for membership of a Legislative Council.

(1) A person shall not be qualified to be chosen to fill a seat in the Legislative Council of a State to be filled by election unless he is an elector for any Assembly constituency in that State.

(2) A person shall not be qualified to be chosen to fill a seat in the Legislative Council of a State to be filled by nomination by the Governor [34]* * * unless he is ordinarily resident in the State.

[35][CHAPTER - III : DISQUALIFICATIONS FOR MEMBERSHIP OF PARLIAMENT AND STATE LEGISLATURES

7. Definition. In this Chapter,

(a) "appropriate Government" means in relation to any disqualification for being chosen as or for being a member of either House of Parliament, the Central Government, and in relation to any disqualification for being chosen as or for being a member of the Legislative Assembly or Legislative Council of a State, the State Government;

(b) "disqualified" means disqualified for being chosen as, and for being, a member of either House of Parliament or of the Legislative Assembly or Legislative Council of a State.

8. Disqualification on conviction for certain offences.

[36][(1) A person convicted of an offence punishable under—

(a) section 153A (offence of promoting enmity between different groups on ground of religion, race, place of birth, residence, language, etc., and doing acts prejudicial to maintenance of harmony) or Section 171E (offence of bribery) or Section 171F (offence of undue influence or personation at an election) or sub-section (1) or sub-section (2) of Section 376 or Section 376A or Section 376B or Section 376C or Section 376D (offences relating to rape) or Section 498A (offence of cruelty towards a woman by husband or relative of a husband) or sub-section (2) or sub-section (3) of Section 505 (offence of making statement creating or promoting enmity, hatred or ill-will between classes or offence relating to such statement in any place of worship or in any assembly engaged in the performance of religious worship or religious ceremonies) of the Indian Penal Code (45 of 1860); or

(b) the Protection of Civil Rights Act, 1955 (22 of 1955) which provides for punishment for the preaching and practice of "untouchability", and for the enforcement of any disability arising therefrom; or

(c) Section 11 (offence of importing or exporting prohibited goods) of the Customs Act, 1962 (52 of 1962); or

(d) Sections 10 to 12 (offence of being a member of an association declared unlawful, offence relating to dealing with funds of an unlawful association or offence relating to contravention of an order made in respect of a notified place) of the Unlawful Activities (Prevention) Act, 1967 (37 of 1967); or

(e) the Foreign Exchange (Regulation) Act, 1973 (46 of 1973); or

(f) the Narcotic Drugs and Psychotropic Substances Act, 1985 (61 of 1985); or

(g) Section 3 (offence of committing terrorist acts) or Section 4 (offence of committing disruptive activities) of the Terrorist and Disruptive Activities (Prevention) Act, 1987 (28 of 1987); or

(h) Section 7 (offence of contravention of the provisions of Sections 3 to 6) of the Religious Institutions (Prevention of Misuse) Act, 1988 (41 of 1988); or

(i) Section 125 (offence of promoting enmity between classes in connection with the election) or Section 135 (offence of removal of ballot papers from polling stations) or Section 135A (offence of booth capturing) of clause (a) of sub-section (2) of Section 136 (offence of fraudulently defacing or fraudulently destroying any nomination paper) of this Act;

[38][or]

[37][(j) Section 6 (offence of conversion of a place of worship) of the Places of Worship (Special Provisions) Act, 1991];

[39][(k) Section 2 (offence of insulting the Indian National Flag or the Constitution of India) or Section 3 (offence of preventing singing of National Anthem) of the Prevention of Insults to National Honour Act, 1971 (69 of 1971),]

[40][(l) the Commission of Sati (Prevention) Act, 1987 (3 of 1988); or

(m) the Prevention of Corruption Act, 1988 (49 of 1988); or

(n) the Prevention of Terrorism Act, 2002 (15 of 2002),]

[41][shall be disqualified, where the convicted person is sentenced to—

(i) only fine, for a period of six years from the date of such conviction;

(ii) imprisonment, from the date of such conviction and shall continue to be disqualified for a further period of six years since his release.]

(2) A person convicted for the contravention of—

(a) any law providing for the prevention of hoarding or profiteering; or

(b) any law relating to the adulteration of food or drugs; or

(c) any provisions of the Dowry Prohibition Act, 1961 (28 of 1961);

[42]* * * * *

(3) A person convicted of any offence and sentenced to imprisonment for not less than two years [other than any offence referred to in sub-section (1) or sub-section (2)] shall be disqualified from the date of such conviction and shall continue to be disqualified for a further period of six years since his release.]

[43][(4)] Notwithstanding anything [44][in sub-section (1), sub-section (2) or sub-section (3)] a disqualification under either sub-section shall not, in the case of a person who on the date of the conviction is a member of Parliament or the Legislature of a State, take effect until three months have elapsed from that date or, if within that period an appeal or application for revision is brought in respect of the conviction or the sentence, until that appeal or application is disposed of by the court.

EXPLANATION. In this Section, —

(a) "law providing for the prevention of hoarding or profiteering" means any law, or any order, rule or notification having the force of law, providing for—

(i) the regulation of production or manufacture of any essential commodity;

(ii) the control of price at which any essential commodity may be bought or sold;

(iii) the regulation of acquisition, possession, storage, transport, distribution, disposal, use or consumption of any essential commodity;

(iv) the prohibition of the withholding from sale of any essential commodity ordinarily kept for sale;

(b) "drug" has the meaning assigned to it in the Durgs and Cosmetics Act, 1940 (23 of 1940);

(c) "essential commodity" has the meaning assigned to it in the Essential Commodity Act, 1955 (10 of 1955);

(d) "food" has the meaning assigned to it in the Prevention of Food Adulteration Act, 1954 (37 of 1954).

[45][**8A. Disqualification on ground of corrupt practices.**

(1) The case of every person found guilty of a corrupt practice by an order under Section 99 shall be submitted, as soon as may be, after such order takes effect, by such authority as the Central Government may specify in this behalf, to the President for determination of the question as to whether such person shall be disqualified and if so, for what period:

PROVIDED that the period for which any person may be disqualified under this sub-section shall in no case exceed six years from the date on which the order made in relation to him under Section 99 takes effect.

(2) Any person who stands disqualified under Section 8A of this Act as it stood immediately before the commencement of the Election Laws (Amendment) Act, 1975 (40 of 1975), may, if the period of such disqualification has not expired, submit a petition to the President for the removal of such disqualification for the unexpired portion of the said period.

(3) Before giving his decision on any question mentioned in sub-section (1) or on any petition submitted under sub-section (2), the President shall obtain the opinion of the Election Commission on such question or petition and shall act according to such opinion.]

9. Disqualification for dismissal for corruption or disloyalty.

(1) A person who having held an office under the Government of India or under the Government of any State has been dismissed for corruption or for disloyalty to the State shall be disqualified for a period of five years from the date of such dismissal.

(2) For the purposes of sub-section (1), a certificate issued by the Election Commission to the effect that a person having held office under the Government of India or under the Government of a State, has or has not been dismissed for corruption or for disloyalty to the State shall be conclusive proof of the fact:

PROVIDED that no certificate to the effect that a person has been dismissed for corruption or for disloyalty to the State shall be issued unless an opportunity of being heard has been given to the said person.

9A. Disqualification for Government contracts, etc. A person shall be disqualified if, and for so long as, there subsists a contract entered into by him in the course of his trade or business with the appropriate Government for the supply of goods to, or for the execution of any works undertaken by, that Government.

EXPLANATION: For the purposes of this Section, where a contract has been fully performed by the person by whom it has been entered into with the appropriate Government, the contract shall be deemed not to subsist by reason only of the fact that the Government has not performed its part of the contract either wholly or in part.

10. Disqualification for office under Government company. A person shall be disqualified if, and for so long as, he is a managing agent, manager or secretary of any company or corporation (other than a cooperative society) in the capital of which the appropriate Government has not less than twenty-five per cent. share.

10A. Disqualification for failure to lodge account of election expenses. If the Election Commission is satisfied that a person—

(a) has failed to lodge an account of election expenses within the time and in the manner required by or under this Act; and

(b) has no good reason or justification for the failure, the Election Commission shall, by order published in the Official Gazette, declare him to be disqualified and any such person shall be disqualified for a period of three years from the date of the order.

11. Removal or reduction of period of disqualification. The Election Commission may, for reasons to be recorded, remove any disqualification under this Chapter [46][(except under Section 8A)] or reduce the period of any such disqualification.

CHAPTER - IV : DISQUALIFICATIONS FOR VOTING

11A. Disqualification arising out of conviction and corrupt practices.

[47][(1)] If any person, after the commencement of this Act,—

[48]* * * is convicted of an offence punishable under Section 171E or Section 171F of the Indian Penal Code (45 of 1860), or under Section 125 or Section 135 or clause (a) of sub-section (2) of Section 136 of this Act, [49]* * *

[50]* * * * *

he shall, for a period of six years from the date of the conviction or from the date on which the order takes effect, be is qualified for voting at any election.

[51][(2) Any person disqualified by a decision of the President under sub-section (1) of Section 8A for any period shall be disqualified for the same period for voting at any election.

(3) The decision of the President on a petition submitted by any person under sub-section (2) of Section 8A in respect of any disqualification for being chosen as, and for being, a member of either House of Parliament or of the Legislative Assembly or Legislative Council of a State shall, so far as may be, apply in respect of the disqualification for voting at any election incurred by him under clause (b) of sub-section (1) of Section 11A of this Act as it stood immediately before the commencement of the Election Laws (Amendment) Act, 1975 (40 of 1975), as if such decision were a decision in respect of the said disqualification for voting also.]

11B. Removal of Disqualifications. The Election Commission may, for reasons to be recorded, remove [52][any disqualification under sub-section (1) of Section 11A].]

[53][PART - III : NOTIFICATION OF GENERAL ELECTIONS

12. Notification for biennial election to the Council of States. For the purpose of filling the seats of members of the Council of States retiring on the expiration of their term of office the President shall, by one or more notifications published in the Gazette of India on such date or dates as may be recommended by the Election Commission, call upon the elected members of the Legislative Assembly or, as the case may be, the members of the electoral college, of each State concerned to elect members in accordance with the provisions of this Act and of the rules and orders made thereunder :

PROVIDED that no notification under this Section shall be issued more than three months prior to the date on which the term of office of the retiring members is due to expire.

[54][**12A. Notification for election to fill the seat allotted to the State of Sikkim in the Council of States.** For the purpose of filling for the first time the seat allotted to the State of Sikkim by the Constitution (Thirty-sixth Amendment) Act, 1975 in the Council of States, the President shall, by a notification published in the Gazette of India, on such date as may be recommended by Election Commission, call upon the elected members of the Legislative Assembly of the State of Sikkim to elect a member in accordance with the provisions of this Act and of the rules and orders made thereunder and the election so held shall for all purposes and intent be deemed to have been held under Section 12.]

13. [Notification for reconstitution of electoral colleges for certain Union territories.] *Rep. by the Territorial Councils Act, 1956 (103 of 1956), s. 66.*

14. Notification for general election to the House of the People.

(1) A general election shall be held for the purpose of constituting a new House of the People on the expiration of the duration of the existing House or on its dissolution.

(2) For the said purpose the President shall, by one or more notifications published in the Gazette of India on such date or dates as may be recommended by the Election Commission, call upon all parliamentary constituencies to elect members in accordance with the provisions of this Act and of the rules and orders made thereunder:

PROVIDED that where a general election is held otherwise than on the dissolution of the existing House of the People, no such notification shall be issued at any time earlier than six months prior to the date on which the duration of that House would expire under the provisions of clause (2) of article 83.

[54][**14A. Notification for electing the representative of the State of Sikkim to the existing House of the People.** For the purpose of electing a representative of the State of Sikkim to the House of the People, specified in clause (e) of article 371F of the Constitution, the Election Commission shall call upon the members of the Legislative Assembly of the State of Sikkim to elect the representative in accordance with such of the provisions of this Act, and the rules and orders made thereunder, as are applicable to the election of the members of the Council of States.]

15. Notification for general election to a State Legislative Assembly.

(1) A general election shall be held for the purpose of constituting a new Legislative Assembly on the expiration of the duration of the existing Assembly or on its dissolution.

(2) For the said purpose, [55][the Governor or Administrator, as the case may be], [56]* * * shall by one or more notifications published in the Official Gazette of the State on such date or dates as may be recommended by the Election Commission, call upon all Assembly constituencies in the State to elect members in accordance with the provisions of this Act and of the rules and orders made thereunder:

*PROVIDED that where a general election is held otherwise than on the dissolution of the existing Legislative Assembly, no such notification shall be issued at any time earlier than six months prior to the date on which the duration of that Assembly would expire under the provisions of clause (1), of article 172 3 * * * [57][or under the provisions of Section 5 of the Government of Union Territories Act, 1963 (20 of 1963), as the case may be.]*

[58][**15A. Notification for certain elections to Legislative Councils.** For the purpose of constituting the Legislative Council of the State of Madhya Pradesh under the States Reorganisation Act, 1956 (37 of 1956), and constituting the Legislative Council of the State of Andhra Pradesh under the Legislative Councils Act, 1957 (37 of 1957), the Governor of each of the aforesaid States shall, by one or more notifications published in the Official

Gazette of the State on such date or dates as may be recommended by the Election Commission, call upon the members of the Legislative Assembly of the State and all the Council constituencies to elect members in accordance with the provisions of this Act and of the rules and orders made thereunder.]

16. Notification for biennial election to a State Legislative Council. For the purpose of filling the seats of members of the Legislative Council of a State retiring on the expiration of their term of office, the Governor [59]* * * shall, by one or more notifications published in the Official Gazette of the State on such date or dates as may be recommended by the Election Commission call upon the members of the Legislative Assembly of the State and all the Council constituencies concerned to elect members in accordance with the provisions of this Act and of the rules and orders made thereunder:

PROVIDED that no notification under this Section shall be issued more than three months prior to the date on which the term of office of the retiring members is due to expire.]

PART - IV : ADMINISTRATIVE MACHINERY FOR THE CONDUCT OF ELECTIONS

19. Definition. In this Part and in Part V, unless the context otherwise requires, "constituency" means [60]* * * a Parliamentary constituency or an Assembly constituency or a Council constituency.

[61][**19A. Delegation of functions of Election Commission**. The functions of the Election Commission under the Constitution, the Representation of the People Act, 1950 (43 of 1950), and this Act or under the rules made thereunder may, subject to such general or special directions, if any, as may be given by the Election Commission in this behalf, be performed also by a Deputy Election Commissioner or by the Secretary to the Election Commission.]

[62][**20. General duties of chief electoral officers.** Subject to the superintendence, direction and control of the Election Commission, the chief electoral officer of each State shall supervise the conduct of all elections in the State under this Act.

[63][**20A. General duties of district election officer.**

(1) Subject to the superintendence, direction and control of the chief electoral officer, the district election officer shall coordinate and supervise all work in the district or in the area within his jurisdiction in connection with the conduct of all elections to Parliament and the Legislature of the State.

(2) The district election officer shall also perform such other functions as may be entrusted to him by the Election Commission and the chief electoral officer.]

[64][**20B. Observers.**

(1) The Election Commission may nominate an Observer who shall be an officer of Government to watch the conduct of election or elections in a constituency or a group of constituencies and to perform such other functions as may be entrusted to him by the Election Commission.

(2) The Observer nominated under sub-section (1) shall have the power to direct the returning officer for the constituency or for any of the constituencies for which he has been nominated, to stop the counting of votes at any time before

the declaration of the result or not to declare the result if in the opinion of the Observer booth capturing has taken place at a large number of polling stations or at places fixed for the poll or counting of votes or any ballot papers used at a polling station or at a place fixed for the poll are unlawfully taken out of the custody of the returning officer or are accidentally or intentionally destroyed or lost or are damaged or tampered with to such an extent that the result of the poll at that polling station or place cannot be ascertained.

(3) Where an Observer has directed the returning officer under this Section to stop counting of votes or not to declare the result, the Observer shall forthwith report the matter to the Election Commission and thereupon the Election Commission shall, after taking all material circumstances into account, issue appropriate directions under Section 58A or Section 64A or Section 66.

EXPLANATION: For the purposes of sub-section (2) and sub-section (3), "Observer" shall include a Regional Commissioner or any such officer of the Election Commission as has been assigned under this Section the duty of watching the conduct of election or elections in a constituency or group of constituencies by the Commission.]

21. Returning officers. For every constituency, for every election to fill a seat or seats in the Council of States and for every election by the members of the Legislative Assembly of a State to fill a seat or seats in the Legislative Council of the State, the Election Commission shall, in consultation with the Government of the State, designate or nominate a returning officer who shall be 1[an officer of Government or of a local authority]:

PROVIDED that nothing in this Section shall prevent the Election Commission from designating or nominating the same person to be the returning officer for more than one constituency.]

22. Assistant returning officers.

(1) The Election Commission may appoint one or more persons to assist any returning officer in the performance of his functions:

PROVIDED that every such person shall be [65][an officer of Government or of a local authority].

(2) Every assistant returning officer shall, subject to the control of the returning officer, be competent to perform all or any of the functions of the returning officer:

PROVIDED that no assistant returning officer shall perform any of the functions of the returning officer which relate [66] * * to the scrutiny of nominations [67]* * * unless the returning officer is unavoidably prevented from performing the said function.*

23. Returning officer to include assistant returning officers performing the functions of the returning officer. References in this Act to the returning officer shall, unless the context otherwise requires, be deemed to include an assistant returning officer performing any function which he is authorised to perform under sub-section (2) of Section 22.

24. General duty of the returning officer. It shall be the general duty of the returning officer at any election to do all such acts and things as may be necessary for effectually conducting the election in the manner provided by this Act and rules or orders made thereunder.

[68][**25. Provision of polling stations for constituencies**. The district election officer shall, with the previous approval of the Election Commission, provide a sufficient number of polling stations for every constituency the whole or greater part of which lies within his jurisdiction, and shall publish, in such manner as the Election Commission may direct, a list showing the polling stations so provided and the polling areas or groups of voters for which they have respectively been provided.]

26. Appointment of presiding officers for polling stations.

(1) The [69][district election officer] shall appoint a presiding officer for each polling station and such polling officer or officers as he thinks necessary, but he shall not appoint any person who has been employed by or on behalf of, or has been otherwise working for, a candidate in or about the election:

PROVIDED that if a polling officer is absent from the polling station, the presiding officer may appoint any person who is present at the polling station other than a person who has been employed by or on behalf of, or has been otherwise working for, a candidate in or about the election, to be the polling officer during the absence of the former officer, and inform the 5[district election officer] accordingly:

[70][PROVIDED FURTHER that nothing in this sub-section shall prevent the 5[district election officer] from appointing the same person to be the presiding officer for more than one polling station in the same premises.]

(2) A polling officer shall, if so directed by the presiding officer, perform all or any of the functions of a presiding officer under this Act or any rules or orders made thereunder.

(3) If the presiding officer, owing to illness or other unavoidable cause, is obliged to absent himself from the polling station, his functions shall be performed by such polling officer as has been previously authorized by the [71][district election officer] to perform such functions during any such absence.

(4) References in this Act to the presiding officer shall, unless the context otherwise requires, be deemed to include any person performing any function which he is authorized to perform under sub-section (2) or sub-section (3), as the case may be.

[72]* * * * *

27. General duty of the presiding officer. It shall be the general duty of the presiding officer at a polling station to keep order thereat and to see that the poll is fairly taken.

28. Duties of a polling officer. —It shall be the duty of the polling officers at a polling station to assist the presiding officer for such station in the performance of his functions.

[73][**28A. Returning officer, presiding officer, etc., deemed to be on deputation to Election Commission**. —The returning officer, assistant returning officer, presiding officer, polling officer, and any other officer appointed under this Part, and any police officer designated for the time being by the State Government, for the conduct of any

election shall be deemed to be on deputation to the Election Commission for the period commencing on and from the date of the notification calling for such election and ending with the date of declaration of the results of such election and accordingly, such officers shall, during that period, be subject to the control, superintendence and discipline of the Election Commission.

29. Special provisions in the case of certain elections.

(1) The returning officer for an election [74]* * * to fill a seat or seats in the Council of States or for an election by the members of the Legislative Assembly of a State to fill a seat or seats in the Legislative Council of the State shall, with the previous approval of the Election Commission, fix the place at which the poll will be taken for such election and shall notify the place so fixed in such manner as the Election Commission may direct.

(2) The returning officer shall preside over such election at the place so fixed and shall appoint such polling officer or officers to assist him as he thinks necessary but he shall not appoint any person who has been employed by or on behalf of, or has been otherwise working for, a candidate in or about the election.

[75][PART - IVA : REGISTRATION OF POLITICAL PARTIES

29A. Registration with the Election Commission of associations and bodies as political parties.

(1) Any association or body of individual citizens of India calling itself a political party and intending to avail itself of the provisions of this Part shall make an application to the Election Commission for its registration as a political party for the purposes of this Act.

(2) Every such application shall be made,—

(a) if the association or body is in existence at the commencement of the Representation of the People (Amendment) Act, 1988 (1 of 1989), within sixty days next following such commencement;

(b) if the association or body is formed after such commencement, within thirty days next following the date of its formation.

(3) Every application under sub-section (1) shall be signed by the chief executive officer of the association or body (whether such chief executive officer is known as Secretary or by any other designation) and presented to the Secretary to the Commission or sent to such Secretary by registered post.

(4) Every such application shall contain the following particulars, namely:—

(a) the name of the association or body;

(b) the State in which its head office is situate;

(c) the address to which letters and other communications meant for it should be sent;

(d) the names of its president, secretary, treasurer and other office-bearers;

(e) the numerical strength of its members, and if there are categories of its members, the numerical strength in each category;

(f) whether it has any local units; if so, at what levels;

(g) whether it is represented by any member or members in either House of Parliament or of any State Legislature; if so, the number of such member or members.

(5) The application under sub-section (1) shall be accompanied by a copy of the memorandum or rules and regulations of the association or body, by whatever name called, and such memorandum or rules and regulations shall contain a specific provision that the association or body shall bear true faith and allegiance to the Constitution of India as by law established, and to the principles of socialism, secularism and democracy, and would uphold the sovereignty, unity and integrity of India.

(6) The Commission may call for such other particulars as it may deem fit from the association or body.

(7) After considering all the particulars as aforesaid in its possession and any other necessary and relevant factors and after giving the representatives of the association or body reasonable opportunity of being heard, the Commission shall decide either to register the association or body as a political party for the purposes of this Part, or not so to register it; and the Commission shall communicate its decision to the association or body:

PROVIDED that no association or body shall be registered as a political party under this sub-section unless the memorandum or rules and regulations of such association or body conform to the provisions of sub-section (5).

(8) The decision of the Commission shall be final.

(9) After an association or body has been registered as a political party as aforesaid, any change in its name, head office, office-bearers, address or in any other material matters shall be communicated to the Commission without delay.]

[76][**29B. Political parties entitled to accept contribution.** Subject to the provisions of the Companies Act, 1956 (1 of 1956), every political party may accept any amount of contribution voluntarily offered to it by any person or company other than a Government company:

PROVIDED that no political party shall be eligible to accept any contribution from any foreign source defined under clause (e) of Section 2 of the Foreign Contribution (Regulation) Act, 1976 (49 of 1976).

EXPLANATION: For the purposes of this Section and Section 29C,—

(a) "company" means a company as defined in Section 3;

(b) "Government company" means a company within the meaning of Section 617; and

(c) "contribution" has the meaning assigned to it under Section 293A, of the Companies Act, 1956 (1 of 1956) and includes any donation or subscription offered by any person to a political party; and

(d) "person" has the meaning assigned to it under clause (31) of Section 2 of the Income-tax Act, 1961 (43 of 1961), but does not include Government company, local authority and every artificial juridical person wholly or partially funded by the Government.

29C. Declaration of donation received by the political parties.

(1) The treasurer of a political party or any other person authorised by the political party in this behalf shall, in each financial year, prepare a report in respect of the following, namely:

(a) the contribution in excess of twenty thousand rupees received by such political party from any person in that financial year;

(b) the contribution in excess of twenty thousand rupees received by such political party from companies other than Government companies in that financial year.

(2) The report under sub-section (1) shall be in such form as may be prescribed.

(3) The report for a financial year under sub-section (1) shall be submitted by the treasurer of a political party or any other person authorised by the political party in this behalf before the due date for furnishing a return of its income of that financial year under Section 139 of the Income-tax Act, 1961 (43 of 1961), to the Election Commission.

(4) Where the treasurer of any political party or any other person authorised by the political party in this behalf fails to submit a report under sub-section (3) then, notwithstanding anything contained in the Income-tax Act, 1961 (43 of 1961), such political party shall not be entitled to any tax relief under that Act.]

PART - V : CONDUCT OF ELECTIONS
CHAPTER - I : NOMINATION OF CANDIDATES

[77][**30. Appointment of dates for nominations, etc**. As soon as the notification calling upon a constituency to elect a member or members is issued, the Election Commission shall, by notification in the Official Gazette, appoint —

(a) the last date for making nominations, which shall be the [78][seventh day] after the date of publication of the first-mentioned notification or, if that day is a public holiday, the next succeeding day which is not a public holiday;

(b) the date for the scrutiny of nominations, which shall be [79][the day immediately following] the last date for making nominations or, if that day is a public holiday, the next succeeding day which is not a public holiday ;

(c) the last date for the withdrawal of candidatures, which shall be [80][the second day] after the date for the scrutiny of nominations or, if that day is a public holiday, the next succeeding day which is not a public holiday;

(d) the date or dates on which a poll shall, if necessary, be taken, which or the first of which shall be a date not earlier than the [81][fourteenth day] after the last date for the withdrawal of candidatures; and

(e) the date before which the election shall be completed.

[82]* * * * *]

31. Public notice of election. On the issue of a notification under Section 30, the returning officer [83]*** shall give public notice of the intended election in such form and manner as may be prescribed, inviting nominations of candidates for such election and specifying the place at which the nomination papers are to be delivered.

32. Nomination of candidates for election. Any person may be nominated as a candidate for election to fill a seat [84]*** if he is qualified to be chosen to fill that seat under the provisions of the Constitution and this Act [85]*** [86][or under the provisions of the Government of Union Territories Act, 1963 (20 of 1963), as the case may be.]

[87][**33. Presentation of nomination paper and requirements for a valid nomination.**

(1) On or before the date appointed under clause (a) of Section 30 each candidate shall, either in person or by his proposer, between the hours of eleven o'clock in the forenoon and three o'clock in the afternoon deliver to the returning officer at the place specified in this behalf in the notice issued under Section 31 a nomination paper completed in the prescribed form and signed by the candidate and by an elector of the constituency as proposer :

[88][PROVIDED that a candidate not set up by a recognised political party, shall not be deemed to be duly nominated for election form a constituency unless the nomination paper is subscribed by ten proposers being electors of the constituency:

PROVIDED FURTHER that no nomination paper shall be delivered to the returning officer on a day which is a public holiday:

PROVIDED ALSO that in the case of a local authorities' constituency, graduates' constituency or teachers' constituency, the reference to "an elector of the constituency as proposer" shall be construed as a reference to ten per cent. of the electors of the constituency or ten such electors, whichever is less, as proposers.]

[89][(1A) Notwithstanding anything contained in sub-section (1) for election to the Legislative Assembly of Sikkim (deemed to be the Legislative Assembly of that State duly constituted under the Constitution), the nomination paper to be delivered to the returning officer shall be in such form and manner as may be prescribed :

PROVIDED that the said nomination paper shall be subscribed by the candidate as assenting to the nomination, and—

(a) in the case of a seat reserved for Sikkimese of Bhutia-Lepcha origin, also by at least twenty electors of the constituency as proposers and twenty electors of the constituency as seconders;

(b) in the case of a seat reserved for Sanghas, also by at least twenty electors of the constituency as proposers and at least twenty electors of the constituency as seconders;

(c) in the case of a seat reserved for Sikkimese of Nepali origin, by an elector of the constituency as proposer:

PROVIDED FURTHER that no nomination paper shall be delivered to the returning officer on a day which is a public holiday.]

(2) In a constituency where any seat is reserved, a candidate shall not be deemed to be qualified to be chosen to fill that seat unless his nomination paper contains a declaration by him specifying the particular caste or tribe of which he is a member and the area in relation to which that caste or tribe is a Scheduled Caste or, as the case may be, a Scheduled Tribe of the State.

(3) Where the candidate is a person who, having held any office referred to in [90][Section 9] has been dismissed and a period of five years has not elapsed since the dismissal, such person shall not be deemed to be duly nominated as a candidate unless his nomination paper is accompanied by a certificate issued in the prescribed manner by the Election Commission to the effect that he has not been dismissed for corruption or disloyalty to the State.

(4) On the presentation of a nomination paper, the returning officer shall satisfy himself that the names and electoral roll numbers of the candidate and his proposer as entered in the nomination paper are the same as those entered in the electoral rolls:

[91][PROVIDED that no misnomer or inaccurate description or clerical, technical or printing error in regard to the name of the candidate or his proposer or any other person, or in regard to any place, mentioned in the electoral roll or the nomination paper and no clerical, technical or printing error in regard to the electoral roll numbers of any such person in the electoral roll or the nomination paper, shall affect the full operation of the electoral roll or the nomination paper with respect to such person or place in any case where the description in regard to the name of the person or place is such as to be commonly understood; and the returning officer shall permit any such misnomer or inaccurate description or clerical, technical or printing error to be corrected and where necessary, direct that any such misnomer, inaccurate description, clerical, technical or printing error in the electoral roll or in the nomination paper shall be overlooked.]

(5) Where the candidate is an elector of a different constituency, a copy of the electoral roll of that constituency or of the relevant part thereof or a certified copy of the relevant entries in such roll shall, unless it has been filed along with the nomination paper, be produced before the returning officer at the time of scrutiny.

[92][(6) Nothing in this Section shall prevent any candidate from being nominated by more than one nomination paper:

PROVIDED that not more than four nomination papers shall be presented by or on behalf of any candidate or accepted by the returning officer for election in the same constituency.]

[93][(7) Notwithstanding anything contained in sub-section (6) or in any other provisions of this Act, a person shall not be nominated as a candidate for election,—

(a) in the case of a general election to the House of the People (whether or not held simultaneously from all Parliamentary constituencies), from more than two Parliamentary constituencies;

(b) in the case of a general election to the Legislative Assembly of a State (whether or not held simultaneously from all Assembly constituencies), from more than two Assembly constituencies in that State;

(c) in the case of a biennial election to the Legislative Council of a State having such Council, from more than two Council constituencies in the State;

(d) in the case of a biennial election to the Council of States for filling two or more seats allotted to a State, for filling more than two such seats;

(e) in the case of bye-elections to the House of the People from two or more Parliamentary constituencies which are held simultaneously, from more than two such Parliamentary constituencies;

(f) in the case of bye-elections to the Legislative Assembly of a State from two or more Assembly constituencies which are held simultaneously, from more than two such Assembly constituencies;

(g) in the case of bye-elections to the Council of States for filling two or more seats allotted to a State, which are held simultaneously, for filling more than two such seats;

(h) in the case of bye-elections to the Legislative Council of a State having such Council from two or more Council constituencies which are held simultaneously, from more than two such Council constituencies.

EXPLANATION: For the purposes of this sub-section, two or more bye-elections shall be deemed to be held simultaneously where the notification calling such bye-elections are issued by the Election Commission under Section 147, Section 149, Section 150 or, as the case may be, Section 151 on the same date.]

[94][**33A. Right to information.**

(1) A candidate shall, apart from any information which he is required to furnish, under this Act or the rules made thereunder, in his nomination paper delivered under sub-section (1) or Section 33, also furnish the information as to whether –

(i) he is accused of any offence punishable with imprisonment for two years or more in a pending case in which a charge has been framed by the court of competent jurisdiction;

(ii) he has been convicted of an offence [other than any offence referred to in sub-section (1) or sub-section (2), or covered in sub-section (3), of Section 8] and sentenced to imprisonment for one year or more.

(2) The candidate of his proposer, as the case may be, shall, at the time of delivering to the returning officer the nomination paper under sub-section (1) of Section 33, also deliver to him an affidavit sworn by the candidate in a prescribed form very fine the information specified in sub-section (1).

(3) The returning officer shall, as soon as may be after the furnishing of information to him under sub-section (1), display the aforesaid information by affixing a copy of the affidavit, delivered under sub-section (2), at a conspicuous place at his office for the information of the electors relating to a constituency for

which the nomination paper is delivered.]

[95][**33B. Candidate to furnish information only under the Act and the rules.** Notwithstanding anything contained in any judgment, decree or order of any court or any direction, order or any other instruction issued by the Election Commission, no candidate shall be liable to disclose or furnish any such information, in respect of his election which is not required to be disclosed or furnished under this Act or the rules made thereunder.]

34. Deposits.

[96][(1) A candidate shall not be deemed to be duly nominated for election from a constituency unless he deposits or causes to be deposited,—

(a) in the case of an election from a Parliamentary constituency, a sum of ten thousand rupees or where the candidate is a member of a Scheduled Caste or Scheduled Tribe, a sum of five thausand rupees; and

(b) in the case of an election from an Assembly or Council constituency, a sum of five thousand rupees or where the candidate is a member of a Scheduled Caste or Scheduled Tribe, a sum of two thousand and five hundred rupees :

PROVIDED that where a candidate has been nominated by more than one nomination paper for election in the same constituency, not more than one deposit shall be required of him under this sub-section.]

(2) Any sum required to be deposited under sub-section (1) shall not be deemed to have been deposited under that sub-section unless at the time of delivery of the nomination paper [97][under sub-section (1) or, as the case may be, sub-section (1A) of Section 33] the candidate has either deposited or caused to be deposited that sum with the returning officer in cash or enclosed with the nomination paper a receipt showing that the said sum has been deposited by him or on his behalf in the Reserve Bank of India or in a Government Treasury.

35. Notice of nominations and the time and place for their Scrutiny. The returning officer shall, on receiving the nomination paper [97][under sub-section (1) or, as the case may be, sub-section (1A) of Section 33], inform the person or persons delivering the same of the date, time and place fixed for the scrutiny of nominations and shall enter on the nomination paper its serial number, and shall sign thereon a certificate stating the date on which and the hour at which the nomination paper has been delivered to him; and shall, as soon as may be thereafter, cause to be affixed in some conspicuous place in his office a notice of the nomination containing descriptions similar to those contained in the nomination paper, both of the candidate and of [98][the proposer].

36. Scrutiny of nominations.

(1) On the date fixed for the scrutiny of nominations under Section 30, the candidates, their election agents, one proposer [99]* * * of each candidate, and one other person duly authorized in writing by each candidate, but no other person, may attend at such time and place as the returning officer may appoint; and the returning officer shall give them all reasonable facilities for examining the nomination papers of all candidates which have been delivered within the time and in the manner laid down in Section 33.

(2) The returning officer shall then examine the nomination papers and shall

decide all objections which may be made to any nomination and may, either on such objection or on his own motion, after such summary inquiry, if any, as he thinks necessary, [100][reject] any nomination on any of the following grounds:—

[101][(a) [102][that on the date fixed for the scrutiny of nominations the candidate] either is not qualified or is disqualified for being chosen to fill the seat under any of the following provisions that may be applicable, namely:—

Articles 84, 102, 173 and 191, [103]* * *

[104][Part II of this Act, and Sections 4 and 14 of the Government of Union Territories Act, 1963 (20 of 1963)] [105]***; or

(b) that there has been a failure to comply with any of the provisions of Section 33 or Section 34 ; or

(c) that the signature of the candidate or the proposer on the nomination paper is not genuine.

(3) Nothing contained in [106][clause (b) or clause (c)] of sub-section (2) shall be deemed to authorize the [107][rejection] of the nomination of any candidate on the ground of any irregularity in respect of a nomination paper, if the candidate has been duly nominated by means of another nomination paper in respect of which no irregularity has been committed.

(4) The returning officer shall not reject any nomination paper on the ground of any [108]* * * defect which is not of a substantial character.

(5) The returning officer shall hold the scrutiny on the date appointed in this behalf under clause (b) of Section 30 and shall not allow any adjournment of the proceedings except when such proceedings are interrupted or obstructed by riot or open violence or by causes beyond his control:

PROVIDED that in case [109][an objection is raised by the returning officer or is made by any other person] the candidate concerned may be allowed time to rebut it not later than the next day but one following the date fixed for scrutiny, and the returning officer shall record his decision on the date to which the proceedings have been adjourned.

(6) The returning officer shall endorse on each nomination paper his decision accepting or rejecting the same and, if the nomination paper is rejected, shall record in writing a brief statement of his reasons for such rejection.

[110][(7) For the purposes of this Section, a certified copy of an entry in the electoral roll for the time being in force of a constituency shall be conclusive evidence of the fact that the person referred to in that entry is an elector for that constituency, unless it is proved that he is subject to a disqualification mentioned in Section 16 of the Representation of the People Act, 1950 (43 of 1950).

(8) Immediately after all the nomination papers have been scrutinized and decisions accepting or ejecting the same have been recorded, the returning officer shall prepare a list of validly nominated candidates, that is to say,

candidates whose nominations have been found valid, and affix it to his notice board.]

37. Withdrawal of candidature.

(1) Any candidate may withdraw his candidature by a notice in writing which shall contain such particulars as may be prescribed and shall be subscribed by him and delivered before three o'clock in the afternoon on the day fixed under clause (c) of Section 30 to the returning officer either by such candidate in person or by his proposer, [111]* * * or election agent who has been authorized in this behalf in writing by such candidate.

[111]* * * * *

(2) No person who has given a notice of withdrawal of his candidature under sub-section (1) shall be allowed to cancel the notice.

[112][(3) The returning officer shall, on being satisfied as to the genuineness of a notice of withdrawal and the identity of the person delivering it under sub-section (1), cause the notice to be affixed in some conspicuous place in his office.]

[113][**38. Publication of list of contesting candidates.**

(1) Immediately after the expiry of the period within which candidatures may be withdrawn under sub-section (1) of Section 37, the returning officer shall prepare and publish in such form and manner as may be prescribed a list of contesting candidates, that is to say, candidates who were included in the list of validily nominated candidates and who have not withdrawn their candidature within the said period.

[114][(2) For the purpose of listing the names under sub-section (1), the candidates shall be classified as follows, namely:

(i) candidates of recognised political parties;

(ii) candidates of registered political parties other than those mentioned in clause (i);

(iii) other candidates.

(3) The categories mentioned in sub-section (2) shall be arranged in the order specified therein and the names of candidates in each category shall be arranged in alphabetical order and the addresses of the contesting candidates as given in the nomination papers together with such other particulars as may be prescribed.]

[115][**39. Nomination of candidates at other elections.**

(1) As soon as the notification calling upon the elected members or the members of the Legislative Assembly of a State or the members of the electoral college of a [116][Union territory] to elect a member or members is issued, the Election Commission shall, by notification in the Official Gazette, appoint—

(a) the last date of making nominations, which shall be the [117][seventh day] after the date of publication of the first mentioned notification or, if that day is a public holiday, the next succeeding day which is not a public holiday;

(b) the date for the scrutiny of nominations, which shall be [118][the day immediately following] the last date for making nominations or, if that day is a public holiday, the next succeeding day which is not a public holiday;

(c) the last date for the withdrawal of candidatures, which shall be [119][the second day] after the date for the scrutiny of nominations or, if that day is a public holiday, the next succeeding day which is not a public holiday;

(d) the date or dates on which a poll shall, if necessary, be taken, which or the first of which shall be a date not earlier than the seventh day after the last date for the withdrawal of candidatures; and

(e) the date before which the election shall be completed.

[120]* * * * *

(2) The provisions of Sections 31 to 38, excluding sub-sections (2) and (5) of Section 33 and [121][clause (a) of sub-section (1) of Section 34], shall apply in relation to any such election as they apply in relation to an election in any constituency :

PROVIDED that—

(a) any references in the said provisions to the electoral roll of the constituency shall, unless the context otherwise requires, be construed, in the case of an election by the members or the elected members of the Legislative Assembly of the State, as references to the list of members or elected members, as the case may be, of that Assembly maintained under sub-section (1) of Section 152, and in the case of an election by the members of the electoral college of a [122][Union territory], as references to the list of members of such electoral college maintained under sub-section (2) of that Section;

[123][*(aa) the reference in the opening paragraph of sub-section (1) of Section 33 to "an elector of the constituency as proposer" shall be construed as a reference to "ten per cent. of the elected members or of the members of the Legislative Assembly of a State or of the members of the electoral college of a Union territory, as the case may be, or ten members concerned, whichever is less, as proposers":*

PROVIDED that where as a result of the calculation of the percentage referred to in this clause, the number of members arrived at is a fraction and if the fraction so arrived at is more than one-half it shall be counted as one, and if the fraction so arrived at is less than one-half it shall be ignored];

[124][[125][(ab)] in the case of an election to the Legislative Council of a State by the members of the Legislative Assembly of that State, clause (a) of sub-section (2) of Section 36 shall be construed as including a reference to sub-clause (d) of clause (3) of article 171];

(b) any reference in the said provisions to Section 30 shall be construed as references to sub-section (1) of this Section; and

(c) at the time of presenting the nomination paper, the returning officer may require the person presenting the same to produce either a copy of the electoral roll, or part of the electoral roll, in which the name of the candidate is included or a certified copy of the relevant entries in such roll.]

[126][**39A. Allocation of equitable sharing of time.**

(1) Notwithstanding anything contained in any other law for the time being in force, the Election Commission shall, on the basis of the past performance of a recognised political party, during elections, allocate equitable sharing of time on the cable television network and other electronic media in such manner as may be prescribed to display or propagate any election matter or to address public in connection with an election.

(2) The allocation of equitable sharing of time under sub-section (1), in respect of an election, shall be made after the publication of list of contesting candidates under Section 38 for the election and shall be valid till forty-eight ours before the hour fixed for poll for such election.

(3) The allocation of equitable sharing of time under sub-section (1) shall be binding on all political parties concerned.

(4) The Election commission may, for the purpose of this Section, make code of conduct for cable operators and electronic media and the cable operators and every person managing or responsible for the management of the electronic media shall abide by such code of conduct.

EXPLANATION: For the purposes of this Section —

(a) "electronic media" includes radio and any other broadcasting media notified by the Central Government in the Official Gazette;

(b) "cable television network" and "cable operator" have the meanings respectively assigned to them under the cable Television Networks (Regulation) Act, 1995 (7 of 1995).

CHAPTER - II : CANDIDATES AND THEIR AGENTS

[127][**40. Election agents.** A candidate at an election may appoint in the prescribed manner any one person other than himself to be his election agent and when any such appointment is made, notice of the appointment shall be given in the prescribed manner to the returning officer.]

[128][**41. Disqualification for being an election agent.** Any person who is for the time being disqualified under the Constitution or under this Act for being a member of either House of Parliament or the House or either House of the Legislature of a State or for voting at elections, shall, so long as the disqualification subsists, also be disqualified for being an election agent at any election.]

42. Revocation of the appointment, or death, of an election agent.

(1) Any revocation of the appointment of an election agent, shall be signed by the candidate, and shall operate from the date on which it is lodged with the returning officer.

[129][(2) In the event of such a revocation or of the death of an election agent whether that event occurs before or during the election, or after the election but before

the account of the candidate's election expenses has been lodged in accordance with the provisions of Section 78, the candidate may appoint in the prescribed manner another person to be his election agent and when such appointment is made notice of the appointment shall be given in the prescribed manner to the returning officer.]

43. [Effect of default in appointment of election agent under Section 42.] Rep. by the Representation of the People (Second Amendment) Act, 1956 (27 of 1956), s. 25.

44. [Duty of the election agent to keep accounts.] Rep. by s. 25, *ibid.*

[130][**45. Functions of election agents.** An election agent may perform such functions in connection with the election as are authorised by or under this Act to be performed by an election agent.]

[131][**46. Appointment of polling agents.** A contesting candidate or his election agent may appoint in the prescribed manner such number of agents and relief agents as may be prescribed to act as polling agents of such candidate at each polling station provided under Section 25 or at the place fixed under sub-section (1) of Section 29 for the poll.]

[132][**47. Appointment of counting agents.** A contesting candidate or his election agent may appoint in the prescri bed manner one or more persons, but not exceeding such number as may be prescribed, to be present as his counting agent or agents at the counting of votes, and when any such appointment is made notice of the appointment shall be given in the prescribed manner to the returning officer.]

48. Revocation of the appointment or death of a polling agent or counting agent.

(1) Any revocation of the appointment of a polling agent shall be signed by the candidate or his election agent and shall operate from the date on which it is lodged with such officer as may be prescribed, and in the event of such a revocation or of the death of a polling agent before the close of the poll, the candidate or his election agent may appoint in the prescribed manner another polling agent at any time before the poll is closed and shall forthwith give notice of such appointment in the prescribed manner to such officer as may be prescribed.

(2) Any revocation of the appointment of a counting agent shall be signed by the candidate or his election agent and shall operate from the date on which it is lodged with the returning officer, and in the event of such a revocation or of the death of a counting agent before the commencement of the counting of votes, the candidate or his election agent may appoint in the prescribed manner another counting agent at any time before the counting of votes is commenced and shall forthwith give notice of such appointment in the prescribed manner to the returning officer.

49. Functions of polling agents and counting agents.

(1) A polling agent may perform such functions in connection with the poll as are authorised by or under this Act to be performed by a polling agent.

(2) A counting agent may perform such functions in connection with the counting

of votes as are authorised by or under this Act to be performed by a counting agent.

50. Attendance of contesting candidate or his election agent at polling stations, and performance by him of the functions of a polling agent or counting agent.

(1) At every election where a poll is taken, each [133][contesting candidate] at such election and his election agent shall have a right to be present at any polling station provided under Section 25 for the taking of the poll or at the place fixed under sub-section (1) of Section 29 for the poll.

(2) A [134][contesting candidate] or his election agent may himself do any act or thing which any polling agent or the counting agent of such 6[contesting candidate] if appointed, would have been authorised by or under this Act to do, or may assist any polling agent or the counting agent of such 2[contesting candidate] in doing any such act or thing.

51. Non-attendance of polling or counting agents. Where any act or thing is required or authorised by or under this Act to be done in the presence of the polling or counting agents, the non-attendance of any such agent or agents at the time and place appointed for the purpose shall not, if the act or thing is otherwise duly done, invalidate the act or thing done.

CHAPTER - III : GENERAL PROCEDURE AT ELECTIONS

[135][**52. Death of candidate of reorganised political party before poll.**

(1) If a candidate, set up by a recognised political party,—

(a) dies at any time after 11 A.M. on the last date for making nomination and his nomination is found valid on scrutiny under Section 36; or

(b) whose nomination has been found valid on scrutiny under Section 36 and who has not withdrawn his candidature under Section 37 dies;

and in either case, a report of his death is received at any time before the publication of the list of contesting candidate under Section 38; or

(c) dies as a contesting candidate and a report of his death is received before the commencement of the poll, the returning officer shall, upon being satisfied about the fact of the death of the candidate, by order announce an adjournment of the poll to a date to be notified later and report the fact to the Election Commission and also to the appropriate authority:

PROVIDED that no order for adjourning a poll should be made in a case referred to in clause (a) except after the scrutiny of all the nominations including the nomination of the deceased candidate:

(2) The Election Commission shall, on receipt of a report from the returning officer under sub-section (1), call upon the recognised political party, whose candidate has died, to nominate another candidate for the said poll within seven days of issue of such notice to such recognised political party and the provisions of Sections 30 to 37 shall, so far as may be, apply in relation to such nomination as they would apply to other nominations:

PROVIDED that no person who has given a notice of withdrawal of his candidature under sub-section (1) of Section 37 before the adjournment of the poll shall be ineligible for being nominated as a candidate for election after such adjournment.

(3) Where a list of contesting candidates had been published under Section 38 before the adjournment of the poll under sub-section (1), the returning officer shall again prepare and publish a fresh list of contesting candidates under that Section so as to include the name of the candidate who has been validly nominated under sub-section (2).

EXPLANATION: For the purposes of this Section, Sections 33 and 38, "recognised political party" means a political party reorganised by the Election Commission under the Election Symbols (Reservation and Allotment) Order, 1968.]

53. Procedure in contested and uncontested elections.

[136][(1) If the number of contesting candidates is more than the number of seats to be filled, a poll shall be taken.]

(2) If the number of such candidates is equal to the number of seats to be filled, the returning officer shall forthwith declare all such candidates to be duly elected to fill those seats.

(3) If the number of such candidates is less than the number of seats to be filled, the returning officer shall forthwith declare all such candidates to be elected and the [137][Election Commission] shall, by notification in the Official Gazette, call upon the constituency or the elected members or the members of the State Legislative Assembly or the members of the electoral college concerned [138]***, as the case may be, to elect a person or persons to fill the remaining seat or seats [139]*** :

*PROVIDED that where the constituency or the elected members or the members of the State Legislative Assembly or the members of the electoral college [138]*** having already been called upon under this sub-section, has or have failed to elect a person or the requisite number of persons, as the case may be, to fill the vacancy or vacancies, the [136][Election Commission] shall not be bound to call again upon the constituency, or such members to elect a person or persons [140][until it is satisfied that if called upon again, there will be no such failure on the part of the constituency or such members].*

54. [Special procedure at elections in constituencies where seats are reserved for Scheduled Castes or Scheduled Tribes.] *Rep. by the Representation of the People (Amendment) Act, 1961 (40 of 1961), s. 12 (w.e.f. 20-9-1961).*

55. Eligibility of members of Scheduled Castes or Scheduled Tribes to hold seats not reserved for those castes or tribes — For the avoidance of doubt it is hereby declared that a member of the Scheduled Castes or of the Scheduled Tribes shall not be disqualified to hold a seat not reserved for members of those castes or tribes, if he is otherwise qualified to hold such seats under the Constitution and this Act [141][or under the Government of Union Territories Act, 1963 (20 of 1963), as the case may be.]

[142]**[55A. [Retirement from contest at elections in Parliamentary and Assembly constituencies.]** *Rep. by the Representation of the People (Amendment) Act, 1958 (58 of 1958), s. 22.*

CHAPTER - IV : THE POLL

56. Fixing time for poll. The [143][Election Commission] shall fix the hours during which the poll will be taken; and the hours so fixed shall be published in such manner as may be prescribed:

PROVIDED that the total period allotted on any one day for polling at an election in [144][a Parliamentary or Assembly constituency] shall not be less than eight hours.

57. Adjournment of poll in emergencies.

(1) If at an election the proceedings at any polling station provided under Section 25 or at the place fixed under sub-section (1) of Section 29 for the poll are interrupted or obstructed by any riot or open violence, or if at an election it is not possible to take the poll at any polling station or such place on account of any natural calamity, or any other sufficient cause, the presiding officer for such polling station or the returning officer presiding over such place, as the case may be, shall announce an adjournment of the poll to a date to be notified later, and where the poll is so adjourned by a presiding officer, he shall forthwith inform the returning officer concerned.

(2) Whenever a poll is adjourned under sub-section (1), the returning officer shall immediately report the circumstances to the appropriate authority and the Election Commission, and shall, as soon as may be, with the previous approval of the Election Commission, appoint the day on which the poll shall recommence, and fix the polling station or place at which and the hours during which the poll will be taken and shall not count the votes cast at such election until such adjourned poll shall have been completed.

(3) In every such case as aforesaid; the returning officer shall notify in such manner as the Election Commission may direct the date, place and hours of polling fixed under sub-section (2).

[145][**58. Fresh poll in the case of destruction, etc., of ballot boxes.**

(1) If at any election,—

(a) any ballot box used at a polling station or at a place fixed for the poll is unlawfully taken out of the custody of the presiding officer or the returning officer, or is accidentally or intentionally destroyed or lost, or is damaged or tampered with, to such an extent, that the result of the poll at that polling station or place cannot be ascertained; or

[146][(aa) any voting machine develops a mechanical failure during the course of the recording of votes; or]

(b) any such error or irregularity in procedure as is likely to vitiate the poll is committed at a polling station or at a place fixed for the poll, the returning officer shall forthwith report the matter to the Election Commission.

(2) Thereupon the Election Commission shall, after taking all material circumstances into account; either—

(a) declare the poll at that polling station or place to be void, appoint a day, and fix the hours, for taking a fresh poll at that polling station or place and notify the day so appointed and the hours so fixed in such manner as it may deem fit, or

(b) if satisfied that the result of a fresh poll at that polling station or place will not, in any way, affect the result of the election or that 5[the mechanical failure of the voting machine or] the error or irregularity in procedure is not material, issue such directions to the returning officer as it may deem proper for the further conduct and completion of the election.

(3) The provisions of this Act and of any rules or orders made thereunder shall apply to every such fresh poll as they apply to the original poll.]

[147][**58A. Adjournment of poll or countermanding of election on the ground of booth capturing.**

(1) If at any election,—

(a) booth capturing has taken place at a polling station or at a place fixed for the poll (hereafter in this Section referred to as a place) in such a manner that the result of the poll at that polling station or place cannot be ascertained; or

(b) booth capturing takes place in any place for counting of votes in such a manner that the result of the counting at that place cannot be ascertained, the returning officer shall forthwith report the matter to the Election Commission.

(2) The Election Commission shall, on the receipt of a report from the returning officer under sub-section (1) and after taking all material circumstances into account, either—

(a) declare that the poll at that polling station or place be void, appoint a day, and fix the hours, for taking fresh poll at that polling station or place and notify the date so appointed and hours so fixed in such manner as it may deem fit; or

(b) if satisfied that in view of the large number of polling stations or places involved in booth capturing the result of the election is likely to be affected, or that booth capturing had affected counting of votes in such a manner as to affect the result of the election, countermand the election in that constituency.

EXPLANATION: In this Section, "booth capturing" shall have the same meaning as in Section 135A.]

59. Manner of voting at elections. At every election where a poll is taken votes shall be given by ballot in such manner as may be prescribed, [148][and, save as expressly provided by this Act, no votes shall be received by proxy:]

> [149]*[PROVIDED that the votes at every election to fill a seat or seats in the Council of States shall be given by open ballot.]*

[150][**60. Special procedure for voting by certain classes of persons.**—Without prejudice to the generality of the provisions contained in Section 59, provision may be made, by rules made under this Act, for enabling,—

(a) any of the persons as is referred to in clause (a) or clause (b) of sub-section (8) of Section 20 of the Representation of the People Act, 1950 (43 of 1950), (hereinafter in this Section referred to as the 1950-Act) to give his vote either in person or by postal ballot or by proxy, and not in any other manner, at an election in a constituency where poll is taken;

(b) any of the following persons to give his vote either in person or by postal ballot, and not in any other manner, at an election in a constituency where a poll is taken, namely:—

(i) any person as is referred to in clause (c) or clause (d) of sub-section (8) of Section 20 of the 1950-Act;

(ii) the wife of any such person to whom the provisions of sub-section (3) of Section 20 of the 1950-Act apply and such wife being ordinarily residing with that person in terms of sub-section (6) of that Section;

(c) any person belonging to a class of persons notified by the Election Commission in consultation with the Government to give his vote by postal ballot, and not in any other manner, at an election in a constituency where a poll is taken subject to the fulfilment of such requirement as may be specified in those rules.

(d) any person subjected to preventive detention under any law for the time being in force to give his vote by postal ballot, and not in any other manner, at an election in a constituency where a poll is taken, subject to the fulfilment of such requirements as may be specified in those rules.]

[151][**61. Special procedure for preventing personation of electors.** With a view to preventing personation of electors provision may be made by rules made under this Act:—

(a) for the marking with indelible ink of the thumb or any other finger of every elector who applies for a ballot paper or ballot papers for the purpose of voting at a polling station before delivery of such paper or papers to him;

(b) for the production before the presiding officer or a polling officer of a polling station by every such elector as aforesaid of his identity card before the delivery of a ballot paper or ballot papers to him if under rules made in that behalf under the Representation of the People Act, 1950 (43 of 1950), electors of the constituency in which the polling station is situated have been supplied with identity cards with or without their respective photographs attached thereto; and

(c) for prohibiting the delivery of any ballot paper to any person for voting at a polling station if at the time such person applies for such paper he has already such a mark on his thumb or any other finger or does not produce on demand his identity card before the presiding officer or a polling officer of the polling station.]

[152][**61A. Voting machines at elections.** Notwithstanding anything contained in this Act or the rules made thereunder, the giving and recording of votes by voting machines in such manner as may be prescribed, may be adopted in such constituency or constituencies as the Election Commission may, having regard to the circumstances of each case, specify.

EXPLANATION: For the purpose of this Section, "voting machine" means any machine or apparatus whether operated electronically or otherwise used for giving or recording of votes and any reference to a ballot box or ballot paper in this Act or the rules made thereunder shall, save as otherwise provided, be construed as including a reference to such voting machine wherever such voting machine is used at any election.]

62. Right to vote.

(1) No person who is not, and except as expressly provided by this Act, every person who is, for the time being entered in the electoral roll of by any constituency shall be entitled to vote in that constituency.

(2) No person shall vote at an election in any constituency if he is subject to any of the disqualifications referred to in Section 16 of the Representation of the People Act, 1950 (43 of 1950).

(3) No person shall vote at a general election in more than one constituency of the same class, and if a person votes in more than one such constituency, his votes in all such constituencies shall be void.

(4) No person shall at any election vote in the same constituency more than once, notwithstanding that his name may have been registered in the electoral roll for that constituency more than once, and if he does so vote, all his votes in that constituency shall be void.

(5) No person shall vote at any election if he is confined in a prison, whether under a sentence of imprisonment or transportation or otherwise, or is in the lawful custody of the police:

PROVIDED that nothing in this sub-section shall apply to a person subjected to preventive detention under any law for the time being in force.

[153][(6) Nothing contained in sub-sections (3) and (4) shall apply to a person who has been authorised to vote as proxy for an elector under this Act in so far as he votes as a proxy for such elector.].

63. [Method of voting.] *Rep. by the Representation of the People (Amendment) Act, 1961 (40 of 1961), s. 14 (w.e.f.20-9-1961).*

CHAPTER - V : COUNTING OF VOTES

64. Counting of votes. At every election where a poll is taken, votes shall be counted by, or under the [154][supervision and direction] of, the returning officer, and each [155][contesting candidate], his election agent and his [156][counting agents], shall have a right to be present at the time of counting.

[157][**64A. Destruction, loss, etc., of ballot papers at the time of counting.**

(1) If at any time before the counting of votes is completed any ballot papers used at a polling station or at a place fixed for the poll are unlawfully taken out of the custody of the returning officer or are accidentally or intentionally destroyed or lost or are damaged or tampered with, to such an extent that the result of the poll at that polling station or place cannot be ascertained, the returning officer shall

forthwith report the matter to the Election Commission.

(2) Thereupon, the Election Commission shall, after taking all material circumstances into account, either—

(a) direct that the counting of votes shall be stopped, declare the poll at that polling station or place to be void, appoint a day, and fix the hours, for taking a fresh poll at that polling station or place and notify the date so appointed and hours so fixed in such manner as it may deem fit, or

(b) if satisfied that the result of a fresh poll at that polling station or place will not, in any way, affect the result of the election, issue such directions to the returning officer as it may deem proper for the resumption and completion of the counting and for the further conduct and completion of the election in relation to which the votes have been counted.

(3) The provisions of this Act and of any rules or orders made thereunder shall apply to every such fresh poll as they apply to the original poll.]

65. Equality of votes. If, after the counting of the votes is completed, an equality of votes is found to exist between any candidates, and the addition of one vote will entitle any of those candidates to be declared elected, the returning officer shall forthwith decide between those candidates by lot, and proceed as if the candidate on whom the lot falls had received an additional vote.

66. Declaration of results. When the counting of the votes has been completed, the returning officer [158][shall, in the absence of any direction by the Election Commission to the contrary, forthwith declare] the result of the election in the manner provided by this Act or the rules made thereunder.

67. Report of the result. As soon as may be after the result of an election has been declared, the returning officer shall report the result to the appropriate authority and the Election Commission, and in the case of an election to a House of Parliament or of the Legislature of a State also to the Secretary of that House, and the appropriate authority shall cause to be published in the Official Gazette the declarations containing the names of the elected candidates.

[159][**67A. Date of election of candidate.** For the purposes of this Act, the date on which a candidate is declared by the returning officer under the provisions of Section 53, [160]***, [161]*** or Section 66, to be elected to a House of Parliament or of the Legislature of a State [162]*** shall be the date of election of that candidate.]

CHAPTER - VI : MULTIPLE ELECTIONS

68. Vacation of seats when elected to both Houses of Parliament.

(1) Any person who is chosen a member of both the Houses of the People and the Council of States and who has not taken his seat in either House may, by notice in writing signed by him and delivered to the Secretary to the Election Commission [163][within ten days from the date, or the later of the dates, on which he is so chosen, intimate] in which of the Houses he wishes to serve,

and thereupon, his seat in the House in which he does not wish to serve shall become vacant.

(2) In default of such intimation within the aforesaid period, his seat in the Council of States shall, at the expiration of that period, become vacant.

(3) Any intimation given under sub-section (1) shall be final and irrevocable.

[164][(4) For the purposes of this Section and of Section 69, the date on which a person is chosen to be a member of either House of Parliament shall be in the case of an elected member, the date of his election and in the case of a nominated member, the date of first publication in the Gazette of India of his nomination.]

69. Vacation of seats by persons already members of one House on election to other House of Parliament.

(1) If a person who is already a member of the House of the People and has taken his seat in such House is chosen a member of the Council of States, his seat in the House of the People shall, [165][on the date on which he is so chosen], become vacant.

(2) If a person who is already a member of the Council of States and has taken his seat in such Council is chosen a member of the House of the People, his seat in the Council of States shall, [165][on the date on which he is so chosen], become vacant.

[168]**70. Election to more than one seat in either House of Parliament or in the House or either House of the legislature of a State.** If a person is elected to more than one seat in either House of Parliament or in the House or either House of the Legislature of a State, then, unless within the prescribed time he resigns all but one of the seats [166][by writing under his hand addressed to the Speaker or Chairman, as the case may be, or to such other authority or officer as may be prescribed], all the seats shall become vacant.

CHAPTER - VII : PUBLICATION OF ELECTION RESULTS AND NOMINATIONS

[167][**71. Publication of results of elections to the Council of States and of names of persons nominated by the President**. After the elections held in any year in pursuance of the notifications issued under Section 12, there shall be notified by the appropriate authority in the Official Gazette the names of members elected by the elected members of the

Legislative Assemblies of the States and by the members of the electoral colleges for the various [169][Union territories] at the said elections together with the names of any persons nominated by the President of the Council of States under sub-clause (a) of clause (1) of article 80 or under any other provisions.

72. [Publication of results of elections for the reconstitution of electoral colleges for certain Union territories.] *Rep. by the Territorial Councils Act, 1956 (103 of 1956), s. 66.*

73. Publication of results of general elections to the House of the People and the State Legislative Assemblies. Where a general election is held for the purpose of constituting a new House of the People or a new State Legislative Assembly, there shall be notified by [170][the Election Commission] in the Official Gazette, as soon as may be after [171][the results of the elections in all the constituencies] [other than those in which the poll could not be taken for any reason on the date originally fixed under clause (d) of Section 30 or for which the time for completion of the election has been extended under the provisions of Section 153] have been declared by the returning officer under the provisions of Section 53 or, as the case may be, Section 66, the names of the members elected for those constituencies] [172]* * * and upon the issue of such notification that House or Assembly shall be deemed to be duly constituted:

PROVIDED that the issue of such notification shall not be deemed—

[173][(a)to preclude— (i) the taking of the poll and the completion of the election in any Parliamentary or Assembly constituency or constituencies in which the poll could not be taken for any reason on the date originally fixed under clause (d) of Section 30; or (ii) the completion of the election in any Parliamentary or Assembly constituency or constituencies for which time has been extended under the provisions of Section 153; or]

(b) to affect the duration of the House of the People or the State Legislative Assembly, if any, functioning immediately before the issue of the said notification.

[174][**73A. Special provisions as to certain elections**. Notwithstanding anything contained in Section 73 or in any other provision of this Act, with respect to the general election for the purpose of constituting a new House of the People upon dissolution of the Ninth House of the People,—

(a) the notification under Section 73 may be issued without taking into account the Parliamentary constituencies in the State of Jammu and Kashmir; and

(b) the Election Commission may take the steps in relation to elections from the Parliamentary constituencies in the State of Jammu and Kashmir separately and in such manner and no such date or dates as it may deem appropriate.]

74. Publication of results of elections to the State Legislative Councils and of names of persons nominated to such Councils.—After the elections held [175][in pursuance of the notifications issued under Section 15A or] in any year in pursuance of the notifications issued under Section 16, there shall be notified by the appropriate authority in the Official Gazette the names of the members elected for the various Council constituencies and by the members of the Legislative Assembly of the State at the said elections together with the names of any persons nominated by the Governor [176]*** under sub-clause (e) of clause (3) of article 171.]

[177][CHAPTER - VIIA : DECLARATION OF ASSETS AND LIABILITIES]

75A. Declaration of assets and liabilities.

(1) Every elected candidate for a House of Parliament shall, within ninety days from the date on which he makes and subscribes an oath or affirmation, according to the form set out for the purpose in the Third Schedule to the Constitution, for taking his seat in either House of Parliament, furnish the information, relating to—

(i) the movable and immovable property of which he, his spouse and his dependant children are jointly or severally owners or beneficiaries;

(ii) his liabilities to any public financial institution; and

(iii) his liabilities to the Central Government or the State Government, to the Chairman of the Council of States or the Speaker of the House of the People, as the case may be.

(2) The information under sub-section (1) shall be furnished in such form and in such manner as may be prescribed in the rules made under sub-section (3).

(3) The Chairman of the Council of States or the Speaker of the House of the People, as the case may be, may make rules for the purposes of sub-section (2).

(4) The rules made by the Chairman of the Council of States or the Speaker of the House of the People, under sub-section (3) shall be laid, as soon as may be after they are made, before the Council of States or the House of the People, as the case may be, for a total period of thirty days which may be comprised in one session or in two or more successive sessions and shall take effect upon the expiry of the said period of thirty days unless they are sooner approved with or without modifications or disapproved by the Council of States or the House of the People and where they are so approved, they shall take effect on such approval in the form in which they were laid or in such modified form, as the case may be, and where they are so disapproved, they shall be of no effect.

(5) The Chairman of the Council of States or the Speaker of the House of the People, as the case may be, may direct that any wilful contravention of the rules made under sub-section (3) by an elected candidate for a House of Parliament referred to in sub-section (1) may be dealt with in the same manner as a breach of privilege of the Council of States or the House of the People, as the case may be.

EXPLANATION: For the purposes of this Section,—

(i) "immovable property" means the land and includes any building or other structure attached to the land or permanently fastened to anything which is attached to the land;

(ii) "movable property" means any other property which is not the immovable property and includes corporeal and incorporeal property of every description;

(iii) "public financial institution" means a public financial institution within the meaning of Section 4A of the Companies Act, 1956 (1of 1956), and includes bank;

(iv) "bank" referred to in clause (iii) means—

(a) State Bank of India constituted under Section 3 of the State Bank of India Act, 1955 (23 of 1955);

(b) subsidiary bank having the meaning assigned to it in clause (k) of Section 2 of the State Bank of India (Subsidiary Banks) Act, 1959 (38 of 1959);

(c) Regional Rural Bank established under Section 3 of the Regional Rural Banks Act, 1976 (21 of 1976);

(d) corresponding new bank having the meaning assigned to it in clause (da) of Section 5 of the Banking Regulation Act, 1949 (10 of 1949); and

(e) co-operative bank having the meaning assigned to it in clause (cci) of Section 5 of the Banking Regulation Act, 1949 (10 of 1949) as modified by sub-clause (i) of clause (c) of Section 56 of that Act; and

(v) "dependant children" means sons and daughters who have no separate means of earning and are wholly dependant on the elected candidate referred to in sub-section (1) for their livelihood.]

CHAPTER - VIII : ELECTION EXPENSES

[178][**76. Application of Chapter.** This Chapter shall apply only to the elections to the House of the People and to the Legislative Assembly of a State.

77. Account of election expenses and maximum thereof.

(1) Every candidate at an election shall, either by himself or by his election agent, keep a separate and correct account of all expenditure in connection with the election incurred or authorized by him or by his election agent between [179][the date on which he has been nominated] and the date of declaration of the result thereof, both dates inclusive.

[180][*EXPLANATION 1:* For the removal of doubts, it is hereby declared that—

(a) the expenditure incurred by leaders of a political party on account of travel by air or by any other means of transport for propagating programme of the political party shall not be deemed to be the expenditure in connection with the election incurred or authorised by a candidate of that political party or his election agent for the purposes of this sub-section.

(b) any expenditure incurred in respect of any arrangements made, facilities provided or any other act or thing done by any person in the service of the Government and belonging to any of the classes mentioned in clause (7) of Section 123 in the discharge or purported discharge of his official duty as mentioned in the proviso to that clause shall not be deemed to be expenditure in connection with the election incurred or authorised by a candidate or by his election agent for the purposes of this sub-section.

EXPLANATION 2: For the purposes of clause (a) of Explanation 1, the expression "leaders of a political party", in respect of any election, means,—

(i) where such political party is a recognised political party, such persons not exceeding forty in number, and

(ii) where such political party is other than a recognised political party, such persons not exceeding twenty in number, whose names have been communicated to the Election Commission and the Chief Electoral Officers of the States by the political party to be leaders for the purposes of such election, within a period of seven days from the date of the notification for such election published in the Gazette of India or Official Gazette of the State, as the case may be, under this Act:

PROVIDED that a political party may, in the case where any of the persons referred to in clause (i) or, as the case may be, in clause (ii) dies or ceases to be a member of such political party, by further communication to the Election Commission and the Chief Electoral Officers of the States, substitute new name, during the period ending immediately before forty-eight hours ending with the hour fixed for the conclusion of the last poll for such election, for the name of such person died or ceased to be a member, for the purposes of designating the new leader in his place.]

(2) The account shall contain such particulars, as may be prescribed.

(3) The total of the said expenditure shall not exceed such amount as may be prescribed.

78. Lodging of account with the district election officer.

[181][(1)] Every contesting candidate at an election shall, within thirty days from the date of election of the returned candidate or, if there are more than one returned candidate at the election and the dates of their election are different, the later of those two dates, lodge with the [182][district election officer] an account of his election expenses which shall be a true copy of the account kept by him or by his election agent under Section 77.]

[183]* * * * *

[184][PART - VA : FREE SUPPLY OF CERTAIN MATERIAL TO CANDIDATES OF RECOGNISED POLITICAL PARTIES

78A. Free supply of copies of electoral rolls.

(1) The Government shall, at any election to be held for the purposes of constituting the House of the People or the Legislative Assembly of a State, supply, free of cost, to the candidates of recognised political parties such number of copies of the electoral roll, as finally published under the Representation of the People Act, 1950 (43 of 1950) and such other material as may be prescribed.

(2) The material referred to in sub-section (1) shall be supplied,—

(i) subject to such conditions as may be imposed by the Central Government in consultation with the Election Commission with respect to the reduction of the maximum expenditure which may be incurred by the candidate under Section 77; and

(ii) through such officers as may be specified by the Election Commission who shall act in accordance with such general or special directions as may be given by the Election Commission.

78B. Supply of certain items to candidates, etc.

(1) The Election Commission shall, at any time between the date of publication of the notification calling the election for the purposes of consitituting the House of the People or the Legislative Assembly of a State and the date on which the poll is to be taken, supply or cause to be supplied, such items as the Central Government may, by order, determine in consultation with the Election Commission, to the electors in the constituencies concerned or to the

candidates set up by the recognised political parties.

(2) Where the Election Commission supplies the items to the candidates under sub-section (1), the Central Government may, in consultation with the Election Commission, impose conditions with respect to the reduction of the maximum expenditure which may be incurred by the candidate under Section 77.

EXPLANATION. For the purposes of Section 39A, this Chapter and clause (hh) of sub-section (2) of Section 169, the expression "recognised political party", has the meaning assigned to it in the Election Symbols (Reservation and Allotment) Order, 1968.].

PART - VI : DISPUTES REGARDING ELECTIONS
CHAPTER - I : INTERPRETATION

79. Definitions. In this Part and in [185][Part VII] unless the context otherwise requires —

[186][(a) any reference to a High Court or to the Chief Justice or Judge of a High Court shall, in relation to a Union territory having a Court of the Judicial Commissioner, be construed as a reference to the said Court of the Judicial Commissioner or to the Judicial Commissioner or any Additional Judicial Commissioner, as the case may be];

[187][(b) "candidate" means a person who has been or claims to have been duly nominated as a candidate at any election];

(c) "costs" means all costs, charges and expenses of, or incidental to, a trial of an election petition;

(d) "electoral right" means the right of a person to stand or not to stand as, or [188][to withdraw or not to withdraw] from being, a candidate, or to vote or refrain from voting at an election;

[189][(e) "High Court" means the High Court within the local limits of whose jurisdiction the election to which the election petition relates has been held];

(f) "returned candidate" means a candidate whose name has been published under Section 67 as duly elected.

CHAPTER - II : PRESENTATION OF ELECTION PETITIONS TO [190][HIGH COURT]

80. Election petitions. No election shall be called in question except by an election petition presented in accordance with the provisions of this Part.

[191][**80A. High Court to try election petitions**.

(1) The Court having jurisdiction to try an election petition shall be the High Court.

(2) Such jurisdiction shall be exercised ordinarily by a single Judge of the High Court and the Chief Justice shall, from time to time, assign one or more Judges for that purpose:

PROVIDED that where the High Court consists only of one Judge, he shall try all election petitions presented to that Court.

(3) The High Court in its discretion may, in the interests of justice or convenience,

try an election petition, wholly or partly, at a place other than the place of seat of the High Court.]

81. Presentation of petitions.

(1) An election petition calling in question any election may be presented on one or more of the grounds specified in [192][sub-section (1)] of Section 100 and Section 101 to the [193][High Court] by any candidate at such election or any elector [194][within forty-five days from, but not earlier than the date of election of the returned candidate, or if there are more than one returned candidate at the election and the dates of their election are different, the later of those two dates].

EXPLANATION. In this sub-section, "elector" means a person who was entitled to vote at the election to which the election petition relates, whether he has voted at such election or not.

[195]* * * * *

[196][(3) Every election petition shall be accompanied by as many copies thereof as there are respondents mentioned in the petition [197]***, and every such copy shall be attested by the petitioner under his own signature to be a true copy of the petition.]

[198][**82. Parties to the petition.** A petitioner shall join as respondents to his petition—

(a) where the petitioner, in addition to claiming a declaration that the election of all or any of the returned candidates is void, claims a further declaration that he himself or any other candidate has been duly elected, all the contesting candidates other than the petitioner, and where no such further declaration is claimed, all the returned candidates; and

(b) any other candidate against whom allegations of any corrupt practice are made in the petition.]

[199][**83. Contents of petition.**

(1) An election petition—

(a) shall contain a concise statement of the material facts on which the petitioner relies;

(b) shall set forth full particulars of any corrupt practice that the petitioner alleges, including as full a statement as possible of the names of the parties alleged to have committed such corrupt practice and the date and place of the commission of each such practice; and

(c) shall be signed by the petitioner and verified in the manner laid down in the Code of Civil Procedure, 1908 (5 of 1908) for the verification of pleadings:

[200]*[PROVIDED that where the petitioner alleges any corrupt practice, the petition shall also be accompanied by an affidavit in the prescribed form in support of the allegation of such corrupt practice and the particulars thereof.]*

(2) Any schedule or annexure to the petition shall also be signed by the petitioner and verified in the same manner as the petition.]

[201][**84. Relief that may be claimed by the petitioner.** A petitioner may, in addition to claiming a declaration that the election of all or any of the returned candidates is void, claim a further declaration that he himself or any other candidate has been duly elected.] s. 40.

85. [Procedure on receiving petition.] *Rep. by the Representation of the People (Amendment) Act, 1966 (47 of 1966),*

CHAPTER - III : TRIAL OF ELECTION PETITIONS

[202][**86. Trial of election petitions.**

(1) The High Court shall dismiss an election petition which does not comply with the provisions of Section 81 or Section 82 or Section 117.

EXPLANATION. An order of the High Court dismissing an election petition under this sub-section shall be deemed to be an order made under clause (a) of Section 98.

(2) As soon as may be after an election petition has been presented to the High Court, it shall be referred to the Judge or one of the Judges who has or have been assigned by the Chief Justice for the trial of election petitions under sub-section (2) of Section 80A.

(3) Where more election petitions than one are presented to the High Court in respect of the same election, all of them shall be referred for trial to the same Judge who may, in his discretion, try them separately or in one or more groups.

(4) Any candidate not already a respondent shall, upon application made by him to the High Court within fourteen days from the date of commencement of the trial and subject to any order as to security for costs which may be made by the High Court, be entitled to be joined as a respondent.

EXPLANATION. For the purposes of this sub-section and of Section 97, the trial of a petition shall be deemed to commence on the date fixed for the respondents to appear before the High Court and answer the claim or claims made in the petition.

(5) The High Court may, upon such terms as to costs and otherwise as it may deem fit, allow the particulars of any corrupt practice alleged in the petition to be amended or amplified in such manner as may in its opinion be necessary for ensuring a fair and effective trial of the petition, but shall not allow any amendment of the petition which will have the effect of introducing particulars of a corrupt practice not previously alleged in the petition.

(6) The trial of an election petition shall, so far as is practicable consistently with the interests of justice in respect of the trial, be continued from day to day until its conclusion, unless the High Court finds the adjournment of the trial beyond the following day to be necessary for reasons to be recorded.

(7) Every election petition shall be tried as expeditiously as possible and endeavour shall be made to conclude the trial within six months from the date on which the election petition is presented to the High Court for trial.

87. Procedure before the High Court.

(1) Subject to the provisions of this Act and of any rules made thereunder, every election petition shall be tried by the High Court, as nearly as may be, in accordance with the procedure applicable under the Code of Civil Procedure, 1908 (5 of 1908) to the trial of suits:

PROVIDED that the High Court shall have the discretion to refuse, for reasons to be recorded in writing, to examine any witness or witnesses if it is of the opinion that the evidence of such witness or witnesses is not material for the decision of the petition or that the party tendering such witness or witnesses is doing so on frivolous grounds or with a view to delay the proceedings.

(2) The provisions of the Indian Evidence Act, 1872 (1 of 1972), shall, subject to the provisions of this Act, be deemed to apply in all respects to the trial of an election petition.]

93. Documentary evidence. Notwithstanding anything in any enactment to the contrary, no document shall be inadmissible in evidence at the trial of an election petition on the ground that it is not duly stamped or registered.

94. Secrecy of voting not to be infringed. No witness or other person shall be required to state for whom he has voted at an election:

[203]*[PROVIDED that this Section shall not apply to such witness or other person where he has voted by open ballot].*

95. Answering of criminating questions and certificate of indemnity.

(1) No witness shall be excused from answering any question as to any matter relevant to a matter in issue in the trial of an election petition upon the ground that the answer to such question may criminate or may tend to criminate him, or that it may expose or may tend to expose him to any penalty or forfeiture:

PROVIDED that—

(a) a witness, who answers truly all questions which he is required to answer shall be entitled to receive a certificate of indemnity from 2[the High Court]; and

(b) an answer given by a witness to a question put by or before 1[the High Court] shall not, except in the case of any criminal proceeding for perjury in respect of the evidence, be admissible in evidence against him in any civil or criminal proceeding.

(2) When a certificate of indemnity has been granted to any witness, it may be pleaded by him in any court and shall be a full and complete defence to or upon any charge under Chapter IXA of the Indian Penal Code, 1860 (45 of 1860), or Part VII of this Act arising out of the matter to which such certificate relates, but it shall not be deemed to relieve him from any disqualification in connection with an election imposed by this Act or any other law.

96. Expenses of witnesses. The reasonable expenses incurred by any person in attending to give evidence may be allowed by [204][the High Court] to such person and shall, unless [204][the High Court] otherwise directs, be deemed to be part of the costs.

97. Recrimination when seat claimed.

(1) When in an election petition a declaration that any candidate other than the returned candidate has been duly elected is claimed, the returned candidate or any other party may give evidence to prove that the election of such candidate would have been void if he had been the returned candidate and a petition had been presented calling in question his election:

PROVIDED that the returned candidate or such other party, as aforesaid shall not be entitled to give such evidence unless he has, within fourteen days from the date of [205][commencement of the trial], given notice to [204][the High Court] of his intention to do so and has also given the security and the further security referred to in Sections 117 and 118 respectively.

(2) Every notice referred to in sub-section (1) shall be accompanied by the statement and [206]* * * particulars required by Section 83 in the case of an election petition and shall be signed and verified in like manner.

98. Decision of the High Court. At the conclusion of the trial of an election petition [204][the High Court] shall make an order—

(a) dismissing the election petition; or

(b) declaring the election of [207][all or any of the returned candidates] to be void; or

(c) declaring the election, of [207][all or any of the returned candidates] to be void and the petitioner or any other candidate to have been duly elected.

[208]* * * * *

99. Other orders to be made by the High Court.

(1) At the time of making an order under Section 98 [209][the High Court] shall also make an order—

[210][(a) where any charge is made in the petition of any corrupt practice having been committed at the election, recording—

(i) a finding whether any corrupt practice has or has not been proved to have been committed [211]*** at the election, and the nature of that corrupt practice; and

(ii) the names of all persons, if any, who have been proved at the trial to have been guilty of any corrupt practice and the nature of that practice; and] paid:

(b) fixing the total amount of costs payable and specifying the persons by and to whom costs shall be

PROVIDED that [212][a person who is not a party to the petition shall not be named] in the order under sub-clause (ii) of clause (a) unless—

(a) he has been given notice to appear before [209][the High Court] and to show cause why he should not be so named; and (b) if he appears in pursuance of the notice, he has been given an opportunity of cross-examining any witness who has already been examined by [209][the High Court] and has given evidence against him, of calling evidence in his defence and of being heard.

[213][(2) In this Section and in Section 100, the expression "agent" has the same meaning as in Section 123.]

100. Grounds for declaring election to be void.

[214][(1) Subject to the provisions of sub-section (2) if [209][the High Court] is of opinion—

(a) that on the date of his election a returned candidate was not qualified, or was disqualified, to be chosen to fill the seat under the Constitution or this Act [215][or the Government of Union Territories Act, 1963 (20 of 1963)]; or

(b) that any corrupt practice has been committed by a returned candidate or his election agent or by any other person with the consent of a returned candidate or his election agent; or

(c) that any nomination has been improperly rejected; or

(d) that the result of the election, in so far as it concerns a returned candidate, has been materially affected—

(i) by the improper acceptance or any nomination, or

(ii) by any corrupt practice committed in the interests of the returned candidate [216][by an agent other than his election agent], or

(iii) by the improper reception, refusal or rejection of any vote or the reception of any vote which is void, or

(iv) by any non—compliance with the provisions of the Constitution or of this Act or of any rules or orders made under this Act, [217][the High Court] shall declare the election of the returned candidate to be void.]

[218][(2)] If in the opinion of [217][the High Court], a returned candidate has been guilty by an agent, other than his election agent, of any corrupt practice [219]*** but [217][the High Court] is satisfied—

(a) that no such corrupt practice was committed at the election by the candidate or his election agent, and every such corrupt practice was committed contrary to the orders, and [220][without the consent], of the candidate or his election agent;

[221]* * * * *

(c) that the candidate and his election agent took all reasonable means for preventing the commission of corrupt [222]*** practices at the election; and

(d) that in all other respects the election was free from any corrupt [222]*** practice on the part of the candidate or any of his agents, then [217][the High Court] may decide that the election of the returned candidate is not void.

101. Grounds for which a candidate other than the returned candidate may be declared to have been elected. If any person who has lodged a petition has, in addition to calling in question the election of the returned candidate, claimed a declaration that he himself or any other candidate has been duly elected and [217][the High Court] is of opinion—

(a) that in fact the petitioner or such other candidate received a majority of the valid votes; or

(b) that but for the votes obtained by the returned candidate by corrupt [223]* * * practices the petitioner or such other candidate would have obtained a majority of the valid votes, [217][the High Court] shall after declaring the election of the returned candidate to be void declare the petitioner or such other candidate, as the case may be, to have been duly elected.

102. Procedure in case of an equality of votes. If during the trial of an election petition it appears that there is an equality of votes between any candidates at the election and that the addition of a vote would entitle any of those candidates —

(a) any decision made by the returning officer under the provisions of this Act shall, in so far as it determines the question between those candidates, be effective also for the purposes of the petition; and

(b) in so far as that question is not determined by such a decision [224][the High Court] shall decide between them by lot and proceed as if the one on whom the lot then falls had received an additional vote,

[225][103. Communication of orders of the High Court. The High Court shall, as soon as may be after the conclusion of the trial of an election petition, intimate the substance of the decision to the Election Commission and the Speaker or Chairman, as the case may be, of the House of Parliament or of the State Legislature concerned and, as soon as may be thereafter, shall send to the Election Commission an authenticated copy of the decision.]

104. [Difference of opinion among the members of the Tribunal.] *Rep. by the Representation of the People (Second Amendment) Act, 1956 (27 of 1956), s. 57.*

105. [Orders of the Tribunal to be final and conclusive.] *Rep. by s. 58, ibid.*

106. Transmission of order to the appropriate authority, etc., and its publication. As soon as may be after the receipt of any order made by [226][the High Court] under Section 98 or Section 99, the Election Commission shall forward copies of the order to the appropriate authority and, in the case where such order relates to an election [227]*** to a House of Parliament or to an election to the House or a House of the Legislature of a State, also to the Speaker or Chairman, as the case may be, of the House concerned and [228][shall cause the order to be published—

(a) where the order relates to an election to a House of Parliament, in the Gazette of India as well as in the Official Gazette of the State concerned; and

(b) where the order relates to an election to the House or a House of the Legislature of the State, in the Official Gazette of the State.]

[229][**107. Effect of orders of the High Court.**

[230][(1) Subject to the provisions contained in Chapter IVA relating to the stay of operation of an order of the High Court under Section 98 or Section 99, every such order shall take effect as soon as it is pronounced by the High Court.]

(2) Where by an order under Section 98 the election of a returned candidate is declared to be void, acts and proceedings in which that returned candidate has, before the date thereof, participated as a member of Parliament or as a member of the Legislature of a State shall not be invalidated by reason of that order, nor shall such candidate be subjected to any liability or penalty on the ground of such participation.]

CHAPTER - IV : WITHDRAWAL AND ABATEMENT OF ELECTION PETITIONS

108. [Withdrawal of petitions before appointment of Tribunal.] *Rep. by the Representation of the People (Amendment) Act, 1966 (47 of 1966), s. 45. Court.*

[231][**109. Withdrawal of election petitions**.

(1) An election petition may be withdrawn only by leave of the High

(2) Where an application for withdrawal is made under sub-section (1), notice thereof fixing a date for the hearing of the application shall be given to all other parties to the petition and shall be published in the Official Gazette.

110. Procedure for withdrawal of election petitions.

(1) If there are more petitioners than one, no application to withdraw an election petition shall be made except with the consent of all the petitioners.

(2) No application for withdrawal shall be granted if, in the opinion of the High Court, such application has been induced by any bargain or consideration which ought not to be allowed.

(3) If the application is granted—

(a) the petitioner shall be ordered to pay the costs of the respondents theretofore incurred or such portion thereof as the High Court may think fit;

(b) the High Court shall direct that the notice of withdrawal shall be published in the Official Gazette and in such other manner as it may specify and thereupon the notice shall be published accordingly;

(c) a person who might himself have been a petitioner may, within fourteen days of such publication, apply to be substituted as petitioner in place of the party withdrawing, and upon compliance with the conditions, if any, as to security, shall be entitled to be so substituted and to continue the proceedings upon such terms as the High Court may deem fit.]

111. Report of withdrawal by the High Court to the Election Commission. When an application for withdrawal is granted by [232][the High Court] and no person has been substituted as petitioner under clause (c) of sub-section (3) of Section 110, in place of the party withdrawing, [232][the High Court] shall report the fact to the Election Commission [233][and thereupon the Election Commission shall publish the report in the Official Gazette].

[234][**112. Abatement of election petitions.**

(1) An election petition shall abate only on the death of a sole petitioner or of the survivor of several petitioners.

(2) Where an election petition abates under sub-section (1), the High Court shall cause the fact to be published in such manner as it may deem fit.

(3) Any person who might himself have been a petitioner may, within fourteen days of such publication, apply to be substituted as petitioner and upon compliance with the conditions, if any, as to security, shall be entitled to be so substituted and to continue the proceedings upon such terms as the High Court may deem fit.]

116. Abatement or substitution on death of respondent. If before the conclusion of the trial of an election petition, the sole respondent dies or gives notice that he does not intend to oppose the petition or any of the respondents dies or gives such notice and there is no other respondent who is opposing the petition, [235][the High Court] shall cause notice of such event to be published in the Official Gazette, and thereupon any person who might have been a petitioner may, within fourteen days of such publication, apply to be substituted in place of such respondent to oppose the petition, and shall be entitled to continue the proceedings upon such terms as [235][the High Court] may think fit.

[236][CHAPTER - IVA : APPEALS

[237][**116A. Appeals to Supreme Court.**

(1) Notwithstanding anything contained in any other law for the time being in force, an appeal shall lie to the Supreme Court on any question (whether of law or fact) from every order made by a High Court under Section 98 or Section 99.

(2) Every appeal under this Chapter shall be preferred within a period of thirty days from the date of the order of the High Court under Section 98 or Section 99:

PROVIDED that the Supreme Court may entertain an appeal after the expiry of the said period of thirty days if it is satisfied that the appellant had sufficient cause for not preferring the appeal within such period.

116B. Stay of operation of order of High Court.

(1) An application may be made to the High Court for stay of operation of an order made by the High Court under Section 98 or Section 99 before the expiration of the time allowed for appealing therefrom and the High Court may, on sufficient cause being shown and on such terms and conditions as it may think fit, stay the operation of the order; but no application for stay shall be made to the High Court after an appeal has been preferred to the Supreme Court.

(2) Where an appeal has been preferred against an order made under Section 98 or Section 99, the Supreme Court may, on sufficient cause being shown and on such terms and conditions as it may think fit, stay the operation of the order appealed from.

(3) When the operation of an order is stayed by the High Court or, as the case may be, the Supreme Court, the order shall be deemed never to have taken effect under sub-section (1) of Section 107; and a copy of the stay order shall

immediately be sent by the High Court or, as the case may be, the Supreme Court, to the Election Commission and the Speaker or Chairman, as the case may be, of the House of Parliament or of the State Legislature concerned.

116C. Procedure in appeal.

(1) Subject to the provisions of this Act and of the rules, if any, made thereunder, every appeal shall be heard and determined by the Supreme Court as nearly as may be in accordance with the procedure applicable to the hearing and determination of an appeal from any final order passed by a High Court in the exercise of its original civil jurisdiction; and all the provisions of the Code of Civil Procedure, 1908 (5 of 1908), and the Rules of the Court (including provisions as to the furnishing of security and the execution of any order of the Court) shall, so far as may be, apply in relation to such appeal.

(2) As soon as an appeal is decided, the Supreme Court shall intimate the substance of the decision to the Election Commission and the Speaker or Chairman, as the case may be, of the House of Parliament or of the State Legislature concerned and as soon as may be thereafter shall send to the Election Commission an authenticated copy of the decision; and upon its receipt, the Election Commission shall—

(a) forward copies thereof to the authorities to which copies of the order of the High Court were forwarded under Section 160; and

(b) cause the decision to be published in the Gazette or Gazettes in which that order was published under the said Section.]]

CHAPTER - V : COST AND SECURITY FOR COSTS

[238][**117. Security for costs.**

(1) At the time of presenting an election petition, the petitioner shall deposit in the High Court in accordance with the rules of the High Court a sum of two thousand rupees as security for the costs of the petition.

(2) During the course of the trial of an election petition, the High Court may, at any time, call upon the petitioner to give such further security for costs as it may direct.

118. Security for costs from a respondent. No person shall be entitled to be joined as a respondent under sub-section (4) of Section 86 unless he has given such security for costs as the High Court may direct.

119. Costs. Costs shall be in the discretion of the High Court:

PROVIDED that where a petition is dismissed under clause (a) of Section 98, the returned candidate shall be entitled to the costs incurred by him in contesting the petition and accordingly the High Court shall make an order for costs in favour of the returned candidate.]

120. * * * * * * *

121. Payment of costs out of security deposits and return of such deposits.

(1) If in any order as to costs under the provisions of this Part there is a direction

for payment of costs by any party to any person, such costs shall, if they have not been already paid, be paid in full, or so far as possible, out of the security deposit and the further security deposit, if any, made by such party under this Part on an application made in writing in that behalf [239][within a period of one year, from the date of such order] to [240][the High Court] by the person in whose favour the costs have been awarded.

(2) If there is any balance left of any of the said security deposits after payment under sub-section (1) of the costs referred to in that sub-section, such balance, or where no costs have been awarded or no application as aforesaid has been made within the said period of [241][one year] the whole of the said security deposits may, on an application made in that behalf in writing to [240][the High Court] by the person by whom the deposits have been made, or if such person dies after making such deposits, by the legal representative of such person, be returned to the said person or to his legal representative, as the case may be.

122. Execution of orders as to costs. Any order as to costs under the provisions of this Part may be produced before the principal civil court of original jurisdiction within the local limits of whose jurisdiction any person directed by such order to pay any sum of money has a place of residence or business, or where such place is within a presidency-town, before the court of small causes having jurisdiction there, and such court shall execute the order or cause the same to be executed in the same manner and by the same procedure as if it were a decree for the payment of money made by itself in a suit:

PROVIDED that where any such costs or any portion thereof may be recovered by an application made under sub-section (1) of Section 121, no application shall lie under this Section [242][within a period of one year from the date of such order] unless it is for the recovery of the balance of any costs which has been left unrealised after an application has been made under that sub-section owing to the insufficiency of the amount of the security deposits referred to in that sub- Section.

PART - VII : [243][CORRUPT PRACTICES AND ELECTORAL OFFENCES]
[244][CHAPTER - I : CORRUPT PRACTICE

123. Corrupt practices.—The following shall be deemed to be corrupt practices for the purposes of this Act:

[245][(1) "Bribery", that is to say—

(A) any gift, offer or promise by a candidate or his agent or by any other person with the consent of a candidate or his election agent of any gratification, to any person whomsoever, with the object, directly or indirectly of inducing—

(a) a person to stand or not to stand as, or [246][to withdraw or not to withdraw] from being a candidate at an election, or

(b) an elector to vote or refrain from voting at an election, or as a reward to—

(i) a person for having so stood or not stood, or for [247][having withdrawn or not having withdrawn] his candidature; or

(ii) an elector for having voted or refrained from voting;

(B) the receipt of, or agreement to receive, any gratification, whether as a motive or a reward—

(a) by a person for standing or not standing as, or for [248][withdrawing or not withdrawing] from being, a candidate; or

(b) by any person whomsoever for himself or any other person for voting or refraining from voting, or inducing or attempting to induce any elector to vote or refrain from voting, or any candidate [246][to withdraw or not to withdraw] his candidature.

EXPLANATION: For the purposes of this clause the term "gratification" is not restricted to pecuniary gratifications or gratifications estimable in money and it includes all forms of entertainment and all forms of employment for reward but it does not include the payment of any expenses bona fide incurred at, or for the purpose of, any election and duly entered in the account of election expenses referred to in Section 78.]

(2) Undue influence, that is to say, any direct or indirect interference or attempt to interfere on the part of the candidate or his agent, or of any other person [249][with the consent of the candidate or his election agent], with the free exercise of any electoral right:

PROVIDED that—

(a) without prejudice to the generality of the provisions of this clause any such person as is referred to therein who—

(i) threatens any candidate or any elector, or any person in whom a candidate or an elector is interested, with injury of any kind including social ostracism and ex-communication or expulsion from any caste or community; or

(ii) induces or attempts to induce a candidate or an elector to believe that he, or any person in whom he is interested, will become or will be rendered an object of divine displeasure or spiritual censure, shall be deemed to interfere with the free exercise of the electoral right of such candidate or elector within the meaning of this clause;

(b) a declaration of public policy, or a promise of public action, or the mere exercise of a legal right without intent to interfere with an electoral right, shall not be deemed to be interference within the meaning of this clause.

[250][(3) The appeal by a candidate or his agent or by any other person with the consent of a candidate or his election agent to vote or refrain from voting for any person on the ground of his religion, race, caste, community or language or the use of, or appeal to religious symbols or the use of, or appeal to, national symbols, such as the national flag or the national emblem, for the furtherance of the prospects of the election of that candidate or for prejudicially affecting the election of any candidate:

[251]*[PROVIDED that no symbol allotted under this Act to a candidate shall be deemed to be a religious symbol or a national symbol for the purposes of this clause.]*

(3A) The promotion of, or attempt to promote, feelings of enmity or hatred between different classes of the citizens of India on grounds of religion, race, caste, community, or language, by a candidate or his agent or any other person with the consent of a candidate or his election agent for the furtherance of the prospects of the election of that candidate or for prejudicially affecting the election of any candidate.]

[252][(3B) The propagation of the practice or the commission of sati or its glorification by a candidate or his agent or any other person with the consent of the candidate or his election agent for the furtherance of the prospects of the election of that candidate or for prejudicially affecting the election of any candidate.

EXPLANATION: For the purposes of this clause, "sati" and "glorification" in relation to sati shall have the meanings respectively assigned to them in the Commission of Sati (Prevention) Act, 1987 (3 of 1988).]

(4) The publication by a candidate or his agent or by any other person [253][with the consent of a candidate or his election agent], of any statement of fact which is false, and which he either believes to be false or does not believe to be true, in relation to the personal character or conduct of any candidate, or in relation to the candidature, or withdrawal, [254]* * * of any candidate, being a statement reasonably calculated to prejudice the prospects of that candidate's election.

(5) The hiring or procuring, whether on payment or otherwise, of any vehicle or vessel by a candidate or his agent or by any other person [253][with the consent of a candidate or his election agent], [255][or the use of such vehicle or vessel for the free conveyance] of any elector (other than the candidate himself, the members of his family or his agent) to or from any polling station provided under Section 25 or a place fixed under sub-section (1) of Section 29 for the poll:

PROVIDED that the hiring of a vehicle or vessel by an elector or by several electors at their joint costs for the purpose of conveying him or them to and from any such polling station or place fixed for the poll shall not be deemed to be a corrupt practice under this clause if the vehicle or vessel so hired is a vehicle or vessel not propelled by mechanical power:

PROVIDED FURTHER that the use of any public transport vehicle or vessel or any tramcar or railway carriage by any elector at his own cost for the purpose of going to or coming from any such polling station or place fixed for the poll shall not be deemed to be a corrupt practice under this clause.

EXPLANATION: In this clause, the expression "vehicle" means any vehicle used or capable of being used for the purpose of road transport, whether propelled by mechanical power or otherwise and whether used for drawing other vehicles or otherwise.

(6) The incurring or authorizing of expenditure in contravention of Section 77.

(7) The obtaining or procuring or abetting or attempting to obtain or procure by a candidate or his agent or, by any other person [256][with the consent of a candidate or his election agent], any assistance (other than the giving of vote) for the furtherance of the prospects of that candidate's election, from any person in

the service of the Government and belonging to any of the following classes, namely:—

(a) gazetted officers;

(b) stipendiary judges and magistrates;

(c) members of the armed forces of the Union;

(d) members of the police forces;

(e) excise officers;

[257][(f) revenue officers other than village revenue officers known as lambardars, malguzars, patels, deshmukhs or by any other name, whose duty is to collect land revenue and who are remunerated by a share of, or commission on, the amount of land revenue collected by them but who do not discharge any police functions; and]

(g) such other class of persons in the service of the Government as may be prescribed:

[258][PROVIDED that where any person, in the service of the Government and belonging to any of the classes aforesaid, in the discharge or purported discharge of his official duty, makes any arrangements or provides any facilities or does any other act or thing, for, to, or in relation to, any candidate or his agent or any other person acting with the consent of /the candidate or his election agent (whether by reason of the office held by the candidate or for any other reason), such arrangements, facilities or act or thing shall not be deemed to be assistance for the furtherance of the prospects of that candidate's election.]

[259][(8) booth capturing by a candidate or his agent or other person.]

EXPLANATION:

(1) In this Section, the expression "agent" includes an election agent, a polling agent and any person who is held to have acted as an agent in connection with the election with the consent of the candidate.

(2) For the purposes of clause (7), a person shall be deemed to assist in the furtherance of the prospects of a candidate's election if he acts as an election agent [260]* * * of that candidate.]

[261][(3) For the purposes of clause (7), notwithstanding anything contained in any other law, the publication in the Official Gazette of the appointment, resignation, termination of service, dismissal or removal from service of a person in the service of the Central Government (including a person serving in connection with the administration of a Union territory) or of a State Government shall be conclusive proof—

(i) of such appointment, resignation, termination of service, dismissal or removal from service, as the case may be, and

(ii) where the date of taking effect of such appointment, resignation, termination of service, dismissal or removal from service, as the case may be, is stated in such publication, also of the fact that such person was appointed with effect from the said date, or in the case of resignation, termination of service, dismissal or removal from service, such person ceased to be in such service with effect from the said date.]

[262][(4) For the purposes of clause (8), "booth capturing" shall have the same meaning as in Section 135A.]

CHAPTER - III : ELECTORAL OFFENCES

[263][**125. Promoting enmity between classes in connection with election.** Any person who in connection with an election under this Act promotes or attempts to promote on grounds of religion, race, caste, community or language, feelings of enmity or hatred, between different classes of the citizens of India shall be punishable, with imprisonment for a term which may extend to three years, or with fine, or with both.]

[264][**125A. Penalty for filing false affidavit, etc.** A candidate who himself or through his proposer, with intent to be elected in an election,—

(i) fails to furnish information relating to sub-section (1) of Section 33A; or

(ii) give false information which he knows or has reason to believe to be false; or

(iii) conceals any information,

in his nomination paper delivered under sub-section (1) of Section 33 or in his affidavit which is required to be delivered under sub-section (2) of Section 33A, as the case may be, shall, notwithstanding anything contained in any other law for the time being in force, be punishable with imprisonment for a term which may extend to six months, or with fine, or with both.].

[265][**126. Prohibition of public meetings during period of forty-eight hours ending with hour fixed for conclusion of poll.**

(1) No person shall—

(a) convene, hold or attend, join or address any public meeting or procession in connection with an election; or

(b) display to the public any election matter by means of cinematograph, television or other similar apparatus; or

(c) propagate any election matter to the public by holding, or by arranging the holding of, any musical concert or any theatrical performance or any other entertainment or amusement with a view to attracting the members of the public thereto, in any polling area during the period of forty-eight hours ending with the fixed for the conclusion of the poll for any election in the polling area.

(2) Any person who contravenes the provisions of sub-section (1) shall be punishable with imprisonment for a term which may extend to two years, or with fine, or with both.

(3) In this Section, the expression "election matter" means any matter intended or calculated to influence or affect the result of an election.].

127. Disturbances at election meetings.

(1) Any person who at a public meeting to which this Section applies acts, or incites others to act, in a disorderly manner for the purpose of preventing the transaction of the business for which the meeting was called together, [266][shall

be punishable with imprisonment for a term which may extend to [267][six months or with fine which may extend to two thousand rupees] or with both.]

[268][(1A) An offence punishable under sub-section (1) shall be cognizable.]

(2) This Section applies to any public meeting of a political character held in any constituency between the date of the issue of a notification under this Act calling upon the constituency to elect a member or members and the date on which such election is held.

(3) If any police officer reasonably suspects any person of committing an offence under sub-section (1), he may, if requested so to do by the chairman of the meeting, require that person to declare to him immediately his name and address and, if that person refuses or fails so to declare his name and address, or if the police officer reasonably suspects him of giving a false name or address, the police officer may arrest him without warrant.

[269][**127A. Restrictions on the printing of pamphlets, posters, etc.**

(1) No person shall print or publish, or cause to be printed or published, any election pamphlet or poster which does not bear on its face the names and addresses of the printer and the publisher thereof.

(2) No person shall print or cause to be printed any election pamphlet or poster—

(a) unless a declaration as to the identity of the publisher thereof, signed by him and attested by two persons to whom he is personally known, is delivered by him to the printer in duplicate; and

(b) unless, within a reasonable time after the printing of the document, one copy of the declaration is sent by the printer, together with one copy of the document —

(i) where it is printed in the capital of the State, to the Chief Electoral Officer; and

(ii) in any other case, to the district magistrate of the district in which it is printed.

(3) For the purposes of this Section,—

(a) any process for multiplying copies of a document, other than copying it by hand, shall be deemed to be printing and the expression "printer" shall be construed accordingly; and

(b) "election pamphlet or poster" means any printed pamphlet, hand-bill or other document distributed for the purpose of promoting or prejudicing the election of a candidate or group of candidates or any placard or poster having reference to an election, but does not include any hand-bill, placard or poster merely announcing the date, time, place and other particulars of an election meeting or routine instructions to election agents or workers.

(4) Any person who contravenes any of the provisions of sub-section (1) or sub-section (2) shall be punishable with imprisonment for a term which may extend

to six months, or with fine which may extend to two thousand rupees, or with both.].

128. Maintenance of Secrecy of voting.

(1) Every officer, clerk, agent or other person who performs any duty in connection with the recording or counting of votes at an election shall maintain, and aid in maintaining, the secrecy of the voting and shall not (except for some purpose authorised by or under any law) communicate to any person any information calculated to violate such secrecy:

[270]*[PROVIDED that the provisions of this sub-section shall not apply to such officer, clerk, agent or other person who performs any such duty at an election to fill a seat or seats in the Council of States.].*

(2) Any person who contravenes the provisions of sub-section (1) shall be punishable with imprisonment for a term which may extend to three months or with fine or with both.

129. Officers, etc., at elections not to act for candidates or to influence voting.

(1) No person who is [271][a district election officer or a returning officer], or an assistant returning officer, or a presiding or polling officer at an election, or an officer or clerk appointed by the returning officer or the presiding officer to perform any duty in connection with an election shall in the conduct or the management of the election do any act (other than the giving of vote) for the furtherance of the prospects of the election of a candidate.

(2) No such person as aforesaid, and no member of a police force, shall endeavour—

(a) to persuade any person to give his vote at an election, or

(b) to dissuade any person from giving his vote at an election, or

(c) to influence the voting of any person at an election in any manner.

(3) Any person who contravenes the provisions of sub-section (1) or sub-section (2) shall be punishable with imprisonment which may extend to six months or with fine or with both.

[272][(4) An offence punishable under sub-section (3) shall be cognizable.]

130. Prohibition of canvassing in or near polling station.

(1) No person shall, on the date or dates on which a poll is taken at any polling station, commit any of the following acts within the polling station or in any public or private place within a distance of [273][one hundred metres] of the polling station, namely:—

(a) canvassing for votes ; or

(b) soliciting the vote of any elector; or

(c) persuading any elector not to vote for any particular candidate; or

(d) persuading any elector not to vote at the election ; or

(e) exhibiting any notice or sign (other than an official notice) relating to the election.

(2) Any person who contravenes the provisions of sub-section (1) shall be punishable with fine which may extend to two hundred and fifty rupees.

(3) An offence punishable under this Section shall be cognizable.

131. Penalty for disorderly conduct in or near polling stations.

(1) No person shall, on the date or dates on which a poll is taken at any polling station,—

(a) use or operate within or at the entrance of the polling station, or in any public or private place in the neighbourhood thereof, any apparatus for amplifying or reproducing the human voice, such as a megaphone or a loudspeaker,or

(b) shout, or otherwise act in a disorderly manner, within or at the entrance of the polling station or in any public or private place in the neighbourhood thereof, so as to cause annoyance to any person visiting the polling station for the poll, or so as to interfere with the work of the officers and other persons on duty at the polling station.

(2) Any person who contravenes, or wilfully aids or abets the contravention of, the provisions of sub-section (1) shall be punishable with imprisonment which may extend to three months or with fine or with both.

(3) If the presiding officer of a polling station has reason to believe that any person is committing or has committed an offence punishable under this Section, he may direct any police officer to arrest such person, and thereupon the police officer shall arrest him.

(4) Any police officer may take such steps, and use such force, as may be reasonably necessary for preventing any contravention of the provisions of sub-section (1), and may seize any apparatus used for such contravention.

132. Penalty for misconduct at the polling station.

(1) Any person who during the hours fixed for the poll at any polling station misconducts himself or fails to obey the lawful directions of the presiding officer may be removed from the polling station by the presiding officer or by any police officer on duty or by any person authorised in this behalf by such presiding officer.

(2) The powers conferred by sub-section (1) shall not be exercised so as to prevent any elector who is otherwise entitled voting at that station.

(3) If any person who has been so removed from a polling station re-enters the polling station without the permission of the presiding officer, he shall be punishable with imprisonment for a term which may extend to three months, or with fine, or with both.

(4) An offence punishable under sub-section (3) shall be cognizable.

[274][**132A. Penalty for failure to observe procedure for voting.** If any elector to whom a ballot paper has been issued, refused to observe the procedure prescribed for voting the ballot paper issued to him shall be liable for cancellation.

[275][**133. Penalty for illegal hiring or procuring of conveyance at elections**. If any person is guilty of any such corrupt practice as is specified in clause (5) of Section 123 at or in connection with an election, he shall be punishable with imprisonment which may extend to three months and with fine.

134. Breaches of official duty in connection with election.

(1) If any person to whom this Section applies is without reasonable cause guilty of any act or omission in breach of his official duty, he shall be punishable with fine which may extend to five hundred rupees.

[276][(1A) An offence punishable under sub-section (1) shall be cognizable.]

(2) No suit or other legal proceedings shall lie against any such person for damages in respect of any such act or omission as aforesaid.

(3) The persons to whom this Section applies are the [277]*** [278][district election officers, returning officers], assistant returning officers, presiding officers, polling officers and any other person appointed to perform any duty in connection with [279]* * * the receipt of nominations or withdrawal of candidatures, or the recording or counting of votes at an election; and the expression "official duty" shall for the purposes of this Section be construed accordingly, but shall not include duties imposed otherwise than by or under this Act [277]***.

[280][**134A. Penalty for Government servants for acting as election agent, polling agent or counting agent.** If any person in the service of the Government acts as an election agent or a polling agent or a counting agent of a candidate at an election, he shall be punishable with imprisonment for a term which may extend to three months, or with fine, or with both.]

[281][**134B. Prohibition of going armed to or near a polling station.**

(1) No person, other than the returning officer, the presiding officer, any police officer and any other person appointed to maintain peace and order, at a polling station who is on duty at the polling station, shall, on a polling day, go armed with arms, as defined in the Arms Act, 1959 (54 of 1959), of any kind within the neighbourhood of a polling station.

(2) If any person contravenes the provisions of sub-section (1), he shall be punishable with imprisonment for a term which may extend to two years, or with fine, or with both.

(3) Notwithstanding anything contained in the Arms Act, 1959 (54 of 1959), where a person is convicted of an offence under this Section, the arms as defined in the said Act found in his possession shall be liable to confiscation and the licence granted in relation to such arms shall be deemed to have been revoked under Section 17 of that Act.

(4) An offence punishable under sub-section (2) shall be cognizable.]

135. Removal of ballot papers from polling station to be an offence.

(1) Any person who at any election [282][unauthorisedly] takes, or attempts to take, a ballot paper out of a polling station, or wilfully aids or abets the doing of any

such act, shall be punishable with imprisonment for a term which may extend to one year or with fine which may extend to five hundred rupees or with both.

(2) If the presiding officer of a polling station has reason to believe that any person is committing or has committed an offence punishable under sub-section (1), such officer may, before such person leaves the polling station, arrest or direct a police officer to arrest such person and may search such person or cause him to be searched by a police officer:

PROVIDED that when it is necessary to cause a woman to be searched, the search shall be made by another woman with strict regard to decency.

(3) Any ballot paper found upon the person arrested on search shall be made over the safe custody to a police officer by the presiding officer, or when the search is made by a police officer, shall be kept by such officer in safe custody.

(4) An offence punishable under sub-section (1) shall be cognizable.

[283][**135A. Offence of booth capturing**.

[284][(1)] Whoever commits an offence of booth capturing shall be punishable with imprisonment for a term which [285][shall not be less than one year but which may extend to three years and with fine, and where such offence is committed by a person in the service of the Government, he shall be punishable with imprisonment for a term which shall not be less than three years but which may extend to five years and with fine].

EXPLANATION: For the purposes of [286][this sub-section and Section 20B], "booth capturing" includes, among other things, all or any of the following activities, namely:—

(a) seizure of a polling station or a place fixed for the poll by any person or persons, making polling authorities surrender the ballot papers or voting machines and doing of any other act which affects the orderly conduct of elections;

(b) taking possession of a polling station or a place fixed for the poll by any person or persons and allowing only his or their own supporters to exercise their right to vote and 6[prevent others from free exercise of their right to vote];

(c) [287][coercing or intimidating or threatening directly or indirectly] any elector and preventing him from going to the polling station or a place fixed for the poll to cast his vote;

(d) seizure of a place for counting of votes by any person or persons, making the counting authorities surrender the ballot papers or voting machines and the doing of anything which affects the orderly counting of votes;

(e) doing by any person in the service of Government, of all or any of the aforesaid activities or aiding or conniving at, any such activity in the furtherance of the prospects of the election of a candidate.]

[288][(2) An offence punishable under sub-section (1) shall be cognizable.]

[289][**135B. Grant of paid holiday to employees on the day of poll**.

(1) Every person employed in any business, trade, industrial undertaking or any other establishment and entitled to vote at an election to the House of the

People or the Legislative Assembly of a State shall, on the day of poll, be granted a holiday.

(2) No deduction or abatement of the wages of any such person shall be made on account of a holiday having been granted in accordance with sub-section (1) and if such person is employed on the basis that he would not ordinarily receive wages for such a day, he shall nonetheless be paid for such day the wages he would have drawn had not a holiday been granted to him on that day.

(3) If an employer contravenes the provisions of sub-section (1) or sub-section (2), then such employer shall be punishable with fine which may extend to five hundred rupees.

(4) This Section shall not apply to any elector whose absence may cause danger or substantial loss in respect of the employment in which he is engaged.

135C. Liquor not to be sold, given or distributed on polling day.

(1) No spirituous, fermented or intoxicating liquors or other substances of a like nature shall be sold, given or distributed at a hotel, eating house, tavern, shop or any other place, public or private, within a polling area during the period of forty-eight hours ending with the hour fixed for the conclusion of the poll for any election in that polling area.

(2) Any person who contravenes the provisions of sub-section (1), shall be punishable with imprisonment for a term which may extend to six months, or with fine, which may extend to two thousand rupees, or with both.

(3) Where a person is convicted of an offence under this Section, the sprituous, fermented or intoxicating liquors or other substances of a like nature found in his possession shall be liable to confiscation and the same shall be disposed of in such manner as may be prescribed.]

136. Other offences and penalties therefor.

(1) A person shall be guilty of an electoral offence if at any election he—

(a) fraudulently defaces or fraudulently destroys any nomination paper; or

(b) fraudulently defaces, destroys or removes any list, notice or other document affixed by or under the authority of a returning officer; or

(c) fraudulently defaces or fraudulently destroys any ballot paper or the official mark on any ballot paper or any declaration of identity or official envelop used in connection with voting by postal ballot; or

(d) without due authority supplies any ballot paper to any person [290][or receives any ballot paper from any person or is in possession of any ballot paper]; or

(e) fraudulently puts into any ballot box anything other than the ballot paper which he is authorised by law to put in; or

(f) without due authority destroys, takes, opens or otherwise interferes with any ballot box or ballot papers then in use for the purposes of the election; or

(g) fraudulently or without due authority, as the case may be, attempts to do any of the foregoing acts or wilfully aids or abets the doing of any such acts.

(2) Any person guilty of an electoral offence under this Section shall,—

(a) if he is a returning officer or an assistant returning officer or a presiding officer at a polling station or any other officer or clerk employed on official duty in connection with the election, be punishable with imprisonment for a term which may extend to two years or with fine or with both;

(b) if he is any other person, be punishable with imprisonment for a term which may extend to six months or with fine or with both.

(3) For the purposes of this Section, a person shall be deemed to be on official duty if his duty is to take part in the conduct of an election or part of an election including the counting of votes or to be responsible after an election for the used ballot papers and other documents in connection with such election, but the expression "official duty" shall not include any duty imposed otherwise than by or under this Act [291]* * *.

[292][(4) An offence punishable under sub-section (2) shall be cognizable.]

137. [Prosecution regarding certain offences.] *Rep. by the Representation of the People (Amendment) Act, 1966 (47 of 1966), s. 61.*

138. [Amendment of Act 5 of 1898.] *Rep. by the Repealing and Amending Act, 1957 (36 of 1957), s. 2 and the First Schedule.*

PART - VIII : DISQUALIFICATIONS

139—145. [Chapters I to III.] *Rep. by the Representation of the People (Amendment) Act, 1966 (47 of 1966), s. 62.*

[293][CHAPTER - IV : POWERS OF ELECTION COMMISSION IN CONNECTION WITH INQUIRIES AS TO DISQUALIFICATIONS OF MEMBERS

146. Powers of Election Commission.

(1) Where in connection with the tendering of any opinion to the President under article 103 or, as the case may be, under sub-section (4) of Section 14 of the Government of Union Territories Act, 1963 (20 of 1963), or to the Governor under article 192, the Election Commission considers it necessary or proper to make an inquiry, and the Commission is satisfied that on the basis of the affidavits filed and the documents produced in such inquiry by the parties concerned of their own accord, it cannot come to a decisive opinion on the matter which is being inquired into, the Commission shall have, for the purposes of such inquiry, the powers of a civil court, while trying a suit under the Code of Civil Procedure, 1908 (5 of 1908), in respect of the following matters, namely:—

(a) summoning and enforcing the attendance of any person and examining him on oath ;

(b) requiring the discovery and production of any document or other material object producible as evidence;

(c) receiving evidence on affidavits;

(d) requisitioning any public record or a copy thereof from any court or office;

(e) issuing commissions for the examination of witnesses or documents.

(2) The Commission shall also have the power to require any person, subject to any privilege which may be claimed by that person under any law for the time being in force, to furnish information on such points or matters as in the opinion of the Commission may be useful for, or relevant to, the subject-matter of the inquiry.

(3) The Commission shall be deemed to be a civil court and when any such offence, as is described in Section 175, Section 178, Section 179, Section 180 or Section 228 of the Indian Penal Code (45 of 1860), is committed in the view or presence of the Commission, the Commission may after recording the facts constituting the offence and the statement of the accused as provided for in the Code of Criminal Procedure, 1898 [294] (5 of 1898), forward the case to a magistrate having jurisdiction to try the same and the magistrate to whom any such case is forwarded shall proceed to hear the complaint against the accused as if the case had been forwarded to him under Section 482 of the Code of Criminal Procedure, 18982 (5 of 1898).

(4) Any proceeding before the Commission shall be deemed to be a judicial proceeding within the meaning of Section 193 and Section 228 of the Indian Penal Code (45 of 1860).

146A. Statements made by persons to the Election Commission. No statement made by a person in the course of giving evidence before the Election Commission shall subject him to, or be used against him in, any civil or criminal proceeding except a prosecution for giving false evidence by such statement:

PROVIDED that the statement—

(a) is made in reply to a question which he is required by the Commission to answer, or

(b) is relevant to the subject-matter of the inquiry.

146B. Procedure to be followed by the Election Commission. The Election Commission shall have the power to regulate its own procedure (including the fixing of places and times of its sittings and deciding whether to sit in public or in private).]

146C. Protection of action taken in good faith. No suit, prosecution or other legal proceeding shall lie against the Commission or any person acting under the direction of the Commission in respect of anything which is in good faith done or intended to be done in pursuance of the foregoing provisions of this Chapter or of any order made thereunder or in respect of the tendering of any opinion by the Commission to the President or, as the case may be, to the Governor or in respect of the publication, by or under the authority of the Commission of any such opinion, paper or proceedings.]

PART - IX : BYE-ELECTIONS

147. Casual vacancies in the Council of States.

[295][(1)] When before the expiration of the term of office of a member elected to the Council of States, his seat becomes vacant or is declared vacant or his election to the Council of States is declared void, the Election Commission shall by a notification in the Gazette of India call upon the elected members of the Legislative Assembly or the members of the electoral college concerned [296]* * *, as the case may be, to elect a person for the purpose of filling the vacancy so caused before such date as may be specified in the notification and the provisions of this Act and of the rules and orders made thereunder shall apply, as far as may be, in relation to the election of a member to fill such vacancy.

[297][(2) As soon as may be after the date of commencement of the Constitution (Seventh Amendment) Act, 1956, bye-elections shall be held to fill the vacancies existing on that date in the seats allotted to the States of Assam, Orissa and Uttar Pradesh and the Union territories of Delhi, Himachal Pradesh[298] and Manipur[298].]

148. [Casual vacancies in the electoral colleges for certain Union territories.] *Rep. by the Territorial Councils Act, 1956 (103 of 1956), s. 66.*

149. Casual vacancies in the House of the People.

(1) When the seat of a member elected to the House of the People becomes vacant or is declared vacant or his election to the House of the People is declared void, the Election Commission shall, subject to the provisions of sub-section (2), by a notification in the Gazette of India, call upon the Parliamentary constituency concerned to elect a person for the purpose of filling the vacancy so caused before such date as may be specified in the notification, and the provisions of this Act and of the rules and orders made thereunder shall apply, as far as may be, in relation to the election of a member to fill such vacancy.

(2) If the vacancy so caused be a vacancy in a seat reserved in any such constituency for the Scheduled Castes or for any Scheduled Tribes, the notification issued under sub-section (1) shall specify that the person to fill that seat shall belong to the Scheduled Castes or to such Scheduled Tribes, as the case may be.

150. Casual vacancies in the State Legislative Assemblies.

(1) When the seat of a member elected to the Legislative Assembly of a State becomes vacant or is declared vacant or his election to the Legislative Assembly is declared void, the Election Commission shall, subject to the provisions of sub-section (2), by a notification in the Official Gazette, call upon the Assembly constituency concerned to elect a person for the purpose of filling the vacancy so caused before such date as may be specified in the notification, and the provisions of this Act and of the rules and orders made thereunder shall apply, as far as may be, in relation to the election of a member to fill such vacancy.

(2) If the vacancy so caused be a vacancy in a seat reserved in any such constituency for the Scheduled Castes or for any Scheduled Tribes, the notification issued under sub-section (1) shall specify that the person to fill that seat shall belong to the Scheduled Castes or to such Scheduled Tribes, as the case may be.

151. Casual vacancies in the State Legislative Councils. When before the expiration of the term of office of a member elected to the Legislative Council of a State, his seat becomes vacant or is declared vacant or his election to the Legislative Council is declared void, the Election Commission shall, by a notification in the Official Gazette, call upon the Council constituency concerned or the members of the Legislative Assembly of the State, as the case may be, to elect a person for the purpose of filling the vacancy so caused, before such date as may be specified in the notification, and the provisions of this Act and of the rules and orders made thereunder shall apply, as far as may be, in relation to the election of a member to fill such vacancy.

[299][**151A. Time limit for filling vacancies referred to in Sections 147, 149, 150 and 151.** Notwithstanding anything contained in Section 147, Section 149, Section 150 and Section 151, a bye-election for filling any vacancy referred to in any of the said Sections shall be held within a period of six months from the date of the occurrence of the vacancy:

PROVIDED that nothing contained in this Section shall apply if—

(a) the remainder of the term of a member in relation to a vacancy is less than one year; or

(b) the Election Commission in consultation with the Central Government certifies that it is difficult to hold the bye-election within the said period.

PART - X : MISCELLANEOUS

152. List of members of the State Legislative Assemblies and electoral colleges to be maintained by the returning officers concerned.

(1) The returning officer for an election by the elected members of the Legislative Assembly of a State to fill a seat or seats in the Council of States or for an election, by the members of the Legislative Assembly of a State to fill a seat or seats in the Legislative Council of the State shall, for the purposes of such election maintain in his office in the prescribed manner and form a list of elected members or a list of members, as the case may be, of that Legislative Assembly.

(2) The returning officer for an election by the members of the electoral college for a [300][Union territory] [301]* * * [302]* * * to fill a seat or seats in the Council of States shall, for the purposes of such election, maintain in his office in the prescribed manner and form a list of members of the electoral college [302]***.

(3) Copies of the lists referred to in sub-sections (1) and (2) shall be made available for sale.

[303][**153. Extention of time for completion of election.** It shall be competent for the Election Commission for reasons which it considers sufficient, to extend the time for the

completion of any election by making necessary amendments in the notification issued by it under Section 30 or sub-section (1) of Section 39.]

154. Term of office of members of the Council of States.

[304][(1) Subject to the provisions of sub-sections (2) and (2A), the term of office of a member of the Council of States, other than a member chosen to fill a casual vacancy, shall be six years.]

(2) [305]* * Upon the first constitution of the Council of States the President shall, after consultation with the Election Commission, make by order such provision as he thinks fit for curtailing the term of office of some of the members then chosen in order that, as nearly as may be, one-third of the members holding seats of each class shall retire in every second year thereafter.

[306][(2A) In order that, as nearly as may be, one-third of the members may retire on the second day of April, 1958, and on the expiration of every second year thereafter, the President shall, as soon as may be after the commencement of the Constitution (Seventh Amendment) Act, 1956, after consultation with the Election Commission, make by order such provisions as he thinks fit in regard to the terms of office of the members elected under sub-section (2) of Section 147.]

(3) A member chosen to fill a casual vacancy shall be chosen to serve for the remainder of his predecessor's term of office.

155. Commencement of the term of office of members of the Council of States.

(1) The term of office of a member of the Council of States whose name is required to be notified in the Official Gazette under Section 71 shall begin on the date of such notification.

(2) The term of office of a member of the Council of States whose name is not required to be notified under Section 71 shall begin on the date of publication in the Official Gazette of the declaration containing the name of such person as elected under Section 67 or of the notification issued under sub-clause (a) of clause (1) of article 80 or under any other provision announcing the nomination of such person to the Council of States, as the case may be.

156. Term of office of members of State Legislative Councils.

(1) The term of office of a member of the Legislative Council of a State, other than a member chosen to fill a casual vacancy, shall be six years, but upon the first constitution of the Council the Governor [307]* * shall, after consultation with the Election Commission, make by order such provision as he thinks fit for curtailing the term of office of some of the members then chosen in order that, as nearly as may be, one-third of the members holding seats of each class shall retire in every second year thereafter.

(2) A member chosen to fill a casual vacancy shall be chosen to serve for the remainder of his predecessor's term of office.

157. Commencement of the term of office of members of the Legislative Councils.

(1) The term of office of a member of the Legislative Council of a State whose

name is required to be notified in the Official Gazette under [308] [section 74] shall begin on the date of such notification.

(2) The term of office of a member of the Legislative Council of a State whose name is not required to be notified under [308][section 74] shall begin on the date of publication in the Official Gazette of the declaration containing the name of such person as elected under Section 67 or of the notification issued under sub-clause (e) of clause (3) of article 171, announcing the nomination of such person to the Council, as the case may be.

[309][**158. Return of forfeiture of candidate's deposit.**

(1) The deposit made under Section 34 or under that Section read with sub-section (2) of Section 39 shall either be returned to the person making it or his legal representative or be forfeited to the appropriate authority in accordance with the provisions of this Section.

(2) Except in cases hereafter mentioned in this Section, the deposit shall be returned as soon as practicable after the result of the election is declared.

(3) If the candidate is not shown in the list of contesting candidates, or if he dies before the commencement of the poll, the deposit shall be returned as soon as practicable after the publication of the list or after his death, as the case may be.

(4) Subject to the provisions of sub-section (3), the deposit shall be forfeited if at an election where a poll has been taken, the candidate is not elected and the number of valid votes polled by him does not exceed one-sixth of the total number of valid votes polled by all the candidates or in the case of election of more than one member at the election, one-sixth of the total number of valid votes so polled divided by the number of members to be elected:

PROVIDED that where at an election held in, accordance with the system of proportional representation by means of the single transferable vote, a candidate is not elected, the deposit made by him shall be forfeited if he does not get more than one-sixth of the number of votes prescribed in this behalf as sufficient to secure the return of a candidate.

(5) Notwithstanding anything in sub-sections (2), (3) and (4),—

(a) if at a general election, the candidate is a contesting candidate in more than one parliamentary constituency or in more than one assembly constituency, not more than one of the deposits shall be returned, and the others shall be forfeited.

(b) if the candidate is a contesting candidate at an election in more than one council constituency or at an election in a council constituency and at an election by the members of the State Legislative Assembly to fill seats in the Legislative Council, not more than one of the deposits shall be returned, and the others shall be forfeited.]

[310][**159. Staff of certain authorities to be made available for election work.**

(1) The authorities specified in sub-section (2) shall, when so requested by a Regional Commissioner appointed under clause (4) of article 324 or the Chief

Electoral Officer of the State, make available to any returning officer such staff as may be necessary for the performance of any duties in connection with an election.

(2) The following shall be the authorities for the purpose of sub-section (1), namely:—

(i) every local authority;

(ii) every university established or incorporated by or under a Central, Provincial or State Act;

(iii) a Government company as defined in Section 617 of the Companies Act, 1956 (1 of 1956);

(iv) any other institution, concern or undertaking which is established by or under a Central, Provincial or State Act or which is controlled, or financed wholly or substantially by funds provided, directly or indirectly, by the Central Government or a State Government.]

160. Requisitioning of premises, vehicles, etc., for election purposes.

(1) If it appears to the State Government that in connection with an election held within the State—

(a) any premises are needed or are likely to be needed for the purpose of being used as a polling station or for the storage of ballot boxes after a poll has been taken, or

(b) any vehicle, vessel or animal is needed or is likely to be needed for the purpose of transport of ballot boxes to or from any polling station, or transport of members of the police force for maintaining order during the conduct of such election, or transport of any officer or other person for performance of any duties in connection with such election, that Government may by order in writing requisition such premises, or such vehicle, vessel or animal, as the case may be, and may make such further orders as may appear to it to be necessary or expedient in connection with the requisitioning:

PROVIDED that no vehicle, vessel or animal which is being lawfully used by a candidate or his agent for any purpose connected with the election of such candidate shall be requisitioned under this sub-section until the completion of the poll at such election.

(2) The requisition shall be effected by an order in writing addressed to the person deemed by the State Government to be the owner or person in possession of the property, and such order shall be served in the prescribed manner on the person to whom it is addressed.

(3) Whenever any property is requisitioned under sub-section (1), the period of such requisition shall not extend beyond the period for which such property is required for any of the purposes mentioned in that sub-section.

(4) In this Section —

(a) "premises" means any land, building or part of a building and includes a hut, shed or other structure or any part thereof;

(b) "vehicle" means any vehicle used or capable of being used for the purpose of road transport, whether propelled by mechanical power or otherwise.

161. Payment of compensation.

(1) Whenever in pursuance of Section 160 the State Government requisitions any premises, there shall be paid to the persons interested compensation the amount of which shall be determined by taking into consideration the following, namely:—

(i) the rent payable in respect of the premises or if no rent is so payable, the rent payable for similar premises in the locality;

(ii) if any consequence of the requisition of the premises the person interested is compelled to change his residence or place of business, the reasonable expenses (if any) incidental to such change:

PROVIDED that where any person interested being aggrieved by the amount of compensation so determined makes an application within the prescribed time to the State Government for referring the matter to an arbitrator, the amount of compensation to be paid shall be such as the arbitrator appointed in this behalf by the State Government may determine:

PROVIDED FURTHER that where there is any dispute as to the title to receive the compensation or as to the apportionment of the amount of compensation, it shall be referred by the State Government to an arbitrator appointed in this behalf by that Government for determination, and shall be determined in accordance with the decision of such arbitrator.

EXPLANATION: In this sub-section, the expression "person interested" means the person who was in actual possession of the premises requisitioned under Section 160 immediately before the requisition, or where no person was in such actual possession, the owner of such premises.

(2) Whenever in pursuance of Section 160 the State Government requisitions any vehicle, vessel or animal, there shall be paid to the owner thereof compensation the amount of which shall be determined by the State Government on the basis of the fares or rates prevailing in the locality for the hire of such vehicle, vessel or animal:

PROVIDED that where the owner of such vehicle, vessel or animal being aggrieved by the amount of compensation so determined makes an application within the prescribed time to the State Government for referring the matter to an arbitrator, the amount of compensation to be paid shall be such as the arbitrator appointed in this behalf by the State Government may determine:

PROVIDED FURTHER that where immediately before the requisitioning the vehicle or vessel was by virtue of a hire-purchase agreement in the possession of a person other than the owner, the amount determined under this sub-section as the total compensation payable in respect of the requisition shall be apportioned between that person and the owner in such manner as they may agree upon, and in default of agreement, in such manner as an arbitrator appointed by the State Government in this behalf may decide.

162. Power to obtain information. The State Government may with a view to requisitioning any property under Section 160 or determining the compensation payable under Section 161, by order, require any person to furnish to such authority as may be specified in the order such information in his possession relating to such property as may be so specified.

163. Powers of entry into and inspection of premises, etc.

(1) Any person authorized in this behalf by the State Government may enter into any premises and inspect such premises and any vehicle, vessel or animal therein for the purpose of determining whether, and if so in what manner, an order under Section 160 should be made in relation to such premises, vehicle, vessel or animal, or with a view to securing compliance with any order made under that Section.

(2) In this Section, the expressions "premises" and "vehicle" have the same meanings as in Section 160.

164. Eviction from requisitioned premises.

(1) Any person remaining in possession of any requisitioned premises in contravention of any order made under Section 160 may be summarily evicted from the premises by any officer empowered by the State Government in this behalf.

(2) Any officer so empowered may, after giving to any woman not appearing in public reasonable warning and facility to withdraw, remove or open any lock or bolt or break open any door of any building or do any other act necessary for effecting such eviction.

165. Release of premises from requisition.

(1) When any premises requisitioned under Section 160 are to be released from requisition, the possession thereof shall be delivered to the person from whom possession was taken at the time when the premises were requisitioned, or if there were no such person, to the person deemed by the State Government to be the owner of such premises, and such delivery of possession shall be a full discharge of the State Government from all liabilities in respect of such delivery, but shall not prejudice any rights in respect of the premises which any other person may be entitled by due process of law to enforce against the person to whom possession of the premises is so delivered.

(2) Where the person to whom possession of any premises requisitioned under Section 160 is to be given under sub-section (1) cannot be found or is not readily ascertainable or has no agent or any other person empowered to accept delivery on his behalf, the State Government shall cause a notice declaring that such premises are released from requisition to be affixed on some conspicuous part of such premises and publish the notice in the Official Gazette.

(3) When a notice referred to in sub-section (2) is published in the Official Gazette, the premises specified in such notice shall cease to be subject to requisition

on and from the date of such publication and be deemed to have been delivered to the person entitled to possession thereof; and the State Government shall not be liable for any compensation or other claim in respect of such premises for any period after the said date.

166. Delegation of functions of the State Government with regard to requisitioning. The State Government may, by notification in the Official Gazette, direct that any powers conferred or any duty imposed on that Government by any of the provisions of Sections 160 to 165 shall, under such conditions, if any, as may be specified in the direction, be exercised or discharged by such officer or class of officers as may be so specified.

167. Penalty for contravention of any order regarding requisitioning. If any person contravenes any order made under Section 160 or Section 162, he shall be punishable with imprisonment for a term which may extend to one year or with fine or with both.

168. ***[Special provisions with respect to Rulers of former Indian States.]*** *Rep. by the Rulers of Indian States (Abolition of Privileges) Act, 1972 (54 of 1972), s. 4 (w.e.f. 9-9-1972).*

PART - XI : GENERAL

169. Power to make rules.

(1) The Central Government may, after consulting the Election Commission, by notification in the Official Gazette, make rules[311] for carrying out the purposes of this Act.

(2) In particular, and without prejudice to the generality of the foregoing power, such rules may provide for all or any of the following matters, namely:—

[312][(a) the form of affidavit under sub-section (2) of Section 33A];

[313][(aa)] the duties of presiding officers and polling officers at polling stations;

[314][(aaa) the form of contribution report];

(b) the checking of voters by reference to the electoral roll;

[315][(bb) the manner of allocation of equitable sharing of time on the cable television network and other electronic media];;

(c) the manner in which votes are to be given both generally and in the case of illiterate voters or voters under physical or other disability ;

(d) the manner in which votes are to be given by a presiding officer, polling officer, polling agent or any other person, who being an elector for a constituency is authorised or appointed for duty at a polling station at which he is not entitled to vote;

(e) the procedure to be followed in respect of the tender of vote by a person representing himself to be an elector after another person has voted as such elector;

[316][(ee) the manner of giving and recording of votes by means of voting machines and the procedure as to voting to be followed at poling stations where such machines are used];

(f) the procedure as to voting to be followed at elections held in accordance with the system of proportional representation by means of the single transferable vote;

(g) the scrutiny and counting of votes including cases in which a recount of the votes may be made before the declaration of the result of the election;

[316][(gg) the procedure as to counting of votes recorded by means of voting machines];

(h) the safe custody of [317][ballot boxes, voting machines], ballot papers and other election papers, the period for which such papers shall be preserved and the inspection and production of such papers;

[315][(hh) the material to be supplied by the Government to the candidates of recognised political parties at any election to be held for the purposes of constituting the House of the People or the Legislative Assembly of a State];

(i) any other matter required to be prescribed by this Act.

[318][(3) Every rule made under this Act shall be laid as soon as may be after it is made before each House of Parliament while it is in session for a total period of thirty days which may be comprised in one session or [319][in two or more successive sessions, and if, before the expiry of the session immediately following the session or the successive sessions aforesaid, both Houses agree in making any modification in the rule or both Houses agree that the rule should not be made,] the rule shall thereafter have effect only in such modified form or be of no effect, as the case may be; so, however, that any such modification or annulment shall be without prejudice to the validity of anything previously done under that rule.].

170. Jurisdiction of civil courts barred. No civil court shall have jurisdiction to question the legality of any action taken or of any decision given by the returning officer or by any other person appointed under this Act in connection with an election.

171. [Repeal of Act 39 of 1920.] *Rep. by the Repealing and A mending Act, 1957 (36 of 1957), s. 2 and Sch. I.*

❑❑❑

ENDNOTES

1. The words "and illegal" omitted by Act 27 of 1956, s. 2.
2. Certain words omitted by Act 103 of 1956, s. 66.
3. Ins. by Act 27 of 1956, s. 3.
4. The words and figures "or Section 124" omitted by s. 3, *ibid.*
5. Ins. by Act 47 of 1966, s. 15 (w.e.f. 14-12-1966).
6. Certain words omitted by Act 58 of 1958, s. 14.
7. Subs. by Act 27 of 1956, s. 3, for cl. (e).

8. Cl.(f) which was omitted by Act 27 of 1956, s. 3, and ins. by Act 1 of 1989, s. 3 (w.e.f. 15-6-1989).
9. Ins. by Act 47 of 1966, s. 15 (w.e.f. 14-12-1966).
10. Cls. (h) and (i) omitted by Act 27 of 1956, s. 3.
11. Cl. (i) re-lettered as cl. (h) by s. 3, *ibid.*, omitted by the Adaptation of Laws (No. 2) Order, 1956.
12. Cls. (k) and (i) re-lettered as cls. (i) and (k) by Act 27 of 1956, s. 3.
13. Cl. (j) ins. by s. 3, *ibid.*, and omitted by the Adaptation of Laws (No. 2) Order, 1956.
14. Cl. (k) omitted by Act 47 of 1966, s. 15 (w.e.f. 14-12-1966).
15. Certain words omitted by Act 103 of 1956, s. 66.
16. Sub-sections (5) and (7) omitted and sub-section (6) renumbered as sub-section (5) by Act 27 of 1956, s. 3.
17. Subs. by Act 47 of 1966, s. 15, for sub-section (5).
18. Subs. by s. 16, *ibid.*, for the previous heading (w.e.f. 14-12-1966).
19. Subs. by the Adaptation of Laws (No. 2) Order, 1956, for s. 3.
20. Certain words omitted by Act 47 of 1966, s. 17 (w.e.f. 14-12-1966).
21. Subs. by Act 40 of 2003, s. 2.
22. Certain words omitted by Act 29 of 1975, s. 12 (w.e.f. 15-8-1975).
23. The word "and" omitted by Act 47 of 1966, s. 18 (w.e.f. 14-12-1966).
24. Ins. by s. 18, *ibid.* (w.e.f. 14-12-1966).
25. Subs. by the Laccadive, Minicoy and Amindivi Islands (Alteration of Name) Adaptation of Laws Order, 1974 (w.e.f. 1-11-1973).
26. The word "and" omitted by Act 10 of 1976, s. 2 and Sch. (w.e.f. 9-9-1975).
27. Ins. by s. 2 and Sch., *ibid.* (w.e.f. 9-9-1975).
28. Certain words omitted by the North-Eastern Areas (Reorganisation) (Adaptation of Laws on Union Subjects) Order, 1974 (w.e.f. 21-1-1972).
29. Subs. by Act 47 of 1966, s. 19, for "Scheduled Tribe of that district" (w.e.f. 14-12-1966).
30. Ins. by Act 27 of 1962, s. 11.
31. Ins. by Act 10 of 1976, s. 2 and Sch. (w.e.f. 9-9-1975).
32. S. 5A renumbered as sub-section (1) of that Section by Act 8 of 1980, s. 3 (w.e.f. 1-9-1979).
33. Ins. by s..3, *ibid.* (w.e.f. 1-9-1979).
34. The words "or the Rajpramukh, as the case may be" omitted by the Adaptation of Laws (No. 2) Order, 1956.
35. Subs. by Act 47 of 1966, s. 20, for Chapter III (w.e.f. 14-12-1966). Previous Chapter IV (ss. 10 and 11) was rep. by Act 103 of 1956, s. 66.
36. Subs. by Act 1 of 1989, s. 4, for sub-sections (1) and (2) (w.e.f. 15-3-1989).
37. Ins. by Act 42 of 1991, s. 8 (w.e.f. 18-9-1991).
38. Added by Act 21 of 1996, s. 3 (w.e.f.1-8-1996).
39. Ins. by s. 3, *ibid.* (w.e.f. 1-8-1996).
40. Ins. by Act 9 of 2003, s. 2 (w.e.f. 7-1-2003).
41. Subs. by s. 2, *ibid.* (w.e.f. 7-1-2003).
42. Cl. (d) omitted by s. 2, *ibid.* (w.e.f. 7-1-2003).
43. Sub-section (3) renumbered as sub-section (4) by Act 1 of 1989, s. 4 (w.e.f. 15-3-1989).

44. Subs. by s. 4, *ibid.*, for certain words (w.e.f.15-3-1989).
45. Subs. by Act 40 of 1975, s. 2, for s. 8A.
46. Ins. by Act 40 of 1975, s. 3.
47. S. 11A re-numbered as sub-section (1) thereof by s. 4, *ibid.*
48. The brackets and letter "(a)" omitted by Act 38 of 1978, s. 3 and the Second Sch.
49. The word "or" omitted by s. 3 and the Second Sch. *ibid.*
50. Cl.(b) omitted by Act 40 of 1975, s. 4.
51. Ins. by s. 4, *ibid.*
52. Subs. by s. 5, *ibid.*, for certain words.
53. Subs. by Act 27 of 1956, s. 7, for Part III (ss. 12 to 18).
54. Ins. by Act 10 of 1976, s. 2 and Sch. (w.e.f. 9-9-1975).
55. Subs. by Act 20 of 1963, s. 57 and the Second Sch., for "the Governor".
56. The words "Rajpramukh, Lieutenant-Governor or Chief Commissioner, as the case may be, omitted by the Adaptation of Laws (No. 2) Order, 1956.
57. Ins. by Act 20 of 1963, s. 57 and the Second Sch.
58. Ins. by Act 37 of 1957. s. 13.
59. The words "or Rajpramukh, as the case may be," omitted by the Adaptation of Laws (No. 2) Order, 1956.
60. Certain words omitted by Act 103 of 1956, s. 66.
61. Ins. by Act 47 of 1966, s. 21 (w.e.f. 14-12-1966).
62. Subs. by Act 27 of 1956, s. 9, for ss. 20 and 21.
63. Ins. by Act 47 of 1966, s. 22 (w.e.f. 14-12-1966).
64. Ins. by Act 21 of 1996, s. 4 (w.e.f. 1-8-1996).
65. Subs. by Act 47 of 1966, s. 23, for "an officer of Government".
66. Certain words omitted by Act 27 of 1956, s.10.
67. The words "or to the counting of votes" omitted by s. 10, *ibid.*
68. Subs. by Act 47 of 1966, s. 25, for s. 25 (w.e.f. 14-12-1966).
69 Subs. by s. 26, *ibid.*, for "returning officer" (w.e.f. 14-12-1966).
70. Ins. by Act 27 of 1956, s.12.
71. Subs. by Act 47 of 1966, s. 26, for "returning officer" (w.e.f. 14 -12-1966).
72. Sub-section (5), ins. by s. 12, *ibid.* (w.e.f. 14-12-1966) and omitted by Act 2 of 2004, s.3.
73. Ins. by Act 1 of 1989, s. 5 (w.e.f. 15-3-1989).
74. The words and brackets "(other than a primary election)" omitted by Act 27 of 1956, s. 13.
75. Ins. by Act 1 of 1989, s. 6 (w.e.f. 15-6-1989).
76. Ins. by Act 46 of 2003, s. 2.
77. Subs. by Act 27 of 1956, s. 14, for s. 30.
78. Subs. by Act 40 of 1961, s. 7, for "tenth day" (w.e.f. 20-9-1961).
79. Subs. by Act 47 of 1966, s. 27, for "the second day after" (w.e.f. 14-12-1966).
80. Subs. by s. 27, *ibid.*, for "the third day" (w.e.f. 14-12-1966).
81. Subs. by Act 21 of 1996, s. 5, for "twentieth day" (w.e.f. 1-8-1996).
82. Explanation omitted by Act 47 of 1966, s. 27 (w.e.f. 14-12-1966).
83. The words "for the constituency" omitted by s. 28, *ibid.* (w.e.f. 14-12-1966).

84. The words "in any constituency" omitted by Act 27 of 1956, s. 15.
85. Certain words ins. by s. 15, *ibid.*, and omitted by the Adaptation of Laws (No. 2) Order, 1956.
86. Ins. by Act 20 of 1963, s. 57 and the Second Sch.
87. Subs. by Act 27 of 1956, s. 16, for s. 33.
88. Subs. by Act 21 of 1996, s. 6, for the provisos (w.e.f. 1-8-1996).
89. Ins. by Act 10 of 1976, s. 2 and Sch. (w.e.f. 9-9-1975).
90. Subs. by Act 38 of 1978, s. 3 and the Second Sch., for "clause (f) of Section 7".
91. Subs. by Act 47 of 1966, s. 29, for the proviso (w.e.f. 14-12-1966).
92. Subs. by Act 40 of 1961, s. 8, for sub-section (6) (w.e.f. 20-9-1961).
93. Ins. by Act 21 of 1996, s. 6 (w.e.f. 1-8-1996).
94. Ins. by Act 72 of 2002, s. 2 (w.e.f. 24-8-2002).
95. Subs. by s. 3, *ibid.* (w.e.f. 2-5-2002).
96. Subs. by Act 21 of 1996, s. 7, for sub-section (1) (w.e.f. 1-8-1996).
97. Subs. by Act 10 of 1976, s. 2 and Sch., for certain words (w.e.f. 9-9-1975).
98. Subs. by Act 27 of 1956, s. 18, for certain words.
99. The words "and one seconder" omitted by s. 19, *ibid.*
100. Subs. by Act 27 of 1956, s. 19, for "refuse".
101. Subs. by s. 19, *ibid.*, for cls. (a) to (e).
102. Subs. by Act 40 of 1961, s. 9, for "that the candidate" (w.e.f. 20-9-1961).
103. The word "and" ins. by the Adaptation of Laws (No. 2) Order, 1956 and omitted by Act 20 of 1963, s. 57 and the Second Sch.
104. Subs. by Act 20 of 1963, s. 57 and the Second Sch. for certain words.
105. Certain words omitted by the Adaptation of Laws (No. 2) Order, 1956.
106. Subs. by Act 27 of 1956, s. 19. for "clause (c), clause (d) or clause (e)".
107. Subs. by s. 19, *ibid.*, for "refusal".
108. The word "technical" omitted by Act 27 of 1956, s. 19.
109. Subs. by Act 40 of 1961, s. 9, for "an objection is made" (w.e.f. 20-9-1961).
110. Subs. by Act 27 of 1956, s. 19, for sub-section (7).
111. The word "seconder" and the proviso omitted by s. 20, *ibid.*
112. Subs. by Act 40 of 1961, s. 10, for sub-section (3) (w.e.f. 20-9-1961).
113. Subs. by Act 27 of 1956, s. 21, for s. 38.
114. Subs. by Act 21 of 1996, s. 8, for sub-section (2) (w.e.f. 1-8-1996).
115. Subs. by Act 27 of 1956, s. 22, for s. 39.
116. Subs. by the Adaptation of Laws (No. 2) Order, 1956, for "Part C State".
117. Subs. by Act 40 of 1961, s. 11, for "tenth day" (w.e.f. 20-9-1961).
118. Subs. by Act 47 of 1966, s. 30, for "the second day after" (w.e.f. 14-12-1966).
119. Subs. by s. 30, *ibid.*, for "the third day" (w.e.f. 14-12-1966).
120. Explanation omitted by s. 30, *ibid.* (w.e.f. 14-12-1966).
121. Subs. by Act 58 of 1958, s. 19, for " Section 34".
122. Subs. by the Adaptation of Laws (No. 2) Order, 1956, for "Part C State".
123. Ins. by Act 1 of 1989, s. 8 (w.e.f. 1-4-1989).
123. Ins. by Act 47 of 1966, s. 30 (w.e.f. 14-12-1966).

124. Cl.(aa) relettered as cl. (ab) by Act 1 of 1989, s. 8 (w.e.f. 1-4-1989).
125. Ins. by Act 46 of 2003, s. 3 (w.e.f. 24-9-2003).
126. Subs. by Act 27 of 1956, s. 23, for s. 40.
127. Subs. by Act 47 of 1966, s. 31, for s. 41 (w.e.f. 14-12-1966).
128. The words "whether he be the candidate himself or not" omitted by Act 27 of 1956, s. 24.
129. Subs. by s. 24, *ibid.*, for sub-section (2).
130. Subs. by s. 26, *ibid.*, for s. 45.
131. Subs. by s. 27, for s. 46, *ibid.*
132. Subs. by Act 27 of 1956, s. 28, *ibid.*, for s. 47.
133. Subs. by Act 58 of 1958, s. 20, for "candidate".
134. Subs. by Act 58 of 1958, s. 20, for "candidate".
135. Subs. by Act 2 of 1992, s. 2, for s. 52 and again subs. by Act 21 of 1996, s. 9 (w.e.f.1-8-1996).
136. Subs. by Act 27 of 1956, s. 30, for sub-section (1).
137. Subs. by s. 30, *ibid.*, for "appropriate authority".
138. The words "or the elected members of the Coorg Legislative Council" omitted by Act 49 of 1951, s. 44 and the Fifth Sch.
139. The words "before such date as may be appointed in this behalf by the Election Commission and specified in the notification " omitted by Act 27 of 1956, s. 30.
140. Subs. by s. 30, *ibid.*, for "until such date as the Election Commission may specify in this behalf".
141. Ins. by Act 20 of 1963, s. 57 and the Second Schedule. The words "or under the Government of Part C States Act, 1951 (49 of 1951), as the case may be" ins. by Act 27 of 1956, s. 32, and omitted by the Adaptation of Laws (No. 2) Order, 1956.
142. Ins. by Act 27 of 1956, s. 33.
143. Subs. by s. 34, *ibid.*, for "appropriate authority".
144. Subs. by Act 58 of 1958, s. 23, for "a constituency".
145. Subs. by Act 40 of 1961, s. 13, for s. 58 (w.e.f. 20-9-1961).
146. Ins. by Act 1 of 1989, s. 9 (w.e.f. 15-3-1989).
147. Ins. by Act 1 of 1989, s. 10, *ibid.* (w.e.f. 15-3-1989).
148. Subs. by Act 24 of 2003, s. 2 (w.e.f. 22-9-2003).
149. Ins. by Act 40 of 2003, s. 3.
150. Subs. by Act 24 of 2003, s. 3, (w.e.f. 22-9-2003).
151. Subs. by Act 58 of 1958, s. 25, for s. 61.
152. Ins. by Act 1 of 1989, s. 11 (w.e.f. 15-3-1989).
153. Ins. by Act 24 of 2003, s. 4 (w.e.f. 22-9-2003).
154. Subs. by Act 27 of 1956, s. 36, for "supervision".
155. Subs. by Act 58 of 1958, s. 26, for "candidate".
156. Subs. by Act 27 of 1956, s. 36, for "counting agent".
157. Ins. by Act 47 of 1966, s. 34 (w.e.f. 14-12-1966).
158. Subs. by s. 35, *ibid.*, for "shall forthwith declare" (w.e.f. 14-12-1966).
159. Ins. by Act 27 of 1956, s. 37.
160. The word and figures "section 54" omitted by Act 40 of 1961, s. 15 (w.e.f. 20-9-1961).
161. The word, figures and letter " Section 55A " omitted by Act 58 of 1958, s. 27.

162. Certain words omitted by Act 103 of 1956, s. 66.
163. Subs. by Act 27 of 1956, s. 38, for certain words.
164. Ins. by s. 38, *ibid.*
165. Subs. by s. 39, *ibid.*, for "on the publication in the Gazette of India of the declaration that he hits been so chosen".
166. Ins. by s. 40, *ibid.*
167. Subs. by s. 41, *ibid.*, for ss. 71 to 75.
168. See rule 91 of the Conduct of Election Rules, 1961 (page 76 of Vol. II). In relation to Prohibition relating to membership both of Parliament and of a House of the Legislature of a State, see also the Prohibition of Simultaneous Membership Rules, 1950 published under articles 101(2) and 190(2) of the Constitution vide Notification No.F.46/50—C, dated 26th January, 1950, in the Gazette of India, Extraordinary, page 678 (Pages 140 of Vol. I).
169. Subs. by the Adaptation of Laws (No. 2) Order, 1956, for "Part C States".
170. Subs. by Act 40 of 1961, s. 16, for "the appropriate authority" (w.e.f. 20-9-1961).
171. Subs. by Act 10 of 1967, s. 2, for certain words.
172. Certain words omitted by Act 40 of 1961, s. 16 (w.e.f. 20-9-1961).
173. Subs. by Act 10 of 1967, s. 2, for cl. (a).
174. Subs. by Act 31 of 1991, s. 2, for ss 73A and 73AA (w.e.f. 18-4-1991).
175. Ins. by Act 37 of 1957, s. 13.
176. The words " or Rajpramukh, as the case may be" omitted by the Adapatation of Laws (No. 2) Order, 1956.
177. Ins. by Act 72 of 2002, s. 4 (w.e.f. 24-8-2002).
178. Subs. by Act 27 of 1956, s. 42, for ss. 76 to 78.
179. Subs. by Act 40 of 1975, s. 6, for certain words (retrospectively).
180. Subs. by Act 46 of 2003, s. 4, for the Explanation.
181. S. 78 re-numbered as sub-section (1) of that Section by Act 47 of 1966, s. 36.
182. Subs. by Act 47 of 1966, s. 36, for "returning officer".
183. Ins. by s. 36, *ibid.* (w.e.f. 14-12-1966) and omitted by Act 2 of 2004, s. 3(b).
184. Ins. by Act 46 of 2003, s. 5.
185. Subs. by Act 47 of 1966, s. 37, for Parts VII and VIII.
186. Ins. by s. 37, *ibid.*, Original cl. (a) was omitted by Act 27 of 1956, s. 43.
187. Subs. by Act 40 of 1975, s. 7, for cl. (b) (retrospectively).
188. Subs. by Act 47 of 1966, s. 37, for "to withdraw" (w.e.f. 14-12-1966).
189. Subs. by s. 37, *ibid.*, for cl. (e) (w.e.f. 14-12-1966).
190. Subs. by Act 47 of 1966, s. 39, for "Election Commission" (w.e.f. 14-12-1966).
191. Ins. by s. 38, *ibid.* (w.e.f. 14-12-1966).
192. Subs. by Act 27 of 1956, s. 44, for "sub-sections (1) and (2)".
193. Subs. by Act 47 of 1966, s. 39, for "Election Commission" (w.e.f.14-12-1966).
194. Subs. by Act 27 of 1956, s. 44, for certain words.
195. Sub-section (2) omitted by Act 47 of 1966, s. 39 (w.e.f. 14-12-1966).
196. Ins. by Act 40 of 1961, s. 17 (w.e.f. 20-9-1961).
197. Certain words omitted by Act 47 of 1966, s. 39 (w.e.f. 14-12-1966).
198. Subs. by Act 27 of 1956, s. 45, for s. 82.

199. Subs. by s. 46, *ibid.*, for s. 83.
200. Ins. by Act 40 of 1961, s. 18 (w.e.f. 20-9-1961).
201. Subs. by Act 27 of 1956, s. 47, for s. 84.
202. Subs. by Act 47 of 1966, s. 41, for ss. 86 to 92 (w.e.f. 14-12-1966).
203. Ins. by Act 40 of 2003, s. 4.
204. Subs. by Act 47 of 1966, s. 42, for "the Tribunal" (w.e.f. 14-12-1966).
205. Subs. by Act 27 of 1956, s. 52, for "the publication of the election petition under Section 90".
206. The words "list of" omitted by s. 52, *ibid.*
207. Subs. by Act 27 of 1956, s. 53, for "the returned candidate".
208. The word "or" and clause (d) omitted by s. 53, *ibid.*
209. Subs. by Act 47 of 1966, s. 42, for "the Tribunal" (w.e.f. 14-12-1966).
210. Subs. by Act 27 of 1956, s. 54, for cl. (a).
211. Certain words omitted by Act 58 of 1958, s. 29.
212. Subs. by Act 27 of 1956, s. 54, for " no person shall be named".
213. Subs. by s. 54, *ibid.*, for sub-section (2).
214. Subs. by s. 55, *ibid.*, for sub-sections (1) and (2).
215. Ins. by Act 20 of 1963, s. 57 and the Second Sch. the words "or the Government of Part C States Act, 1951 (49 of 1951)" were omitted by the Adaptation of Laws (No. 2) Order, 1956.
216. Subs. by Act 58 of 1958, s. 30, for certain words.
217. Subs. by Act 47 of 1966, s. 42, for "the Tribunal" (w.e.f. 14-12-1966).
218. Sub-section (3) re-numbered as sub-section (2) by Act 27 of 1956, s. 55.
219. The words and figures "specified in Section 123 " omitted by s. 55, *ibid.*
220. Subs. by s. 55, *ibid.*, for " without the sanction or connivance".
221. Cl. (b) omitted by Act 58 of 1958, s. 30.
222. The words "or illegal" omitted by Act 27 of 1956, s. 55.
223. The words "or illegal" omitted by s. 56, *ibid.*
224. Subs. by Act 47 of 1966, s. 42, for "the Tribunal" (w.e.f. 14-12-1966).
225. Subs. by s. 43, *ibid.*, for s. 103 (w.e.f. 14-12-1966).
226. Subs. by s. 44, *ibid.*, for "the Tribunal " (w.e.f. 14-12-1966).
227. The words and brackets "(other than a primary election)" omitted by Act 27 of 1956, s. 59.
228. Subs. by s. 59, *ibid.*, for certain words.
229. Subs. by s. 60, *ibid.*, for s. 107.
230. Subs. by Act 47 of 1966, s. 44, for sub-section (1) (w.e.f. 14-12-1966).
231. Subs. by Act 47 of 1966, s. 46, for ss. 109 and 110 (w.e.f. 14-12-1966).
232. Subs. by s. 47, *ibid.*, for "the Tribunal" (w.e.f. 14-12-1966).
233. Ins. by Act 27 of 1956, s. 61.
234. Subs. by Act 47 of 1966, s. 48, for ss. 112 to 115 (w.e.f. 14-12-1966).
235. Subs. by s. 49, *ibid.*, for "the Tribunal" (w.e.f. 14-12-1966).
236. Ins. by Act 27 of 1956, s. 62.
237. Subs. by Act 47 of 1966, s. 50, for ss. 116A and 116B (w.e.f. 14-12-1966).
238. Subs. by Act 47 of 1966, s. 51, for ss. 117, 118, 119, 119A and 120 (w.e.f. 14-12-1966).
239. Subs. by Act 58 of 1958, s. 34, for certain words.

240. Subs. by Act 47 of 1966, s. 52, for "the Election Commission" (w.e.f. 14-12-1966).
241. Subs. by Act 58 of 1958, s. 34, for "six months".
242. Subs. by s. 35, *ibid.*, for certain words.
243. Subs. by Act 27 of 1956, s. 65, for the heading "CORRUPT AND ILLEGAL PRACTICES AND ELECTORAL OFFENCES".
244. Subs. by s. 66, *ibid.*, for Chapters I and II (ss. 123 to 125).
245. Subs. by Act 58 of 1958, s. 36, for cl. (1).
246. Subs. by Act 47 of 1966, s. 53, for "to withdraw" (w.e.f. 14-12-1966).
247. Subs. by s. 53, *ibid.*, for "having withdrawn" (w.e.f. 14-12-1966).
248. Subs. by s. 53, *ibid.*, for "withdrawing" (w.e.f. 14-12-1966).
249. Ins. by Act 58 of 1958, s. 36.
250. Subs. by Act 40 of 1961, s. 23, for cl. (3) (w.e.f. 20-9-1961).
251. Ins. by Act 40 of 1975, s. 8 (retrospectively).
252. Ins. by Act 3 of 1988, s. 19 (retrospectively).
253. Ins. by Act 58 of 1958, s. 36.
254. The words "or retirement from contest " omitted by s. 36, *ibid.*
255. Subs. by Act 47 of 1966, s. 53, for "for the conveyance" (w.e.f. 14-12-1966).
256 Ins. by Act 58 of 1958, s. 36.
257 Subs. by s. 36, *ibid.*, for clause (f).
258 Ins. by Act 40 of 1975, s. 8 (retrospectively).
259. Ins. by Act 1 of 1989, s. 13 (w.e.f. 15-3-1989).
260. The words "or a polling agent or a counting agent" omitted by Act 47 of 1966, s. 53 (w.e.f. 14-12-1966).
261. Added by Act 40 of 1975, s. 8 (retrospectively).
262. Ins. by Act 1 of 1989, s.13 (w.e.f. 15-3-1989).
263. Ins. by Act 40 of 1961, s. 24 (w.e.f. 20-9-1961).
264. Ins. by Act 72 of 2002, s.5 (w.e.f. 24-8-2002).
265. Subs. by Act 21 of 1996, s. 10, for s. 126 (w.e.f. 1-8-1969).
266. Subs. by Act 1 of 1989, s. 14, for certain words (w.e.f. 15-3-1989).
267. Subs. by Act 21 of 1996, s. 11, for certain words (w.e.f. 1-8-1996).
268. Ins. by s. 11, *ibid.* (w.e.f. 1-8-1996).
269. Ins. by Act 40 of 1961, s. 26 (w.e.f. 20-9-1961).
270. Ins. by Act 40 of 2003, s. 5.
271. Subs. by Act 47 of 1966, s. 55, for "a returning officer " (w.e.f. 14-12-1966).
272. Ins. by s. 55, *ibid.* (w.e.f. 14-12-1966).
273. Subs. by s. 56, *ibid.*, for " one hundred yards " (w.e.f. 14-12-1966).
274. Ins. by Act 4 of 1986, s. 2 and Sch. (w.e.f.15-5-1986).
275. Subs. by Act 21 of 1996, s. 12, for s. 133 (w.e.f. 1-8-1996).
276. Ins. by Act 47 of 1966, s. 58 (w.e.f. 14-12-1966).
277. Certain words omitted by Act 58 of 1958, s. 37.
278. Subs. by Act 47 of 1966, s. 58, for "returning officers" (w.e.f. 14-12-1966).
279. The words "the preparation of an electoral roll" omitted by Act 58 of 1958, s. 37.

280. Ins. by Act 47 of 1966, s. 59 (w.e.f. 14-12-1966).
281. Ins. by Act 21 of 1996, s. 13 (w.e.f. 1-8-1996).
282. Subs. by s. 14, *ibid.*, for "fraudulently" (w.e.f. 1-8-1996).
283. Ins. by Act 1 of 1989, s. 15 (w.e.f. 15-3-1989).
284. S. 135A renumbered as sub-section (1) thereof by Act 21 of 1996, s. 15 (w.e.f. 1-8-1996).
285. Subs. by s. 15, *ibid.*, for certain words (w.e.f. 1-8-1996).
286. Subs. by s. 15, *ibid.*, for "this Section" (w.e.f. 1-8-1996).
287. Subs. by s. 15, *ibid.*, for "threatening" (w.e.f. 1-8-1996).
288. Ins. by s. 15, *ibid.* (w.e.f. 1-8-1996).
289. Ins. by Act 21 of 1996, s. 16 (w.e.f. 1-8-1996).
290. Ins. by Act 27 of 1956, s. 70.
291. The words and figures "or by or under the Representation of the People Act, 1950 " omitted by Act 58 of 1958, s. 38.
292. Subs. by Act 47 of 1966, s. 60, for sub-section (4) (w.e.f. 14-12-1966).
293. Ins. by Act 17 of 1965, s. 2.
294. See now the corresponding provision of the Code of Criminal Procedure, 1973 (2 of 1974).
295. S. 147 re-numbered as sub-section (1) of that Section by the Adaptation of Laws (No. 2) Order, 1956.
296. The words "or the elected members of the Coorg Legislative Council" omitted by Act 49 of 1951, s. 44 and the Fifth Schedule.
297. Ins. by the Adaptation of Laws (No. 2) Order, 1956.
298. Now it has become State.
299. Ins. by Act 21 of 1996, s. 17 (w.e.f. 1-8-1996).
300. Subs. by the Adaptation of Laws (No. 2) Order, 1956, for "Part C State".
301. The words "or group of such States" omitted by Act 27 of 1956, s. 77.
302. Certain words omitted by Act 49 of 1951, s. 44 and the Fifth Schedule.
303. Subs. by Act 27 of 1956, s. 78, for s. 153.
304. Subs. by the Adaptation of Laws (No. 2) Order, 1956, for sub-section (1).
305. Certain words omitted, *ibid.*
306. Ins., *ibid.*
307. The words "or the Rajpramukh, as the case may be" omitted by the Adaptation of Laws (No. 2) Order, 1956.
308. Subs. by Act 27 of 1956, s. 79, for " Section 75".
309. Subs. by Act 58 of 1958, s. 39, for s. 158.
310. Subs. by Act 12 of 1998, s. 2 (w.e.f. 23-12-1997).
311. See the Conduct of Election Rules, 1961, in Vol. II.
312. Ins. by Act 72 of 2002, s. 6 (w.e.f. 24-8-2002).
313. Renumbered by s. 6, *ibid.* (w.e.f. 24-8-2002).
314. Ins. by Act 46 of 2003, s. 6.
315. Ins. by Act 46 of 2003, s. 6.
316. Ins. by Act 1 of 1989, s. 16 (w.e.f. 15-3-1989).
317. Subs. by s. 16, *ibid.*, for "ballot boxes" (w.e.f. 15-3-1989).

318. Subs. by Act 40 of 1961, s. 29, for sub-section (3) (w.e.f. 20-9-1961), which was ins. by Act 27 of 1956, s. 82.
319. Subs. by Act 4 of 1986, s. 2 and Sch. (w.e.f. 15-5-1986).

39

The Salary, Allowances and Pension of Members of Parliament (Amendment) Act, 2006

No. 40 of 2006 [12th September, 2006]

AN ACT further to amend the Salary, Allowances and Pension of Members of Parliament Act, 1954.

Be it enacted by Parliament in the Fifty-seventh Year of the Republic of India as follows:-

1. Short title and commencement.

(1) This Act may be called the Salary, Allowances and Pension of Members of Parliament (Amendment) Act, 2006.

(2) Save as otherwise provided, it shall come into force on such date as the Central Government may, by notification in the Official Gazette, appoint; and different dates may be appointed for different provisions of this Act.

2. Amendment of Section 3. In Section 3 of the Salary, Allowances and Pension of Members of Parliament Act, 1954 (hereinafter referred to as the principal Act), -

(a) for the words "at the rate of four thousand rupees per mensem", the words "at the rate of sixteen thousand rupees per mensem" shall be substituted;

(b) for the words "at the rate of four hundred rupees for each day", the words "at the rate of one thousand rupees for each day" shall be substituted;

(c) for the second and third provison, the following proviso shall be substituted, namely: -

"PROVIDED FURTHER that the rates of salary and allowance specified in this section shall be applicable for a period of five years from the 14th day of September, 2006 or until it is refixed, whichever is later.".

3. Amendment of Section 4. In Section 4 of the principal Act, in sub-section (1), -

(a) in clause (c), in sub-clause (ii), for the words "at the rate of eight rupees per kilometre", the words "at the rate of thirteen rupees per kilometre" shall be substituted;

(b) after the second proviso, and before the Explanation, the following proviso shall be inserted, namely: -

"PROVIDED ALSO that the rate specified in sub-clause (ii) of clause (c) of this sub-section shall be applicable for a period of five years from the date of commencement of the Salary, Allowances and Pension of Members of Parliament (Amendment) Act, 2006.";

(c) in sub-section (2), after the second proviso, the following proviso shall be inserted, namely:-

"PROVIDED ALSO that the first proviso shall not be applicable to a member who, in the opinion of the Chairman of the Council of States or, as the case may be, the Speaker of the House of the People, is so incapacitated physically and cannot travel by air or train.".

4. Amendment of Section 5. In Section 5 of the principal Act,-

(a) in sub-section (1A), for the words "seven days", the words "five days" shall be substituted;

(b) in sub-section (2),-

(i) for the first proviso, the following proviso shall be substituted, namely:

"PROVIDED that the total number of such journeys under this sub-section shall be thirty-four journeys per year";

(ii) in the second proviso, for the words "less than thirty-two", the words "less than thirty-four" shall be substituted;

(iii) in the third proviso, for the words "thirty-two journeys", the words "thirty-four journeys" shall be substituted;

(iv) after the third proviso, the following proviso shall be inserted, namely:-

"PROVIDED ALSO that in case any member avails a total number of journeys by air more than thirty-four, such journeys permissible to him, in the year, he may be allowed to adjust not exceeding eight such journeys from the entitled number of journeys which may accrue in his credit in the next following year.";

(c) after sub-section (2) and before Explanation I, the following sub-section shall be inserted, namely:-

"(3) Notwithstanding anything contained in sub-section (2), there shall be paid to a member who, in the opinion of the Chairman of the Council of States or, as the case may be, the Speaker of the House of the People, is so incapacitated physically and therefore cannot perform air or train journey, road mileage for the entire road journey";

(d) in Explanation III, for the words "thirty-two journeys", the words "thirty-four journeys" shall be substituted.

5. Amendment of Section 6D. In Section 6D of the principal Act, after clause (ii), the following clause shall be added and shall be deemed to have been added with effect from the 17th day of May, 2004, namely:-

"(iii) by road as is referred to in Section 4 or Section 5, be entitled to an amount equal to one road mileage".

6. Amendment of Section 7. In Section 7 of the principal Act, for the words "seven days", the words "five days" shall be substituted.

7. Amendment of Section 8A. In Section 8A of the principal Act,–

(a) for sub-section (1) and the proviso thereto, the following shall be substituted, namely:-

"(1) With effect from the commencement of the Salary, Allowances and Pension of Members of Parliament (Amendment) Act, 2006, there shall be paid a pension of eight thousand rupees per mensem to every person who has served for any period as a member of the Provisional Parliament or either House of Parliament:

PROVIDED that where a person has served as a member of the Provisional Parliament or either House of Parliament for a period exceeding five years, there shall be paid to him an additional pension of eight hundred rupees per mensem for every year served in excess of five years";

(b) sub-section (1A) and the Explanation thereunder shall be omitted.

8. Amendment of Section 8AA. Section 8AA of the principal Act shall be numbered as sub-section (1) thereof and after sub-section (1) as so numbered, the following sub-section shall be inserted, namely: -

"(2) Every person who is not a sitting member but has served for any period as a member from the Andaman and Nicobar Islands or the Lakshadweep, shall be entitled to travel by the highest class of accommodation in any steamer sailing between the Andaman and Nicobar Islands or, as the case may be, the Lakshadweep and the main land territory of India in addition to the facilities available to such member under sub-section (1), without payment of any charges on the basis of an authorisation issued for this purpose by the Secretariat of either House of Parliament".

9. Insertion of new Section 8AC. After Section 8AB of the principal Act, the following section shall be inserted, namely:-

8AC. Family pension.

(1) On the death of a member of either House of Parliament during his term of office, his spouse, if any, or dependent of such member shall be paid during the remaining period of life of such spouse or, as the case may be, such dependent so long as such dependent continues to be a dependent within the meaning of clause (aa) of Section 2, family pension equivalent to one-half of the pension which such member of Parliament would have received had he retired:

PROVIDED that no such family pension shall be payable to a dependent if such dependent is a sitting member of Parliament or is drawing pension under Section 8A.

(2) The family pension payable under sub-section (1) shall also be payable to the spouse or dependent of a person who was a member of either House of Parliament or the Provisional Parliament at any time before the commencement of the Salary, Allowances and Pension of Members of Parliament (Amendment) Act, 2006 and died after serving as such member:

PROVIDED that such spouse or dependent is not drawing any pension under this Act or is not entitled to draw family pension under the proviso to sub-section (1):

PROVIDED FURTHER that no person shall be entitled to claim arrears of any family pension under this sub-section in respect of a period before the commencement of the Salary, Allowances and Pension of Members of Parliament (Amendment) Act, 2006.

EXPLANATION: For the purposes of this section, "Provisional Parliament" shall include the body which functioned as the Constituent Assembly of the Dominion of India immediately before the commencement of the Constitution.

❑❑❑

40

The Sixth Schedule to the Constitution (Amendment) Act, 2003

[Act, No. 44 of 2003] [7th September, 2003]

Preamble

Further to amend the Constitution of India in its application to the State of Assam.

Be it enacted by Parliament in the Fifty-fourth Year of the Republic of India as follows:—

1. Short title. This Act may be called the Sixth Schedule to the Constitution (Amendment) Act, 2003.

2. Amendment of Sixth Schedule to the Constitution. The Sixth Schedule to the Constitution shall, in its application to the State of Assam, have effect subject to the following modifications, namely —

(1) In paragraph 1, after sub-paragraph (2), the following proviso shall be inserted, namely —

"PROVIDED that nothing in this sub-paragraph shall apply to the Bodoland Territorial Areas District";

(2) In paragraph 2, after sub-paragraph (1), the following proviso shall be inserted, namely —

"PROVIDED that the Bodoland Territorial Council shall consist of not more than forty-six members of whom forty shall be elected on the basis of adult suffrage, of whom thirty shall be reserved for the Scheduled Tribes, five for non-tribal communities, five open for all communities and the remaining six shall be nom mated by the Governor having same rights and privileges as other members, including voting rights, from amongst the un-

represented communities of the Bodoland Territorial Areas District, of which at least two shall be women."

(3) In paragraph 2, in sub-paragraph (3), after the proviso, the following proviso shall be inserted, namely —

"PROVIDED FURTHER that the District Council constituted for the Bodoland Territorial Areas District shall be called the Bodoland Territorial Council."

(4) In paragraph 3, for sub-paragraph (3), the following sub-paragraph shall be substituted, namely —

"(3) Save as otherwise provided in sub-paragraph (2) of paragraph 3A or sub-paragraph (2) of paragraph 3B, all laws made under this paragraph or sub-paragraph (1) of paragraph 3A or sub-paragraph (1) of paragraph 3B shall be submitted forthwith to the Governor and, until assented to by him, shall have no effect."

(5) After paragraph 3A, the following paragraph shall be inserted, namely —

"3B. Additional powers of the Bodoland Territorial Council to make laws.

(1) Without prejudice to the provisions of paragraph 3, the Bodoland Territorial Council within its areas shall have power to make laws with respect to:

(i) Agriculture, including agricultural education and research, protection against pests and prevention of plant diseases;

(ii) Animal husbandry and veterinary, that is to say, preservation, protection and improvement of stock and prevention of animal diseases, veterinary training and practice, cattle pounds;

(iii) Cooperation;

(iv) Cultural affairs;

(v) Education, that is to say, primary education, higher secondary including vocational training, adult education, college education (general);

(vi) Fisheries;

(vii) Flood control for protection of village, paddy fields, markets and towns (not of technical nature);

(viii) Food and civil supply;

(ix) Forests (other than reserved forests);

(x) Handloom and textile;

(xi) Health and family welfare;

(xii) Intoxicating liquors, opium and derivatives, subject to the provisions of entry 84 of List I of the Seventh Schedule;

(xiii) Irrigation;

(xiv) Labour and employment;

(xv) Land and Revenue;

(xvi) Library services (financed and controlled by the State Government);

(xvii) Lotteries (subject to the provisions of entry 40 of List I of the Seventh Schedule), theatres, dramatic performances and cinemas (subject to the provisions of entry 60 of List I of the Seventh Schedule);

(xviii) Markets and fairs;

(xix) Municipal corporation, improvement trust, district boards and other local authorities;

(xx) Museum and archaeology institutions controlled or financed by the State, ancient and historical monuments and records other than those declared by or under any law made by Parliament to be of national importance;

(xxi) Panchayat and rural development;

(xxii) Planning and development;

(xxiii) Printing and stationery;

(xxiv) Public health engineering;

(xxv) Public works department;

(xxvi) Publicity and public relations;

(xxvii) Registration of births and deaths;

(xxviii) Relief and rehabilitation;

(xxix) Sericulture;

(xxx) Small, cottage and rural industry subject to the provisions of entries 7 and 52 of List I of the Seventh Schedule;

(xxxi) Social welfare;

(xxxii) Soil conservation;

(xxxiii) Sports and youth welfare;

(xxxiv) Statistics;

(xxxv) Tourism;

(xxxvi) Transport '(roads, bridges, ferries and other, means of communications not specified in List I of the Seventh Schedule, municipal tramways, ropeways, inland waterways and traffic thereon subject to the provision of List I and List III of the Seventh Schedule with regard to such waterways, vehicles other than mechanically propelled vehicles);

(xxxvii) Tribal research institute controlled and financed by the State Government;

(xxxviii) Urban development—town and country planning;

(xxxix) Weights and measures subject to the provisions of entry 50 of List I of the Seventh Schedule; and

(xl) Welfare of plain tribes and backward classes:

PROVIDED that nothing in such laws shall—

(a) extinguish or modify the existing rights and privileges of any citizen in respect of his land at the date of commencement of this Act; and

(b) disallow any citizen from acquiring land either by way of inheritance, allotment, settlement or by any other way of transfer if such citizen is otherwise

eligible for such acquisition of land within the Bodoland Territorial Areas District.

(2) All laws made under paragraph 3 or under this paragraph shall in so far as they relate to matters specified in List III of the Seventh Schedule. be submitted forthwith to the Governor who shall reserve the same for the consideration of the President.

(3) When a law is reserved for the consideration of the President, the President shall declare either that he assents to the said law or that he withholds assent therefrom:

PROVIDED that the President may direct the Governor to return the law to the Bodoland Territorial Council, together with the message requesting that the said Council will reconsider the law or any specified provisions thereof and, in particular, will consider the desirability of introducing any such amendments as he may recommend in his message and, when the law is so returned, the said Council shall consider the law accordingly within a period of six months from the date of receipt of such message and, if the law is again passed by the said Council with or without amendment it shall be presented again to the President for his consideration."

(6) In paragraph 4, after sub-paragraph (5), the following sub-paragraph shall be inserted, namely:—

"(6) Nothing in this paragraph shall apply to the Bodoland Territorial Council constituted under the proviso to sub-paragraph (3) of paragraph 2 of this Schedule."

(7) In paragraph 10, after sub-paragraph (3), the following sub-paragraph shall be inserted, namely —

"(4) Nothing in this paragraph shall apply to the Bodoland Territorial Council constituted under the proviso to sub-paragraph (3) of paragraph 2 of this Schedule";

(8) In paragraph 12, in sub-paragraph (1), in clause (a), for the words, figures and letter "matters specified in paragraph 3 or paragraph 3 A of this Schedule", the words, figures and letters "matters specified in paragraph 3 or paragraph 3A or paragraph 3B of this Schedule" shall be substituted;

(9) In paragraph 17, the following proviso shall be inserted, namely:—

"PROVIDED that nothing in this paragraph shall apply to the Bodoland Territorial Areas District."

(10) In paragraph 19, after sub-paragraph (3), the following sub-paragraph shall be inserted, namely —

"(4) As soon as possible after the commencement of this Act, an Interim Executive Council for Bodoland Territorial Areas District in Assam shall be formed by the Governor from amongst leaders of the Bodo movement, including the signatories to the Memorandum of Settlement, and shall provide adequate representation to the non-tribal communities in that area:

PROVIDED that the Interim Council shall be for a period of six months during which endeavour to hold the election to the Council shall be made.

EXPLANATION: For the purposes of this sub-paragraph, the expression "Memorandum of Settlement" means the Memorandum signed on the 10th day of February,. 2003 between Government of India, Government of Assam and Bddo Liberation Tigers.";

(11) In paragraph 20, in Part I of the Table, after entry 2, the following entry shall be inserted, namely:—

"3. The Bodoland Territorial Areas District".

□□□

41

The Two-Member Constituencies (Abolition) Act, 1961

ACT NO. OF 1961 [9TH MARCH, 1961]

AN ACT to provide for the abolition of two-member parliamentary and assembly constituencies and for the creation of single-member constituencies in their place.

Be it enacted by Parliament in the Twelfth Year of the Republic of India as follows:-

1. Short title. This Act may be called the Two-Member Constituencies (Abolition) Act, 1961.

2. Definition. In this Act, unless the context otherwise requires,-

(a) "Commission" means the Election Commission appointed by the President under article 324 of the Constitution ;

(b) "Delimitation Order" means the Delimitation of Parliamentary and Assembly Constituencies Order, 1956;

(c) "sitting member" means a person who, immediately before the date of publication of a notification under clause (c) of Section 4 in the Official Gazette of the State concerned, is a member of the House of the People from that State or, as the case may be, of the Legislative Assembly of that State;

(d) "State" includes a Union territory;

(e) "two-member constituency" means a two-member parliamentary constituency specified in the First Schedule or a two-member assembly constituency specified in the Second Schedule, to the Delimitation Order.

3. Division of two member constituencies. The Commission shall, as soon as may be practicable and in the manner herein provided, divide every two-member constituency (other than a two-member assembly constituency in the State of Gujarat) into two single-member constituencies, delimit their extent and decide in which of them the seat shall be reserved for the Scheduled castes or, as the case may be, for the scheduled tribes, having regarded to the following provisions namely:

(a) all the single member constituencies shall, as far as practicable, be geographically compact areas and in delimiting them regard shall be had to physical features, existing boundaries of administrative units, facilities of communication and public convenience; and

(b) the seat shall be reserved in that single-member constituency which in the opinion of the Commission has the greater concentration of population of the scheduled castes or, as the case may be, of the scheduled tribes.

EXPLANATION. In this section "population" means the population as ascertained at the census held in 1951.

4.Manner of Division. The Commission shall, as respects each State -

(a) formulate its proposals in regard to the matters mentioned in Section 3 and publish them in the Gazette of India, in the Official Gazette of the State and in such newspapers in the regional languages of the State as are considered important by the Commission, together with a notice inviting objections and suggestions in relation to the proposals and specifying a date on or after which the proposals will be further considered by it;

(b) after considering all objections and suggestions which may have been received by it before the date so specified, determine the matters referred to in Section 3; and

(c) direct, by notification published in the Official Gazette of the State and in the Gazette of India, such amendments to be made in the Delimitation Order as appear to it to be necessary for giving effect to its decisions.

5. Effect of Division. As from the date of publication of a notification under clause (c) of Section 4 in the Official Gazette of the State concerned -

(a) every two-member constituency in the State (other than a two-member assembly constituency in the State of Gujarat) shall cease to exist and, in lieu thereof, there shall come into existence two single-member constituencies (hereinafter referred to as "the corresponding new constituencies" as provided in the amended Delimitation Order;

(b) the sitting member of any two-member constituency in the State elected to fill the reserved seat therein shall be deemed to have been elected to the House of the People or as the case may be, of the Scheduled Tribes is from that one of the corresponding new constituencies in which the seat has been reserved, and the other sitting member of that two-member constituency shall be deemed to have been elected from the other of the corresponding new constituencies; and

(c) any casual vacancy existing immediately before the said date in any two-member constituency in the State shall, if it be in the reserved seat, be deemed to be a casual vacancy in that one of the corresponding new constituencies in which the seat has been reserved, and if it be in the other seat, be deemed to be a casual vacancy in the other of the corresponding new constituencies.

6. Special provision for Gujarat; amendment of Section 19 of Act 11 of 1960. In Section 19 of the Bombay Reorganisation Act, 1960 -

(a) in sub-section (2), for clause (b), the following clause shall be substituted, namely-

(b) the assembly constituencies into which the State shall be divided, the extent of each of such constituencies and in which of them seats shall be reserved for the scheduled castes or for the scheduled tribes ; and

(b) for sub-section (3), the following sub-section shall be substituted, namely —

"(3) In determining the matters referred to in clauses (b) and (c) of sub-section (2), the Election Commission hall have regard to the following provisions, namely:-

(i) all the constituencies shall be single-member constituencies ;

(ii) all the constituencies shall, as far as practicable, be geographically compact areas and in delimiting them regard shall be had to physical features, existing boundaries of administrative units, facilities of communication and public convenience; and

(iii) constituencies in which seats are reserved either for the Scheduled Castes or for the Scheduled Tribes shall as far as practicable, be located in the areas in which the population of the Scheduled Castes or, as the case may be, of the Scheduled Tribes is most, concentrated, but in regard to Scheduled Castes, care should be taken to distribute the reserved seats in different areas of the State."

7. Revision of the Delimitation Order.

(1) After all the notifications have been published under clause (c) of Section 4 and the order referred to in sub-section (5) of Section 19 of the Bombay Reorganisation Act, 1960, has been made, the Commission shall-

(a) make such further-amendments in the Delimitation Order as appear to it to be necessary for bringing up-to-date the description of the extent of all constituencies and for better arranging the order in which they are set out in the Schedules to the Delimitation Order; and

(b) send authenticated Copies of the Delimitation Order as so amended and revised to the Central Government and to each of the State Governments.

(2) As soon as may be after the revised Delimitation Order is received by the Central Government or a State Government, it shall be laid before the House of the People or, as the case may be, before the Legislative Assembly of the State.

8. Power to maintain Delimitation Order up-to-date. The Commission may from time to time, by notification published in the Gazette of India and in the Official Gazette of the State Concerned,-

(a) correct any printing, mistake in the revised Delimitation Order or any error arising therein from an inadvertent slip or omission, and

(b) where the boundaries or name of any district or any territorial division mentioned in a Schedule to the said Order are or is altered, make such amendments as appear to it to be necessary or expedient for bringing the Schedule up-to-date.

❑❑❑

42

The Union Territories (Direct Election to the House of the People) Act, 1965

ACT NO. 49 OF 1965 [22ND DECEMBER, 1965]

AN ACT to provide for direct election in certain Union territories for filling the seats allotted to them in the House of the People and for matters connected therewith.

Be it enacted by Parliament in the Sixteenth Year of the Republic of India as follows:-

1. Short title. This Act may be called the Union Territories (Direct Election to the House of the People) Act, 1965.

2. Definitions. In this Act-

(a) "parliamentary constituency" has the same meaning as in the Representation of the People Act, 1950 (43 of 1950);

(b) "sitting member" means a person who immediately before the commencement of this Act is a member of the House of the People;

(c) "Union territory" means any of the Union territories of the Andaman and Nicobar Islands, [1][Lakshadeep] and Dadra and Nagar Haveli.

3. Direct election to fill the seats in the House of the People allotted to certain Union Territories. At the next general election to the House of the People and thereafter, the seats allotted under section 3 of the Representation of the People Act, 1950 (43 of 1950) to the Union territories in the House of the People shall be seats to be filled by persons chosen by direct election and for that purpose each Union territory shall form one parliamentary constituency.

4. [Amendment of Act 43 of 1950.] Not printed.

5. [Amendment of Act 43 of 1951.] Not printed.

6. Provision as to sitting member. The sitting member representing each Union territory shall continue to represent that Union territory until the dissolution of the present House of the People and if before such dissolution the seat allotted to a Union territory in the House of the People becomes vacant it shall be filled by a person nominated by the President and that person shall represent the Union territory in the present House of the People until its dissolution.

❑❑❑

43

The Union Territories (Laws) Act, 1950

ACT NO. 30 OF 1950 [15TH APRIL, 1950]

AN ACT to provide for the extension of laws to certain Union territories.

Be it enacted by Parliament as follows:—

1. Short title and commencement.

(1) This Act may be called the Union territories (Laws) Act, 1950.

(2) It shall come into force on the 16th day of April, 1950.

2. Power to extend enactments to certain Union territories. The Central Government may, by notification in the Official Gazette, extend to the Union territory of Delhi, Himachal Pradesh, Manipur or Tripura or to any part of such territory, with such restrictions and modifications as it thinks fit, any enactment which is in force in a State at the date of the notification;

3. Extension of laws to Tripura, Vindhya Pradesh, and Manipur.

(1) The Acts and Ordinances specified in the Schedule to the Merged States (Laws) Act, 1949 (59 of 1949), are hereby extended to, and shall be in force in, the States of Tripura and Vindhya Pradesh, as they are generally in force in the territories to which they extend immediately before the commencement of this Act.

(2) Subject to the provisions contained in sub-section (2A), the Acts and Ordinances referred to in sub-section (1), are hereby extended to, and shall be in force in, the State of Manipur as they are generally in force in the territories to which they extend immediately before the commencement of this Act:

PROVIDED that the Indian Penal Code (45 of 1860), in its application to the State of Manipur shall have effect as if—

(a) in Section 361, for the word "eighteen" the word "fifteen" had been substituted, and

(b) in Section 375, for the word "sixteen" in clause Fifthly the word "fourteen" had been substituted, and for the word "fifteen" in the Exception the word "thirteen" had been substituted.

(2A) The Acts specified in Part A of the Schedule to this Act shall not extend to the State of Manipur, and the Acts specified in Part B thereof shall extend to, and be in force in, that State only as from the date of commencement of the Union Territories (Laws) Amendment Act, 1956 (68 of 1956), and shall, with effect from that date, be amended in the manner and to the extent specified in the said Part.

(3) For the purpose of facilitating the application in the said States of any such Act or Ordinance as aforesaid, any Court or other authority may construe the Act or Ordinance with such alterations not affecting the substance as may be necessary or proper to adapt it to the matter before the Court or other authority.

EXPLANATION— For the purposes of this section and Section 4, any reference to the State of Manipur or Tripura in relation to any period after the 31st October, 1956, shall be construed as a reference to the Union territory of Manipur or Tripura as the case may be.

4. Repeals and savings. Section 7 of the Delhi Laws Act, 1912 (13 of 1912), the Ajmer-Merwara (Extension of Laws) Act, 1947 (52 of 1947), and any law which immediately before the coming into force of any Act or Ordinance extended by this Act to any of the States of Manipur, Tripura and Vindhya Pradesh is in force in that State and corresponds to the Act or Ordinance as so extended, are hereby repealed:

PROVIDED that the repeal shall not affect—

(a) the previous operation of any such law, or

(b) any penalty, forfeiture or punishment incurred in respect of any offence committed against any such law, or

(c) any investigation, legal proceeding or remedy in respect of any such penalty, forfeiture or punishment, and any such investigation, legal proceeding or remedy may be instituted, continued or enforced, and any such penalty, forfeiture or punishment may be imposed, as if this Act had not been passed: Provided further that, subject to the preceding proviso, anything done or any action taken, including any appointment or delegation made, notification, order, instruction or direction issued, rule, regulation, form, bye- law or scheme framed, certificate, patent, permit or licence granted or registration effected, under such law shall be deemed to have been done or taken under Section 2 or, as the case may be, under the corresponding provision of the Act or Ordinance 3[as extended] to the State by Section 3, and shall continue in force accordingly, unless and until superseded by anything done or any action taken under the said Section 2 or, as the case may be, under the said Act or Ordinance.

❑❑❑

44

The Uttaranchal (Alteration of Name) Act, 2006

(Act No. 52 of 2006)

The Uttaranchal (Alteration of Name) Act, 2006 as passed by the Houses of Parliament Act to alter the name of the State of Uttaranchal.

Be it enacted by Parliament in the Fifty-seventh Year of the Republic of India as follows:

1. Short title and commencement.

(1) This Act may be called the Uttaranchal (Alteration of Name) Act, 2006.

(2) It shall come into force on such date as the Central Government may, by notification in the Official Gazette, appoint.

2. Definitions. In this Act, unless the context otherwise requires,

(a) "appointed day" means the date appointed under sub-section (2) of Section 1 for the coming into force of this Act;

(b) "appropriate Government" means, as respects a law relating to a matter enumerated in List I in the Seventh Schedule to the Constitution, the Central Government, and as respects any other law, the State Government;

(c) "law" includes any enactment, Ordinance, regulation, order, bye-law, rule, scheme, notification or other instrument having the force of law in the whole or any part of the State of Uttaranchal.

3. Alteration of name of the State of Uttaranchal. As from the appointed day, the State of Uttaranchal shall be known as the State of Uttarakhand.

4. Amendment of First Schedule to the Constitution. In the First Schedule to the

Constitution, under the heading "I THE STATES" in entry 27, under the column "Name" for the word "Uttaranchal", the word "Uttarakhand" shall be substituted.

5. Amendment of Fourth Schedule to the Constitution. In the Fourth Schedule to the Constitution, under the heading "TABLE", in entry 18, in the second column, for the word "Uttarachal" the word "Uttarakhand" shall be substituted.

6. Power to adapt laws.

(1) For the purpose of giving effect to the alteration of the name of the State of Uttaranchal by Section 3, the appropriate Government, may, before the expiration of one year from the appointed day, by order, make such adaptations and modifications of any law made before the appointed day, whether by way of repeal or amendment, as may be necessary or expedient, and thereupon every such law shall have effect subject to the adaptations and modifications so made.

(2) Nothing in sub-section (1) shall be deemed to prevent a competent Legislature or other competent authority from repealing or amending any law adapted or modified by the appropriate Government under the said sub-section.

7. Power to construe laws. Notwithstanding that no provision or insufficient provision has been made under Section 6 for the adaptation of a law made before the appointed day, any court, tribunal or authority, required or empowered to enforce such law, may construe the law in such manner, without affecting the substance, as may be necessary or proper in regard to the matter before the court, tribunal or authority.

8. Legal proceedings. Where immediately before the appointed day any legal proceedings are pending to which the State of Uttaranchal is a party, the State of Uttarakhand shall be deemed to be substituted for the state of Uttaranchal in those proceedings.

❑❑❑

Bibliography

Aggarwala, Om Prakash, *Cases on the Law of the Constitution of India* (1952) (Metropolitan Book Co. Ltd., Delhi).

Aggarwala, Om Prakash, *Fundamental Rights and Constitutional Remedies* (1953) (Metropolitan Book Co. Ltd., Delhi).

Austin, Granville, *Working a Democratic Constitution, A History of the Indian Experience* (1999) (Oxford University Press, New Delhi).

Bajpai, S.R., *Methods of Social Survey and Research* (11th ed. 1984) (Kitab Ghar, Kanpur).

Basu, Durga Das, *Cases on the Constitution of India* (1950-1951) (S.C. Sarkar and Sons Pvt. Ltd., Calcutta).

Chakravarti, K.P., *The Constitution of India, Analysis and Interpretation* (1980) (Allahabad Law Agency, Allahabad).

Chandra, U., Human Rights (2nd ed. 1999) (Allahabad Law Agency Publications, Allahabad).

Chitaley, D.V. and S. Appu Rao, *The Constitution of India* (2nd ed. 1970) (The All India Reporter, Ltd., Nagpur).

Dayal, S., *The Constitutional Law of India* (12th ed. 1979) (Allahabad Law Agency, Allahabad).

Dhar, Pannalal, *Preventive Detention under Indian Constitution* (1986) (Deep & Deep Publications, New Delhi).

Dhavan, Rajeev and Alice Jacob – edited by, *Indian Constitution, Trend and Issues* (1978) (The Indian Law Institute, New Delhi).

Dias, R.W.M., Jurisprudence (5th ed. 1985) (Butterworth Law Publishers, Kent, U.K.).

Douglas, William O., *From Marshall to Mukherjea* (1956) (Eastern Law House Ltd., Calcutta).

Franck, Thomas M., *Comparative Constitutional Process, Cases and Materials* (1968) (Sweet and Maxwell, London).

Gledhill, Alan, *Fundamental Rights in India* (1956) (Stevens & Sons Limited, London).

Goode, William J. and Paul K. Hatt, *Methods in Social Research* (1981) (Mc Graw – Hill Book Company, Singapore).

Halsbury, Earl of, *The Laws of England* (1955) (Butterworth & Co. (Publishers) Ltd., London).

Imam, Mohammed, *The Indian Supreme Court and the Constitution* (1973) (Eastern Book Company, Lucknow).

Jain, M.P., *Indian Constitutional Law* (4th ed. 1987) (Wadhwa and Company, Law Publishers, Nagpur)

Jain, S.N., J.K. Mittal, Kusum, P. Kalpakam, edited by, *Legal Research and Methodology* (1983) (The Indian Law Institute, New Delhi).

Joshi, G.N., *Aspects of Indian Constitutional Law* (1965) (University of Bombay).

Kagzi, Mangal Chandra Jain, *The Constitution of India* (4th ed. 1984) (Metropolitan Book Co. Private Ltd., New Delhi).

Kapoor, S.K., *Human Rights under International Law and Indian Law* (1999) (Central Law Agency, Allahabad).

Kulshreshtha, S.K., *Fundamental Rights and the Supreme Court* (1995) (Rawat Publications, Jaipur).

Mahajan, V.D., *Constitutional Law of India* (7th ed. 1991) (Eastern Book Company, Lucknow)

Malik, Surendra, *Supreme Court on Constitutional Law* (1973) (Eastern Book Company, Lucknow).

Mehta, S.M., *Constitution of India and Amendment Acts* (1990) (Deep and Deep Publications, New Delhi).

Nakade, Shivraj B., *Emergency in Indian Constitution* (1990) (Cosmo Publications, New Delhi).

Pandey, J.N., *Constitutional Law of India* (36th ed. 2000) (Central Law Agency, Allahabad)

Phillips, O. Hood, *The Constitutional Law of Great Britain and the Commonwealth* (2nd ed. 1957) (Sweet and Maxwell Limited, London).

Pylee, M.V., *India's Constitution* (2nd ed. 1967) (Asia Publishing House, New York).

Ramachandran, V.G., *Fundamental Rights and Constitutional Remedies,* Vol. II (2nd ed. 1970) (Eastern Book Company, Lucknow).

Ramachandran, V.G., *The Judicial Control* (1964) (Eastern Book Company, Lucknow).

Ray, S.N., *Judicial Review and Fundamental Rights* (1974) (Eastern Law House, Calcutta).

Salmond, ed. by P.J. *Fitzgerald, Jurisprudence* (12th ed. 1966) (N.M. Tripathi Private Ltd., Bombay).

Sarkar, R.C.S., *The Constitution of India* (1991) (National Publishing House, New Delhi).

Sathe, S.P., *Constitutional Amendments 1950-1988, Law and Politics* (1989) (N.M. Tripathi Private Limited, Bombay).

Sathe, S.P., *Judicial Activism in India* (2002) (Oxford University Press, New Delhi).

Tandon, M.P., *Interpretation of Statutes* (8th ed. 1998) (Allahabad Law Agency, Faridabad, Haryana).

Tope, T.K., *Constitutional Law of India* (1982) (Eastern Book Company, Lucknow).

Index

G

H

I

J

K

L

M

N

O

N

R

R